DEVELOPMENT IN THE PRESCHOOL YEARS

Birth to Age Five

EDUCATIONAL PSYCHOLOGY

Allen J. Edwards, Series Editor
Department of Psychology
Southwest Missouri State University
Springfield, Missouri

In preparation:

Dale G. Range and James R. Layton (eds.). Early Childhood Education: Theory to Research to Practice

Merlin C. Wittrock (eds.). The Brain and Psychology

Jean Stockard and Patricia A. Schmuck. Sex Equity in Education

Published

James R. Layton. The Psychology of Learning to Read

Thomas E. Jordan. Development in the Preschool Years: Birth to Age Five

Gary D. Phye and Daniel J. Reschly (eds.). School Psychology: Perspectives and Issues

Norman Steinaker and M. Robert Bell. The Experiential Taxonomy: A New Approach to Teaching and Learning

J. P. Das, John R. Kirby, and Ronald F. Jarman. Simultaneous and Successive Cognitive Processes

Herbert J. Klausmeier and Patricia S. Allen. Cognitive Development of Children and Youth: A Longitudinal Study

Victor M. Agruso, Jr. Learning in the Later Years: Principles of Educational Gerontology

Thomas R. Kratochwill (ed.). Single Subject Research: Strategies for Evaluating Change

Kay Pomerance Torshen. The Mastery Approach to Competency-Based Education

Harvey Lesser. Television and the Preschool Child: A Psychological Theory of Instruction and Curriculum Development

Donald J. Treffinger, J. Kent Davis, and Richard E. Ripple (eds.). Handbook on Teaching Educational Psychology

Harry L. Hom, Jr. and Paul A. Robinson (eds.). Psychological Processes in Early Education

J. Nina Lieberman. Playfulness: Its Relationship to Imagination and Creativity

Samuel Ball (ed.). Motivation in Education

Erness Bright Brody and Nathan Brody. Intelligence: Nature, Determinants, and Consequences

The list of titles in this series continues on the last page of this volume

DEVELOPMENT IN THE PRESCHOOL YEARS
Birth to Age Five

THOMAS E. JORDAN

The Graduate School
University of Missouri
St. Louis, Missouri

1980

ACADEMIC PRESS
A Subsidiary of Harcourt Brace Jovanovich, Publishers
New York   London   Toronto   Sydney   San Francisco

ACADEMIC PRESS, INC.
111 Fifth Avenue, New York, New York 10003

United Kingdom Edition published by
ACADEMIC PRESS, INC. (LONDON) LTD.
24/28 Oval Road, London NW1 7DX

Library of Congress Cataloging in Publication Data

Jordan, Thomas Edward.
     Development in the preschool years.

     (Educational psychology series)
     Bibliography: p.
     Includes index.
     1. Child development––Missouri––St. Louis metropol-
itan area––Longitudinal studies. I. Title.
HQ792.U5J67   649'.122'0977866   79–51678

ISBN 0–12–390450–1

PRINTED IN THE UNITED STATES OF AMERICA

80 81 82   9 8 7 6 5 4 3 2 1

FOR MY GRANDCHILDREN

Contents

Preface

At the end of a decade of studies of children using the classic psychoeducational technique of analyzing children one by one, I concluded that the possibilities of the method were too limited to reach a broader understanding of child development. A by-product of child study designed to produce better social service or education, child study with an N of one seemed to be a dead end. On that premise I began a series of procedural and substantive studies designed to gauge the range of requisite knowledge in child development and to assess methods of approach. Since the early 1960s I have traced the development of several cohorts of children. This book reports on a cohort of 1008 children from birth to age five.

It appears that longitudinal studies are regaining interest, if not popularity. In the area of delinquency, for example, it has become evident that the life course of young offenders prior to adolescence and their appearance in the criminal justice system merits attention. Valid data sets cannot be re-created retrospectively, and yet they represent the necessary antecedent to the phenomenon of adolescent delinquency. Other fields, of which learning disorders are a prime example, are ripe for a bold methodological stroke in order to cut through a miasma of ill-formed concepts and inadequate data. At the same time we are fortunate to witness a revolution in data processing; computers can store huge archives, and innovations in transmission and manipulation of data suggest that manhandling data can be reduced to a minimum. Observing due regard for the confidentiality of data and the right to privacy we note that data banks can be linked, and data can be shared across oceans. We present no brief for megalomania, but note the growth of sophistication in management of information, a requisite for future studies of development.

While new opportunities arise from technology, old problems persist. Despite new designs involving sequential cohorts, longitudinal study still requires permanent interest and stable support. People sensitive to needs of families are essential, and respect for family privacy and confidentiality mandate great care and delicacy as never before.

Longitudinal studies are not easy to fund and I wish to express my thanks to several agencies and, in particular, key administrators for their support. I wish to thank Dr. Max Mueller of the U.S. Bureau for Education of the Handicapped, and Dr. Wade Robinson of CEMREL, Inc. Among my colleagues, Professor Steven Spaner has been especially important since he has mounted all data for computer storage. Not the least of his talents is his swift grasp of my programming errors when processing the data.

Over the years a large number of people have assisted with acquisition of data. I acknowledge with gratitude the help of Ellen Brasunas, Janice Borgmann, Muriel Ehrenberg, Claire Ernhart, Edith Greenfield, Orville Kirk, Arthur Littleton, Judy McNeil, James Owens, Edna Pahl, Walter Peach, Lois Shepherd, and Elizabeth Williamson.

My thanks go to Marjorie Huston, Mary Ellen Heckel, and Linda Reese for their skill and concentration when typing this manuscript through various revisions.

I would like to express my thanks to Jack Edwards and the staff of Academic Press for their assistance and support.

DEVELOPMENT IN THE PRESCHOOL YEARS
Birth to Age Five

Old Man River's Children

1

Introduction

The purpose of this book is to report a prospective longitudinal analysis of influences on development in the years from birth to age 5. While speculation on the ways in which young children grow tends to be in terms of generalities, this volume emphasizes the role of empirical data in such discourse, and attempts to relate observations to an antecedent set of quantitative findings. At a more particular level, the investigation considers six aspects of development; the domains are not treated equally, since some topics are more pressing than others in early development, and some are hard to study. Height and weight data are comparatively easy to gather, given standardization of procedures. However, the range of theoretical influences on child development is enormous. An empirical inquiry is necessarily limited to using concepts which can be treated mathematically. In this report, the influences of interest are grouped into four sets, and each is applied to study of the six areas of child development.

This work is organized into three sections. This and the next two chapters provide an introduction. Chapter 2 reviews the corpus of longitudinal studies, specific approaches, and recent research. Chapter 3 describes the methods used to generate and analyze the data.

Chapters 4 to 9 present multivariate regression analyses of the data in six domains, and constitute the second portion of the report. Finally, Chapter 10 presents a discussion of the findings, and constitutes the third part of the book.

The fundamental intent of this investigation is to make a contribution to policy formation for the early years of life. To date, the preschool years have lacked a corpus of data designed to subvent social policy for metropolitan living. The deficit is that social policy must be formed from fragmentary data over brief spans of time. When data sets have reached a critical mass, they have often been compromised by the narrow range of domains in which relevant data exist. Also, much of the study of little children has, perchance, been piggy-backed on intervention studies. As a consequence, data sets are drawn from groups of children subjected to various intensive programs. To be sure, the data set of this study is not without its limitations. However, it avoids the hazard just mentioned, and it is coherent in its orientation to research rather than to experimental treatment. All things considered, the data set over time may be considered *naturalistic,* since observations were taken purely for intellectual, descriptive purposes at preselected ages and anniversaries.

It is helpful to note that the period of development analyzed here is from birth to 66 months. Data-taking has continued in the several years since the cohort reached age 5; this is an account of one segment of the developmental span since birth, to be followed by others.

The River and the People

The complexities and simplicities of peoples' lives lie, to a considerable extent, in the perspective we bring to bear on them. In the short run even routine human problems—the matters of rising each day, earning a living, and raising children—are exercises in foreseeing the consequences of actions and decisions. In the longer perspective, either that emerging with the passage of time or from the priviledged view of the detached analyst, trends and implications seem a little clearer. Both of these commonplace observations share the fact that they are within the unit of time which is human experience. Lives ebb and flow, generation succeeds generation, and the flux of society sweeps up people within its overarching themes. Within the domain of Nature the proportion is larger. Eons rather than generations set the scale, and miles in thousands rather than the mere handfuls generated by the pace of everyday life create the perspective for events.

It is in harmony with that proposition that the Great River flows. It rises in the northern plains and, fed by substantial rivers, flows southward across the continent. Here and there it has cast a broad design, a floodplain on which the fertile loam of centuries has been deposited. Now narrowly flowing under limestone bluffs it moves with deepening strength toward its ultimate rendezvous with the oceans themselves.

Old Man River is an elemental force in nature. No mere burbling stream once beyond its source, it has carved its way across a continent. Since time immemorial Man has observed with awe its strength, and has felt in misery its fury. Man the observer has been at best a puny witness to its grandeur, and has lived his alloted span of years conscious of the immensity of its silent energy.

To the Osage, Sac, and Fox Indians the great waterway was a key to many streams. The Mississippi river, itself several thousands of miles in length, was a nearby passage to the Missouri river, and so to the plains and the Northwest. At one time, approximately A.D. 1000, Cahokia was the site of a large city, and provided a point of exchange for both goods and cultures where the Missouri joins the Mississippi.

At a later, more recent time, but one preceded by a silence and anonymity only the forces of Nature can suggest, another neighboring stream—the Illinois River—provided a link for the *voyageurs* from French Canada in the north. After traversing the Great Lakes, Joliet and Marquette found that the Illinois River provided a smooth and simple waterway by which they might traverse the continent. This waterway helped establish a trading link with their fellows living in uncertain security where the great river entered the Gulf. It was from the relative security of New Orleans that explorers began to push further north, establishing trading posts and settlements at strategic locations. These villages, which lay in unexplored lands, existed as political territories only on maps. There were rare places where military installations overcame the problems of hostile surroundings, an aboriginal and little known indigenous population, and the immense distances over which supplies and commerce moved.

It was in April 1764 that Auguste Chouteau decided to use a low bluff a few miles south of the Missouri river to found his trading post, naming it for Saint Louis IX. After an uneasy start, including Indian attacks in the early 1780s, the settlement began to prosper. A ferry was in permanent operation by 1797. In 1803 the Louisiana Purchase brought the city and surrounding portion of the continent under the control of the United States. In 1800, the city of St. Louis was incorporated. By 1817 the first steamboat, the *Pike*, arrived from New Orleans, and a cathedral was built in the following year, a charming structure which is still in use.

In the next decades of the nineteenth century waves of German and Irish migration began, to be followed at a much later date by black migration. The present population of the metropolitan area can be described essentially in terms of these three populations, plus a number of smaller groups.

Today, the metropolitan area contains 2.5 million people. For the most part, they are black, German, and Irish in origin. Lutherans and Catholics are a substantial portion of the community, and the Jesuit St. Louis University is the oldest American university west of the Mississippi.

The community interest in educating the young was a distinctive function of nineteenth-century life. In 1873, Susan Blow established the first American kindergarten. The term would have been obvious to the large German-speaking population. It represented an interest in children growing like so many flowers in a garden. We choose the metaphor of the father of Great Waters, and his children, Old Man River's Children, as the motif of this book.

Our intent is to contribute to the understanding of how children grow in the first 5 years of life. We do so by taking children from all walks of life, religions, and races at the moment of birth, and follow their course over the subsequent 5 years.

The Metropolitan Area

Today, the St. Louis metropolitan area is perhaps best described in terms of the Standard Metropolitan Statistical Area (SMSA), as the Census Bureau formulates this area that was once only broad rivers, flowing streams, and wooded hills. In recent years the area has generally lost population, especially the city of St. Louis and the declining city of East St. Louis, Illinois on the east bank of the Mississippi. Between 1960 and 1970 the St. Louis city population decreased by roughly 130,000 people. Conversely, St. Louis county, the surrounding semicircle, grew in population by one-third, and is currently larger in population than the city. St. Charles county, slightly to the west and sitting on the Missouri river, is growing even more rapidly. Our cohort has not been immune to these trends, and many of our former city dwellers now live in the suburbs, and beyond.

In 1970 a quarter-million black Americans lived in the old core city, with another 50,000 living in the surrounding St. Louis county. The median years of schooling in the St. Louis SMSA is 11.9 years for males and 11.5 years for females. This is below the national average for comparable SMSAs. Census data for 1960 and 1970, however, show that the level of years of schooling had risen. For example, the proportion of people with 4 years or more of college rose in the decade from 3.7 to 5.1%.

The life of an area is partly determined by its economic health. The word most applied to the regional economy is "stagnation." Traditionally a "beer, boots, and baseball" community, there have been serious losses in manufacturing jobs and in construction jobs. However, the area has a high concentration of medical and educational resources, and opportunities for the highly educated have not been quite so desperate.

Today, the term *quality of life* is used to sum up the conditions in which children grow. A review of 18 metropolitan areas was made by Flax (1972) at the time the data of this book were collected. At that time the St. Louis area was superior in mental health facilities, public order, and community concern. It was low in air quality, and the previously noted education attainment. In other characteristics contributing to the quality of life, such as health, income, racial equality, and housing it was about average. During the early 1950s the City of St. Louis reached its maximum in population, nearly 900,000 people. In the 1960s nearly one-third of the white population left. The black population reached 270,000 in the late 1960s. It too dropped as the black population also migrated to St. Louis County, having been preceded by the white migrants. Correspondingly the population of St. Louis County has grown. This is a large geographic area balkanized into small governmental units, and lacking a single and consolidated municipal government. The area is a beltlike semicircle surrounding the city from north to south, and touches the Missouri river curving from the west to join the Mississippi.

Morrison (1974) has contrasted the St. Louis SMSA with that of San Jose. The latter draws people from all over the nation, and people migrate from San Francisco to the south. St. Louis city has an aging population, and St. Louis County is the target of both St. Louis city migrants and migrants from other parts of the county who avoid the old, core city.

As a place to live the metropolitan area has many resources. The newly developed riverfront with soaring catenary arch and tourist attractions makes a visit to Old Man River a popular form of recreation. Within the area's rolling hills and remnants of the great oak and hickory forest, once stretching from Michigan to Texas, are many parks. Within the built-up areas are first-class opportunities for theatre, museums, and music. The climate, while running to extremes of heat and cold in due season, encourages vigorous activity for children.

Our population was born in both city and county and has been no exception to patterns of life in metropolitan areas. In this book we look at how the children grew, and what influenced their growth on the banks of the Great River.

Longitudinal Studies

2

This chapter will present information about longitudinal studies, a domain of research that has become popular once more. The resurgence of interest is recognition that longitudinal data provide a way to understand important aspects of human situations. For students of development the first important data set is the set of growth measures gathered on his son by M. Gueneau de Montbeillard. The measures began with the boy's birth on 11 April 1759, and ended on 11 November 1776, when the boy was 16 years and 7 months (16:7). The values are recorded in the pre-metric units *pieds, pouces,* and *lignes* (foot, thumb [inch], and cord). This interesting data set was not published by de Montbeillard, but is extant because it appears in Sonnini's (1799) edition of the works of his colleague, Georges le Clerc, Comte de Buffon. De Montbeillard had previously helped Berryat with his 1754 edition of the early proceedings of the Academie Royale des Sciences.

Today, longitudinal study exercises the minds of people in a variety of fields. In addition to studies in child development, there are major inquiries in schizophrenia (Sartorius, Jablonsky, & Shapiro, 1977; Mednick, Schulsinger, & Venables, 1979), occupational choice (Parnes, 1975), and education (Fetters, 1975). In the abstract this is not surprising, since data over time can lead to fascinating insights. Concretely, there are many practical problems, and the challenge to organizational skill can be enormous. In the past, people used samples that were selected in part because they seemed

7

easy, comparatively speaking, to study. For example, the Oakland–Berkeley studies used protestant, middle-class white families. With equal facility, investigators have chosen to drop certain kinds of children as objects of study (probands). Such groups as the illegitimate and multiple births (Neligan, Kolvin, Scott, & Garside, 1976), adopted children, those without a father figure (Fogelman & Goldstein, 1976), or with congenital defects, as in the Cuban National Study (Jordan *et al.*, 1975), have sometimes been excluded from study groups for procedural reasons. Such population traits are obviously a hazard for retention in a sample. On the other hand, such children are at the greatest developmental risk. The Baltimore group in the National Study of Aging consists of "upper-middle socioeconomic level" males who "are all college graduates, and a large percentage have doctorates [Andres, 1978]." The subjects volunteered in a study whose origins were relatively informal.

Longitudinal study has its intellectual appeal, since it suggests examination of phenomena in a developmental span of interest. Of course, one can go too far in enthusiasm; Zazzo (1967) warned against fantasies of "une methode longitudinale omnipotente," and the advice is sound since people tend to underestimate the hazards. The obstacles are not all procedural: In terms of design, the single cohort followed over time is now less attractive than the newer designs requiring successive groups. At a procedural level there is increasing resistance by groups of interest in the population to be investigated. Finally, we note the hazard of social disorder. As examples we cite our experience with the cohort reported here; the murder of Dr. Martin Luther King in the late 1960s led to a decided, if temporary, drop in efficiency in our case work. Fogelman (1976) reports the spread of negative publicity surrounding a national census for data taking for the British 1958 National Child Development Study (NCDS) cohort. Similarly, Janson (1975) records that a study cohort in Oslo was barely identified when attacks in a newspaper and in the Norwegian parliament caused cancellation of the prospective study.

Finally, we touch on the fiscal and career hazards that longitudinal study poses. In the case of fiscal matters, investigators have substantial costs for salaries, and lesser needs for equipment. In the case of finance, longitudinal study requires commitments of time and energy that must be supported. The chief career hazard is the lack of certainty that longitudinal studies can be carried to completion.

More analytically, management considerations include a pattern of funding that makes recruitment of permanent staff possible, and thereby helps develop the kind of trust that sustained contacts with probands requires over a period of years. In this matter we refer to prospective longitudinal study that is *programmatic*. The investigator identifies a study group at time one (T_1), and follows them through a series of subsequent contacts $(T_1, \ldots, T_n)$ over a span of time. The programmatic aspect means that the plan is to spend a good deal of time, thought, and energy on the venture. A program of research usually consists of projects that share some common characteristic such as the same criterion measures, but that also generates data for analysis on a variety of topics such as delinquency, adolescence, family influences, etc. Perhaps the really distinctive element is the decision to *think* about an intellectual complex in a context of empirical data, and to do so for a long period of time. Such a commitment is not made lightly, since it conjures up a set of problems. Setting apart the practical, procedural aspects, there is the hazard of data measures not available at one time appearing subsequently but too late to cast light on, say, an hypothesis of a critical period in human development. The appearance of innovations in analysis and design can leave a long, prospective enterprise looking just a little bit shabby, intellectually speaking.

It should be noted that it is possible to organize longitudinal study on a *project* basis. That is, the objective can be the generation of a specific corpus of data, which can be compressed procedurally, if not always intellectually. We will have more to say about this shortly.

Terminology

The terminology is not uniform in studies in which time is a major dimension or those in which there is change between scores at two or more points. The result is that some studies are erroneously identified, and some of them are actually better than they seem.

The generic expression is *longitudinal,* and within it the first term we shall consider is *prospective.* This refers to inquiry in which baseline data are defined and then the data set is extended. More precisely, it is an approach in which sampling is conducted via the independent variable. In *retrospective* technique the same data may be sought, but the inquiry hinges on sampling via the dependent variable. Clearly, our conviction is that it is not the technique for generating data, but the element of design evident in the choice of the sample that counts. This may help clear up the matter of use of archival data in which the independent variable exists, regardless of whether one uses more archival data to identify the criterion or undertakes generation of criterion data through follow-up study. In terms of sampling, the key lies in whether or not the subjects are chosen within a design that emphasizes the independent and predictor variables. When this choice is taken, the resulting inquiry may well be quite prospective in logic and sample theory. Interestingly, there are cases of studies identified by their authors as retrospective simply because the investigator went back to the baseline data.

In such cases it is perhaps prudent to label them *anterospective,* but certainly not retrospective.

We continue with the theme of sampling to consider *stratification* as a way to obtain a sample over time for analysis. In this approach, stratification means that a sample contains subsamples or strata, each of which represents an age. In the Cuban National Growth Study (Jordan *et al.,* 1975) the sample was 56,000 young people from birth to 19 years. Different strata received specialized attention; the 13–15-year-olds provided anthropometric measures, and the 3–9-year group was heavily represented. Sampling was also drawn from the six provinces of Cuba. A 30% sample was tested 1 year later. In an Irish study, Simon and Ward (1975) looked into the effect of adolescence on religious beliefs. Instead of waiting for the years of adolescence to wreak their effects on a group of children, Simon and Ward took a single sample containing children at each age from 11 to 15, with obvious economies of time and resistance to shrinkage. The hazard is that each subgroup by age, or substratum, is held to be identical in prior experience to the others, a proposition which does not always hold water. An elaboration of this strategy takes data in cross-sectional form and then takes measures at a later date on the same subjects. In the research by Rao and Rao (1966) the technique is described as "highly compressed, linked cross-sectional." In this approach a group of children at ages 1, 4, 7, and 10 years, if followed for 2 years, would provide prospective data for a 9-year developmental span in 2 years of real time. One can push a good thing too far, of course, and the shaky postulate of identical history prior to the period of interest for each age stratum is central. The fact is that age groups have different experiences. Research by Richman (1975) has shown that 1968 was a unique year for onset of heroin addiction. British research in delinquency suggests that children whose fifth year of life occurred between 1939 and 1945, the war years, have been especially prone to delinquency (Wilkins, 1960). An earlier group prone to delinquency passed their fourth and fifth years in the Depression. Still another variant is stratification with long-term follow-up rather than compressed data-taking. In the Baltimore-based National Study of Aging (Andres, 1978), the subjects are males from the twenties to the nineties.

For samples identified by particular shared traits, such as a common year of births, the word *cohort* is used; apparently, it is because William Beveridge in the 1930s described a study which needed 600 subjects, and recalled that a 600-man regiment of the Roman army was known as a cohort. Presumably, we would use the term *maniple* research had Beveridge's requirements been less demanding, or *legion* research had they been more grandiose. (By inference small sample investigators would be called *Centurions,* etc.)

We note the vague term *follow-up*. In our view it should be applied to studies in which the subjects were originally described or studied for a purpose prior to the investigation in question. Thus, the acquisition of data at one subsequent time point is a secondary, unforseen enterprise. It may well be quite rigorous but, as a sample, has been identified for other purposes. Such research can be quite useful. We wonder about the effects of jail on delinquents (Glueck & Glueck, 1943), and about the effects of schizophrenia in women on their children (Heston & Denny, 1968). Occasionally, follow-up can give credence to otherwise limited data; the work of Rubin and Balow has given a great deal of life to the Minnesota perinatal data from the Collaborative Perinatal Study. Equally, it has been quite useful to know how deprived children studied as probable cases of mental retardation turned out several decades later (Skeels & Skodak, 1965). Finally, we report the word *proband*; it means, as with the related term probate, worthy of critical examination and use. In longitudinal study it connotes not merely a subject, but one worthy of attention because of the richness of data or special relevance to the questions at hand.

Longitudinal study appeals to people around the world. Some places, especially Aberdeen (Tanner, 1956; Birch, 1970; Thompson, 1979) and Newcastle (Spence, Walton, Miller, & Court, 1954; Neligan *et al.*, 1976) in the United Kingdom, and Dunedin in New Zealand (Silva & Ferguson, 1976; Silva, 1979), have generated several useful studies because their populations are stable and their social services and intellectual communities are well integrated. In the case of Aberdeen the population has been studied, and investigators understand the patterns of migration among residents (Illsley, Finlayson, & Thomson, 1963). Other places are suitable because they have definable boundaries, such as the islands of Hawaii (Werner, Bierman, & French, 1971; Werner & Smith, 1977), Mauritius (Mednick & Witkin-Lanoil, 1977), and the Isle of Wight (Rutter, Graham, & Yule, 1970). Other places are more clearly the locus of professional activities for career investigators. Examples are the cities of Boulder (Jessor & Jessor, 1977), Berkeley (Block, 1971), Zurich (Bleuler, 1968), and Baltimore (Hardy & Mellitts, 1972; Gerstenblith *et al.*, 1977). Mednick's (1979) work was an exposition of longitudinal studies in eastern and western Europe, with appraisals of the studies presented by their authors.

Retrospective Study

Many investigations are studies of problem situations; that is, conditions have proved unsatisfactory and then lead us to search for causes. At first glance the sensible thing to do is to find examples of such conditions and, hence, their antecedents. Such thinking has the ring of common sense when we consider conditions such as leukemia (Ford, Patterson, & Treuting, 1959), cerebral palsy (Eastman, 1962), and kidney disease (Rous & Turner, 1977). Clearly, no one is going to deliberately induce such conditions and, so the reasoning goes, we find examples and construct the disease process ad hoc by looking into the history of the patient.

Clearly, it is the latter portion of the thought which creates the trouble. In some instances we look into records and reconstruct the causative events. Unfortunately, the variables we can consider are limited to those in the records, although the file may have recorded variables salient for another purpose. In the absence of objective data we may have to ask people to recall events and facts in order to create a corpus of data (anamnesis). A number of inquiries have examined the value of such information. Bradshaw, Ley, Kincey, and Bradshaw (1975) have shown in a formal experiment on recall of medical data that the choice of language when giving information materially affects subsequent recall. In another experiment Ley (1972) found that recall was influenced by what was told to people first, and then by what the person's selective perceptions judged to be salient for them. In Wenar's (1963) analysis the sex of authority figures providing information affected mothers' recall of their children's weight gains and psychomotor development. Robbins (1963) found that parents' recall of child rearing and child development differed to a significant degree from the objective data.

The topic of recall itself influences retention of information. Finnish data on pregnancy leading to dead or damaged babies was extremely unreliable (Klemmetti & Saxen, 1967), as is the case with bowel histories (Manning & Wyman, 1976). Yet, Damon and Bajeman (1974) found that women's recall of their age for menarche was remarkably accurate, having a mean error after 39 years of only 2.4 months. In the relevant context of maternal recall of children's development, Brekstad (1966) obtained the most accurate recall from women who were older, had more than one child, and were not anxious; there were no effects due to socioeconomic status (SES).

A key question is whether retrospective and prospective inquiry on the same body of information yields similar results. In Burton's (1970) study, mothers recalled children as taller than the children were, and husbands more absent than the husbands actually were. Their children recalled themselves as taller, healthier, and heavier. They too exaggerated their fathers' absence, but less than their mothers exaggerated. In Yarrow, Campbell, and Burton's (1964) analysis, mothers saw their children as healthier and having fewer problems of eating, sleeping, and toileting. Finally, our own study of data on the same children studies prospectively and retrospectively (Jordan, 1967a), showed that retrospective results simply cannot be trusted to the same degree as prospective data. And yet, to quote Mantel and Haenszel (1959), "a primary goal is to reach the same conclusions in a retrospective study as would have been obtained from a forward study, if one had been done [p. 722]." We conclude, accordingly, that retrospective inquiry, despite a grain of common sense and the obvious economy of beginning with criterion measures, has fundamental flaws. When unavoidable, use of multiple rather than single contrast groups helps reduce the possibility of rejecting the null hypothesis (no difference) when it is actually true, and no differences exist. Fundamentally the best choice is prospective study.

Even so, retrospection will continue to play a role in child study. The case study depends on the attempt to reconstruct the past sequence of potentially significant events. Within case studies hypotheses are constructed to guide selection of tests based on the developmental course as we can best understand it. The additional complication of invalidity in maternal reports cannot be set aside; however, effective interviewing generally involves several attempts to check on data elements from informants. In that enterprise there may be no practical alternative, since direct testing of young children may be virtually useless. In that context maternal reports of current and previous attainments and other critical items are a necessity. They also have the value of representing close and sustained observation, which can be fruitful to an experienced interviewer.

Prospective Study

Prospective study describes a class of inquiries in which the sample is formulated in terms of the independent variables. The variables in question may arise at any point in the developmental span. That is, the variables might be characteristics identified at birth, or they might be identified in middle age, as in a study of gerontology. Thus, prospective studies start at the point in the developmental span that the hypotheses dictate. School-based studies of children commonly start when children enter school, as in the Swedish Project Metropolitan directed by Janson (1975), or when they leave school, as in the United States study of the High School Class of 1972 (Fetters, 1976). In the Collaborative Perinatal Study the sample was defined in the pregnancy of 55,000 women (Berendes, 1966). However, prospective studies are better understood in terms of their endings. Few things are more impolitic than announcing the beginning of prospective study when the outcome may be years or decades away. Criterion measures need to be gathered and analyzed in a matrix of early and recent variables. In the interim, data are recorded and analyzed and the data ad hoc become an object of study. For example, the complex of automated data processing absorbs a great deal of energy. Each variable in the study must be described and analyzed, and the usual procedure is to develop a catalogue that lists the statistical properties of each variable. At the time of writing we have 1200 variables on many of the 1000 children in the described cohort. Not every datum is a separate score from a test battery; indeed, some are merely item scores from scales of great interest. Even so, they require analysis and study.

An interesting characteristic of prospective inquiries is their apparent redundance. It seems that everyone begins as if no one else had established anything in other prospective studies. This tendency to start from scratch becomes more understandable when we realize that programmatic research is an attempt to explore a large domain, and that the exploration will be leisurely and detailed. On those premises investigators want to be comprehensive, and plan to explore ideas as well as to gather data for testing specific hypotheses.

We now turn to a brief exposition of several prospective studies. The list is selective since the number of longitudinal studies is large and continues to grow.

OAKLAND-BERKELEY GROWTH STUDIES

This is actually a set of three enterprises. The Berkeley Growth Study was begun in 1928 by Nancy Bayley with the cooperation of 74 boys and girls. The areas of study have been broad with measures of physical and mental development taken on about 60 occasions over the decades. The Guidance Study initiated by Jean MacFarlane in 1928 enrolled every third child born in Berkeley over a period of 19 months. This study combined detailed prospective study to age 18 years with subsequent follow-ups at widely spaced intervals. The Oakland Growth Study began in 1932 by identifying 200 fifth and sixth graders. The probands were also studied in middle age. In all three inquiries the population is in middle age, with the obvious salience of their own children and grandchildren as subjects for inquiry. Block's (1971) monograph, *Lives Through Time*, examined individuals from the 1928 and 1932 cohorts at age 40. In 1974 Elder reported the adult years of the 1932 group as children of the Great Depression. Subjects in both populations had mean IQs as adolescents of 123 and 116.

THE DUNEDIN MULTIDISCIPLINARY CHILD DEVELOPMENT STUDY

In the early 1970s the University of Otago in New Zealand defined a birth cohort of just over 1000 newborns in the city of Dunedin. Funded by several government agencies on a continuous basis the Dunedin Study has the services of several specialities in child development. Papers have appeared on linguistic, pediatric, and medical aspects of child development (Silva & Ferguson, 1976; Silva, 1979).

THE POPULATION INVESTIGATION STUDY COHORT (PIC)

All children born in the United Kingdom in 1 week of March 1946 were potential subjects of this investigation. Once twins and illegitimates were excluded, themselves a major characteristic in a population, a sample of 5000 youngsters was identified. To date this study has produced a number of reports and has carried the birth cohort to maturity. Of particular interest has been Douglas' (1967) *The Home and the School,* an inquiry into scholastic performance at age 11 in light of the social background of the population ($N=5362$). A major conclusion dealt with the loss of talent in the children. In *All Our Future* (Douglas, Ross, & Simpson, 1971) the performance and status of the cohort at age 16 years was investigated. In addition, this study has generated significant papers on prematurity, childhood illnesses, behavior, education, and delinquency.

THE NATIONAL CHILD DEVELOPMENT STUDY (NCDS)

A second major study, also in the United Kingdom, is the 1958 National Child Development Study. Using 16,000 infants and not excluding twins and illegitimates, this program has been quite fruitful. A series of monographs began with *11,000 Seven Year Olds* and analyzed the progress of the cohort. In 1977 Fogelman issued *Britain's Sixteen Year Olds,* carrying analysis through adolescence. In between a series of papers has examined the effects of illegitimacy, adjustment problems in bright children, and hearing loss.

The 1958 NCDS inquiry is an example of large scale prospective study carried to fruition. Its potential for contributing to formation of rational social policy is considerable. The data have been well managed and the entire corpus has enormous potential for future studies of a wide range of problems (Stott, 1978).

THE TERMAN-STANFORD STUDY OF THE GIFTED

In the 1920s Lewis Terman identified 1500 11-year-olds living in California; the youngsters had a mean Binet IQ of 150. Not merely have they been studied over 50 years (vide, Terman, *Mental and Physical Traits of One Thousand Gifted Children* [1925] and Terman & Oden, *The Gifted Group at Mid-Life* [1959]), but their children have been studied, carrying the inquiry across both years and generations. An interesting feature has been retention of cooperation over the remarkable span of time. The basic description is given in a five-volume series entitled *Genetic Studies of Genius.* Subjects in the data set were studied with relation to their life satisfactions by Sears (1977) and Sears and Barbee (1977), when their mean age was 61 years.

CHILDREN OF KAUAI

Werner and colleagues (1968, 1971, 1977) began study of 3000 pregnancies and 1000 live births on the Hawaiian island of Kauai in 1954. From prenatal, prospective data they have generated interesting information on fetal wastage and on life at ages 2, 10, and 18 years. In *Children of Kauai* (1971) they reported that intellectual status and academic achievement at age 10 were well predicted by Cattell IQ at age 2. When SES, pediatric, and psychological data were combined, powerful predictions resulted. For criteria of social and emotional well-being a low standard of living at birth generated powerful predictions. Sex differences exist quite clearly in the published research. In general, this 18-year prospective study of an Oceanic population has been both interesting and productive. Particularly noteworthy is use of the period of gestation for identification of baseline data.

PROJECT METROPOLITAN

Situated in Stockholm, this prospective study is the productive component of what had originally been envisaged as a four-city Scandinavian program of research. The objective has been to define a population of school children and to obtain from bureaucratic records data on family background and school performance. Delinquency, social welfare, and performance in military service were envisaged as later measures. To date monographs have appeared on the cohort, the families, child rearing ideology, juvenile delinquency, and student radicalism (Janson, 1977). The breadth with which this program has formulated its perspective is interesting. Given successful negotiations of the obvious procedural hazards, Project Metropolitan should be one of the more powerful sources of information on human socialization. As Havighurst (1976) has pointed out, the middle class is much the same around the world. On that premise one can imagine a sharing of results from a number of urban centers, the whole being far more than the sum of the parts.

THE NIJMEGEN GROWTH STUDY

The Dutch university town of Nijmegen is the site of Prahl-Anderson and Kowalski's (1973) prospective study of children. The design repeated measures on almost 500 children ($N=486$); however, it is interesting to note that the sample consists of six groups of children, an approach we discuss a little later in this chapter as "contemporary designs." The span of interest in development is the ages 4 to 14 years. An interesting aspect of the study is the range of domains of development. Information has been acquired in the areas of anthropometry, psychology, and school performance. Of particular interest is the acquisition of dental information. This study is also distinguished by the sophistication of measuring procedures and the resultant analysis.

COLLABORATIVE PERINATAL STUDY

In the 1950s the National Institutes of Health described 55,908 pregnancies and deliveries in great detail. The mothers were identified at hospitals in 12 American cities between 1959 and 1965 from a pool of 133,000 relevant admissions. The hospital data are well summarized in Niswander and Gordon (1972), and a series of discrete studies have flowed from the participating university hospitals (Mack & Johnston, 1979; Rubin & Balow, 1979). For students of development useful subsequent studies have come from Johns Hopkins University and the University of Minnesota. Particularly relevant is the work of Broman, Nichols, and Kennedy (1975).

In some ways this program has dispelled three illusions. The first is that data taking equals research. The second is that research under medical auspices is necessarily of good quality. The third is that government-centered research represents a better strategy than university-based research. In view of the enormous costs associated with this data taking enterprise, one can only regret that it has not yielded a proportionate return in results from pooled data. The study has yet to fulfill the promise immanent in the perinatal data.

NATIONAL STUDY OF AGING

This prospective longitudinal study of Baltimore residents uses over 800 males identified between the teen years and the nineties. A variety of papers on the social (Stone & Norris, 1966), physiological (Gerstenblith *et al.*, 1977), and biochemical (Rowe, Andres, Tobin, Norris, & Shork, 1976) aspects of aging have emerged. In recent years the limitations of the male, largely college-educated population have been recognized, and plans for studies of women have been formulated. The cycle of study is that each proband takes 3 days of tests every 2 years.

FRAMINGHAM (MASS.) HEART STUDY

In 1949 prospective study began using 5000 men and women free from heart disease. The subjects have been studied biennially, and useful data have emerged. The psychosocial "Type A" personality prone to disease is a product of this interesting study (Haynes, Levine, Scotch, Feinleib, & Kannel, 1978).

CHILDREN IN AN URBAN COMMUNITY

John and Elizabeth Newson are British research workers in Nottingham. The appearance of *Infant Care in an Urban Community* in 1963 has been followed by other studies (Newson & Newson, 1968, 1976a, 1976b) of 700 mothers and their children. To date information has been taken at ages 1, 4, 11, and 16 years of age. At each age the essential technique has been the interview structured by prepared questions. From a design point of view this interesting series of inquiries appears to be stratified by age, with emphasis on each age in isolation. The data have been gathered prospectively, and analyses do not seem to summate data as much as explore thoroughly each stage. Given the superb feel for the data, that seems quite enough, and succeeding volumes present the temporal progress of Mums and their children in Nottingham. An excellent sense of the process of beginning studies is conveyed in a 1976 paper (Newson & Newson, 1976b).

THE BOGALUSA, LOUISIANA HEART STUDY

The premise of this inquiry, whose longitudinal data began to appear in the late 1970s, is that adult's heart problems have developmental origins, and that study of blood pressure, for example, should begin before maturity. The sample consists of 3524 children first studied at ages 5, 8, 11, and 14 years, which is 93% of the population at those ages (Foster, Voors, Webber, Frerichs, & Berenson, 1978). Subsequent studies at 1 year (Voors, Webber, & Berenson, 1979) and at 3 years have been conducted. From the study should emerge a clearer understanding of the origins of hypertension.

ISLE OF WIGHT STUDIES

Beginning in 1964, Rutter, Tizard, Yale, Graham, and Whitmore (1976) studied the school age population of the Isle of Wight. This epidemiological study began with a survey of handicaps, and there have been selected instances of data collection at subsequent child ages, as in the case of children with psychiatric disorders. In the case of enuresis data were available at child ages 5, 7, 10, and 14 years. Some comparisons have been made with children living in inner London. The primary emphasis has been on children in the school years (Rutter, Tizard, & Whitmore, 1970).

INTERNATIONAL CHILDREN'S CENTER
COORDINATE GROWTH STUDIES

In the 1950s child development workers from several major European cities, two in Africa (Dakar and Kampala), and one in the United States (Louisville), formed a consortium for child research on an international scale. A variety of studies have emerged from the relatively small samples in each country, in which the subjects are now in the adult years. The large corpus of studies from a variety of social contexts have application to social pediatrics, public health, clinical medicine, and teaching. In the early 1970s the Stockholm group reported development of children to age 8 years (Klac-

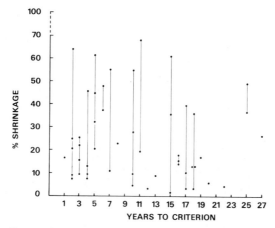

Figure 2.1. Range of sample shrinkage in longitudinal studies (*N* = 50 studies).

kenberg, 1971). A 1977 bibliography lists nearly 1000 publications from this program, which is coordinated from Paris by the Centre International de l'Enfance.

As this review of longitudinal study indicates, apart from the explicit orientation of the research reported in this monograph, we favor prospective longitudinal research that is programmatic. In so doing we are conscious of its hazards, not the least of which is loss of subjects. This may be due to problems of cooperation, and so be procedural; also it can be the case that loss of subjects is an expression of the independent variables or predictors in a research program. This is clearly the hazard in research on aging. In such inquiries frequent testing culminating in a degree of sample attrition may determine when the research must end. On close inspection, however, shrinkage of samples turns out to be less determinate than it seems. In Figure 2.1 we have plotted the shrinkage in percentage of study groups examined over intervals as long as 27 years. The correlation between the length of time a study takes and the loss of subjects is *r* = −.07. Not statistically significant, it shows a clear state of indeterminacy between the two parameters.

Case Studies and Small Sample Studies

Not all prospective studies involve massive samples, just as not all studies cover decades. On this last point there is a perfectly good prospective study of development which lasted 24 hours. That brief span of human time can be enormously significant in the growth of a chick, as Speciale, Nowoczyk, and Jouvet (1976a) have shown. For the nonbiologist it is interesting to see how little attention is paid to describing samples in study of subhuman species. The reason is that the sample is typical of the species; some people believe that it was Piaget's early interest in biology which explains his otherwise inexplicable (and probably unjustifiable) descriptions of samples of children. Other useful studies of small samples over time have been nine former convicts (Glueck & Glueck, 1943), three cases of lobectomy over 16 years (Weiss, 1975), eight people with nutritional problems (Beal, 1965), and dental growth in five people (Lancet, 1930). A particularly interesting small group prospective study is that of a set of five brothers and sisters, first identified by Terman in his earliest studies of the gifted. In the period ending with a 1977 report by Ohanian, information has been reported at intervals, especially on two of the girls.

A number of useful studies over substantial periods of time have reported on only *one* subject in intense case reports. Representative studies are immune deficiency (Williamson, 1977), schizophrenia (Bruch & Cottington, 1942; Takahashi & Gjessing, 1972), and teeth grinding (Hamilton & Whitehead, 1968). In this group we place the original series on human growth by de Montbeillard, gathered between 1759 and 1776.

Commonly, the sample is one person because there is something about the particular individual which is unique. In the case of the study by Williamson, the proband was a child born with no natural immunity to diseases and so forced to live in a sterile atmosphere with a meticulously controlled habitat. Clearly the uniqueness lies in survival to age 4, apart from the nature of the condition.

For the most part, it seems unlikely that studies with small samples will move beyond the realm of curiosities. Today's multivariate statistical analyses requires large rather than small samples. Computers can handle a large number of variables, and the need for substantial subject-to-variable ratios requires that samples be as large as possible. However, the clinical study of a given subject will always be welcome since it is the vehicle for conveying both unique data and special insights.

Contemporary Design

The investigation reported in this volume was designed in the early 1960s, a period in which a series of issues of theoretical importance had yet to be elucidated, let alone resolved. Elsewhere we have touched on the fact that certain cohorts (i.e., children born in a particular year) seem more prone to delinquency than other year-groups. The effect of such empirical outcomes is the realization that it is advisable to separate cohort effects from other effects. Procedurally, Bell (1953) had called for an "accelerated" approach to data taking. As a consequence, single-year age groups have been supplemented by use of several groups on both practical grounds in project research, and on theoretical grounds in the matter of selecting the optimal design for programmatic inquiry. Cohorts might be established at 1-year intervals (e.g., 2, 3, . . . , 6 years, with subsequent cohorts 1 year older) followed for several years by means of annual testing. It is clear that there would be data, eventually, at age 6 on children in several of the annual cohorts. As a consequence one could distinguish whether 6-year-olds were like other 6-year-olds from different cohorts, and cross-validation of any given set of 6-year-olds would be possible.

When this possibility is approached precedurally, we have as an example the study of boys in Calcutta by Rao and Rao (1966). In that inquiry, development from age 6–15 years was accomplished by using several groups for 2 years. By starting on a birthday and taking data on two subsequent birthdays, all data for the developmental span of interest were acquired in 24 months by using several age groups in a *time-lag* design (Baltes, 1968).

In the Nymegen study the "most efficient" arrangement, to use Schaie's approach, was to have six overlapping cohorts with each followed for 5 years. It is clear that that future longitudinal studies will employ consecutive cohorts in order to meet both theoretical and procedural goals. The hazard is that there may be too much compression on grounds of economies in time and money, which might lead to less checks on sources of error due to cohort, age, or the time of measurement. Goldstein (1968) attributes to Tanner the observation that research on body measurements required 20 children measured cross-sectionally to achieve precision in rate of change for each child measured longitudinally.

Archival Studies

The essential property of a data set for longitudinal study is that it be usable for testing hypotheses. By that principle it is not always necessary that the data be gathered by the investigator, or that the data sets have been gathered for the purpose at hand. Data sets which exist in some form, and which are not so asynchronous as to be invalid, occur in many ways. At their weakest, archival data sets consist of information recorded for no intellectual purpose and having few common grounds. At best, there are the data sets in which a principle or organization is recognizable, and from which coherent observations and deductions may flow. As an example of the latter we cite the London Bills of Mortality in the seventeenth century (Graunt, 1662), and of the former the mass of hospital records and vital statistics.

There are times when the obsolete, historical nature of a data set makes it especially suitable for inquiry. Study of children's growth, for example, can be compared from one century to the next. Tanner (1961) has presented data on the height of school boys in a series extending from 1833 to 1958. He also makes comparisons by drawing on data from 1741. Some places are especially fruitful sources of archives. The data presented by Tanner to which we have just referred came from Norway. Public policy in Scandinavia has long favored careful recording of population data. Janson (1975) reports that the first set of regulations to guide creation of accurate demographic data in Sweden were published in 1686. At that same time good public records existed in Dresden and in other population centers. The motives for establishing such records were usually political, since central governments attempted to rationalize their national budgets and to estimate taxation sources and projections. Writing in 1750, Thomas Short thought that the practice of keeping records began with the Bible, saying "The 5th and 11th Chapters of Genesis are *Plain Bills of Mortality.*" For more recent times Short believed public records began in Germany in the fifteenth century. He notes that Henry VIII, on the advice of that zealous civil servant Thomas Cromwell, required in 1538 that every incumbent minister record births, baptisms, weddings, and deaths. Subsequently, Elizabeth refined the system in laws promulgated in 1558 and 1559. Short's own observations followed the pattern set by Graunt a century before; however, he added "New Observations, Natural, Moral, Civil, Political and Medical" on the archival information. Short noted occupational and geographical aspects, items we would describe as demographic, and so contributed to the study of population characteristics.

Overtures into old documents do not qualify as archival research simply because the materials are old. The qualities of precision in reporting and the absence of lacunae (gaps) are also important. Finally, one must be sure that the data are reasonably accurate and not fragmentary.

Records of deaths in the city of York in the sixteenth century do not merely report the date of death, but the hour (Wrigley, 1972). In de Montbeillard's measurements of his son from 1759 to 1776, height is recorded to one-half ligne, a measure which equals 2.25 mm (Sonnini, 1799). Such detail is found because the sensibilities of careful, bookish men tend to be similar in all cultures and in all epochs. Some examples of research in which data over time are an important aspect follow.

GENEALOGY

In the Parma valley of northern Italy meticulous records were kept on births, baptisms, and deaths amid the turbulence of the *cinquecento*. Ten generations of family genealogy can be traced amid 70,000 births. The records of 26 parishes have been linked by Barrai, Moroni, and Cavalli-Sforza (1968), the latter being itself a name rich in associations. In North America the Amish provide a rich vein for tracing pedigrees. Tending to marry only their own (endogamy) and to remain in the areas they originally settled, the Amish have created opportunities for genealogical studies of disease. One-quarter of the Amish in Lancaster County, Pennsylvania, for example, are descended from a man who settled in 1766, Nicholas Stolzfus. McKusick and Cross (1968) have traced several abnormalities of development through archival data on the Amish.

ANTHROPOLOGY

The most longitudinal of data on human affairs are those fragments which tell us about ancient man. Fragments of Amerindian culture have been assembled by Brown and Houart (1975), who used a computer to store their site survey data as an archive. Similarly, the anthropologist Kunter (1976) has extended our knowledge of still more ancient man. Analyzing Lebanese skeletal remains from the Iron Age, he has created a picture of life as brief and tough. Many of the individuals in this skeletal archive were children, and all showed evidence of great physical strain.

HISTORY

Less pathological but no less interesting are the archival data in official records. Thrupp (1977) traced out a picture of the alien population in fifteenth-century England using the archival data of the Public Records Office in London. For later periods, Baulant (1968) has explicated the price of grain in seventeenth-century Paris, shedding a great deal of light on the background to public events.

GENETICS

A most interesting archival set of twin data is reported by Harrald and Hauge (1958). Their data cover all twins born in Denmark between 1870 and 1910. Within the same northern European context, we cite the assembly of data on health problems in Iceland. From Bjarnason and Magnusson's (1975) work we conclude that colossal health archives can be envisaged. Bjarnason, Fridrikson, and Magnusson (1968) have described computer linkage of data sets on pregnancy, death, and blood donations.

PSYCHIATRY

Occasionally, data on individuals are gathered with sufficient care and maintained with long-term outcomes in mind so that, given acquisition of criterion data at a later time, unique insights are possible. Case records on a child guidance population were elaborated by acquisition of adult data in the work of Robbins (1966). The resulting "natural history" has become a landmark of archival investigation. We note, however, that assembling dossiers of a heterogeneous nature leads merely to the trivia of what is called "file-drawer" research. Perhaps the most interesting psychiatric research using archives is that sponsored by the World Health Organization (WHO). This group has assembled data on schizophrenia from several parts of the world, and analyses are far from complete at the moment (Sartorius, Jablensky, & Shapiro, 1977).

SOCIAL PROBLEMS

Human acts of a different quality have also been studied by means of archives. Project Metropolitan (Janson, 1978) has created data on delinquency in Stockholm. Other Swedish data analyzed by Curman and Nylander (1976) have examined delinquency, alcoholism, and related problems in adults who were referred to child guidance clinics a decade before. From Dutch military and social data on 200,000 males, Belmont, Wittes, and Stein (1977) discovered that boys in one-child families at all social levels have the best developmental outcomes.

EDUCATION

Surprisingly, few of the many sets of school records qualify as useable research archives. Education is organized as a decentralized process in many ways, and it is the exceptional situation in which school records turn out to be useful. Some success has been reported from the Follow-Through sequel to Headstart. Ferb, Larson, and Napior (1977), for example, reported that the requirement of complete data reduced 8000 potentially useful pupil records to a usable 2500. On the other hand, Rubin and Balow (1977) have been highly successful at extending perinatal histories through the elementary school years.

GROWTH

Finally, we note the opportunities for studies of how the body develops from archival sets. The Harvard Growth Studies assembled an excellent corpus of information on dental growth (Moorrees, 1959). Falkner (1962) combined data sets from published accounts, and from the aggregate generated physical growth standards for children.

This account of archives would be incomplete without reference to the hazards which mere assembly of data can present. Much of the data from the Collaborative Perinatal Study of 56,000 pregnancies can only be analyzed as geographical subsets, vide the Minneapolis data brought to usefulness by Bruce Balow and Rosalyn Rubin, and the Baltimore data set extended by Janet Hardy. The essential hazards are the loss of a unifying perspective on questions of procedure due to problems of coordination and, more fundamentally, the absence of an overarching intellectual question to guide deductions about methodology and to settle procedural questions. To some extent the state of the art today is a matter of scope. The writer's research archive, from which the data of this report are drawn, contains upward of a million data elements. In addition, we quote Goldstein's (1968) report of 10^7 items in the 1958 NCDS File. Theoretically, there is no limit to how much information is available in computers, and we tend to underestimate the quantity. The International Educational Survey, sponsored by UNESCO and reported in the mid 1970s, assembled 110 million pieces of information from a quarter-million pupils in 20 countries. The entire data set was used as an archival set and lead to the conclusion that the home is consistently the single greatest influence on school achievement.

In the matter of archives Feller assembled in 1976 the first directory of *educational* data in the form of computer tapes held by the Federal government and available to the public. Presumably, personal data could be similarly catalogued on the basis of taxes, social security, and military records. The amount of information held by national, state, and local governments is enormous. Curiously, some of the literature on data banks does not mention questions of privacy and security with regard to national, computer-based archives, although most countries have laws protecting confidentiality of individual records.

We point out that there are procedural problems associated with use of pooled data sets, as the collaborative perinatal study has demonstrated. In reality, there is the practical limit to mastery of the strengths and weaknesses of particular data elements. It is useful to know, for example, that Dr. Jones never assigns Apgar scores of 10 to even perfect newborns, but settles invariably for a high score of 9. Such idiosyncrasies are not critical, but they are interesting, and tend to be lost when data manipulation is undertaken on a large scale. When data sets are credited with accuracy and a misplaced degree of confidence, the reason sometimes turns out to be that users are at a distance, metaphorically, from the reality of assembling data elements case by case. It follows, then, that the increasing popularity and surprising respectability of what is currently called *secondary analysis* of data (Bryant & Wortman, 1978; Burstein, 1978) is a mixed blessing. Reanalysis of data sets can obviously be fruitful, but it is highly unlikely that secondary analysts fully understand the idiosyncracies of data sets.

In all fairness we acknowledge that primary analysts, that is, people analyzing their own data, can be quite taxed in the matter of comprehending special characteristics of variables. The state of the art in computer storage means virtually unlimited capacity. Proportionately, the problem of understanding data increases with the passage of time. When data are gathered and analyzed over decades, the challenge to people joining staffs that have

Procedures

3

Introduction

Having considered the strengths and weaknesses of a large number of longitudinal studies, we now turn to the details of this inquiry. It is an analysis of influences on the first 5 years of life, in a cohort age 13 at the time of writing. The sheer volume of data and the convenience of age 5 years as a developmental milestone for the earliest years account for the time span covered in this report. This report does not stand alone; in communications listed in the Bibliography are other studies on selected aspects of the earliest years of Old Man River's Children.

In this chapter we report the procedures employed. In so doing we are conscious that the procedural aspects of longitudinal study are not as well described in the literature as in theory. We can, however, shed a little light, and share a few hard-earned lessons with the reader. Do all cohorts shrink? Is cooperation a middle-class phenomenon? How does one convert case study data into group data? We engage these and other questions, conscious that they convey the warp and woof of programmatic research on human development in the earliest years.

Finally, we respond to some of the intellectual questions. Is there an alternative to chi-square as a research tool? What multivariate techniques are currently available, and how does one combine discrete and continuous data? By what steps do test results on a given child, plus those from several hundred other boys and girls come together and, in turn, get combined with a data analytic system within a computer?

The Cohort

The birth cohort formed in 1966–1967 was 50% black and 50% white. The full range of socioeconomic status was represented, and the mean occupational level was blue-collar. Subsequent research has shown that maternal educational level is an important influence on children. Table 3.1 shows the characteristics of the cohort. For all subjects the distribution of level of maternal education is essentially a normal curve. For white mothers it is slightly skewed at upper levels, and for black mothers it is substantially skewed toward the lower levels. Thus, the cohort is representative through the influential parameter of maternal educational level. In both racial subgroups there is the full range of parental education. There are

TABLE 3.1

1966-7 COHORT: MATERNAL EDUCATION

(N=1008)

Level of Maternal Education	Race			
	Black	White	Total	All ss.
	%	%	%	%
8th grade or less	15	5	20	8
Part high school	41	18	59	26
High School graduate	35	46	81	42
Part College	8	22	30	17
College	1	10	11	7

black mothers with college experience on the one hand, and there are white mothers with less than 8 years of schooling, on the other.

In the case of perinatal social class, Figure 3.1 illustrates the characteristics of the cohort by summarizing McGuire and White (1955) scores, which are based on source of income, occupation, and education. We see that the theoretical range of scores from 14 to 84 is present in the case of all families. McGuire and White scores are *high* for *low* socioeconomic level, and low for high level, an item which will become important in subsequent chapters. The scores from the entire 1000 subjects have a mean of 56.21, ($\sigma = 15.57$). The deciles from low SES to high SES, expressed in McGuire and White scores, are also given in Figure 3.1, which shows all families, white, and black families. In Figure 3.1 we see the cumulative percentages for the black families are scores of approximately 50 on the McGuire and White scale, which places them in the lower half of the distribution. While the SES scores of white families also extend to the highest SES scores (i.e., lowest status) they also extend as far as the lower twenties which is high status. The mean SES score for whites is 47.70, and the mean for blacks is 65.78. The white SES level is one-half a standard deviation above the grand mean of 56.21 ($\sigma = 15.57$), and the black mean SES level is below the grand mean social level to a slightly larger degree. It is helpful to note that the number of black and white families at birth was almost equal.

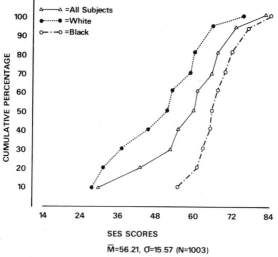

Figure 3.1. Distribution of McGuire and White three-factor SES scores for black families, white families, and all families.

In the matter of perinatal risk, a set of categories was defined using the nomenclature and coding of the International Classification of Diseases (1962). ICDA categories codify, for example, toxaemic and placental disorders, plus child-centered disorders. Selected risk elements were codified using inter alia, the categories 640-, 670-, and 760-. These categories and codes from ICDA were used by obstetric and pediatric staffs in the five hospitals, two of which are teaching hospitals. The writer read all 1000 developmental histories and assigned a 0–5 rating based on separate rating scale of biorisk. The mean level of biorisk is <1, which is good, since we are talking about real children, but does include some infants given the maximum rating of 5, due to their unsatisfactory condition in the perinatal period. We can report that the perinatal phase of the research became the occasion for two hospitals making Apgar ratings (1962) in the first few minutes of life a standard procedure for all deliveries.

A question which arises in all prospective studies is the matter of attrition—the loss of subjects over time. The survey of prospective studies lasting from 1 month to 27 years shown in Figure 2.1 leads to the conclusion

TABLE 3.2

SOCIAL CLASS* DISTRIBUTION (in Percent) BY RACE

Range of SES**	Race		
	Black	White	Total
14-39 (High)	2.3	30.5	17.2
40-56	7.6	31.8	20.4
67-62	25.0	21.1	22.9
63-69	29.0	11.1	16.6
70-84 (Low)	36.0	5.5	19.8
	99.9	100.0	99.9

*A scale devised by McGuire & White (1955) incorporating occupation, education, and income source.

**The interpretation of the scale scores may be facilitated by the following examples:
1. A self employed businessman who had completed college would receive a score of 34.
2. A seasonally employed, semi-skilled worker with only eight grades of education completed would receive a score of 72.

that it is naive to assume that the loss of subjects is a function of years to criterion. Slightly more useful is the number of contacts with a cohort (i.e., attrition is due to repeated contacts) however, that is a generalization which is inadequate. In the 5 years of development of this cohort which are reported here, the dynamics of attrition and expansion were interesting. That is, there was an initial loss of cooperation from about 100 "false cooperatives." In the case of the remaining 900 or so, 700 provided data at age 6 months. However, the data-taking period included the day on which Dr. Martin Luther King was killed. The resulting tension cast a pall on both the efforts of some caseworkers and on the cooperation of some families yet to be contacted. While perhaps 50 of these families were lost to the study for that period, cases in process were disrupted by the reactions of some casework-ers. We mention this not merely to explain attrition, but to convey the sensitivities of field research to the realities of social forces.

In Table 3.3 we see an interesting thing; while the numbers given for children studies are all below 1000 and also below the 900 alluded to earlier, they rise rather than fall beginning after the 12-month testing. The peak for any 12-month period is age 4; the peak for any single testing period after 12 months is the group tested at age 48 months.

In this regard it is important to point out that case-tracing had become quite complex by age 2½ years. Accordingly, the cohort was split into a birthday group tested in the winter, and a half-year group. Thus, from 36 months on, the number of cases found is a proportion not of the entire cohort, but of one-half of it. The $N = 825$ for child age 4 years describes the proportion of the cohort as a whole, and probably should be assessed against or theoretically testable—if traceable—group of 900.

Case-finding prior to testing has been an interesting item. The initial selection of families excluded those who felt they might leave the area soon. Moving beyond the metropolitan area has generally been no great problem for testing purposes. Some of our families have moved to the other side of the world. They generally have given us notice, and usually provided an address. In such cases we use a local university to find testers, and logistics have constituted a minor procedure once they were established. The greater problem has been the inner-city family who move several times a year, but may be merely a few blocks away, shielded by family and friends from prying. Use of recorded "third-parties" who always know where a family is has been helpful. In some instances the corner tavern has been the rendezvous leading to a fully cooperative—if discrete—family. This applied aspect of prospective study contrasts with the accounts of wholly middle-class cohorts dutifully reporting to an academic center in many in-vestigations. Going to them has been the key to developing data on families of lower socioeconomic status and the proband in most instances. It is

TABLE 3.3

COHORT SIZE FROM BIRTH TO AGE SIX YEARS: POPULATION II

Child Age	N Probands	Year Group N
Birth (T$_1$)	1,008	1,008
6 Months (T$_2$)	693	
12 Months (T$_3$)	580	580
24 Months (T$_4$)	724	724
30 Months (T$_5$)	223	
36 Months (T$_6$)	380	
42 Months (T$_7$)	376	756
48 Months (T$_8$)	421	
54 Months (T$_9$)	404	825
60 Months (T$_{10}$)	414	
66 Months (T$_{11}$)	392	806

important to record that social-class level has not differentiated mothers and their interest in child study. For several years the only formal refusal to cooperate came from the wife of a pediatrician.

CHILD ATTAINMENT

We turn now to the matter of what it is we have attempted to study in the form of the child-centered data. Essentially, we wish to convey a degree of self-awareness about the nature of young children. In a primitive way, the criterion measures in Table 3.7 resolve the problem implicitly; a child is what the criterion measures reveal. However, our approach has been more self-conscious than that, starting with the question of the aspects of functioning one needs to study in order to group the process of growth.

A child is as complex as an adult and, from a methodological view, somewhat less easy to analyze. The complexity takes the form of processes. Our datum is, in fact, the headings for Chapters 4 to 9, but that too is a facile way to avoid the central issue in study of development. We start by observing that children have a material, corporal form which grows remarkably in the first two decades of life. The alterations in morphology are many; velocity of change is itself changeable, as at puberty. To assess such matters there is a large set of indices combining external measures of growth in height and weight. Examples go back as far as 1836, and include, for example, the ponderal index, Tuxford's and Quetelet's indexes, and dribble off into endless combinations of measures between points of the skeleton. We have calculated a number of the morphological ratios for our data set, but report here stature in inches and weight in pounds as unequivocal measures of how the physical body changes.

Our data on physical measurement are a modest overture into the growth of St. Louis children, preceded by a study whose logistical aspects alone would require attention. In 1892 W. T. Porter (1894) measured the physical characteristics of 18,059 girls and 16,295 boys in the public schools of St. Louis, and found substantial differences in patterns of growth when height and weight were grouped by fathers' occupation. A remarkable accomplishment is Porter's acquisition of one million pieces of data in 54 days during the winter. Shortly after publication of his research Porter was called to a college in Cambridge, Massachusetts—and never heard from again.

In addition to being physical, children have dynamic properties; they move, they talk, they think, and they behave in relation to other people in ways that express their natures. At this point, however, the would-be inquirer begins to encounter problems. Not all of the processes of expression can be traced back to reified "mind" or "personality," like the operator of a crane dimly perceived in a little box who closely directs the motions of a large machine. And when such motions seeming to indicate hidden states of motivation, attitudes, and self-perceptions are attributed to young children, the leads become hard to trace. We do not say to Tiffy at 3, "How is your self-concept today?" As a consequence, our formulation of a self-conscious, volitional person, however firmly asserted, wilts a little in the face of procedural difficulties. Even so, we press on. If Tiffy cannot report the state of her psyche perhaps she can be led to display it, or her mother can describe indicants of the concept we are after.

In that spirit we view small persons as physical entities with "faculties," to use self-consciously and comfortably the idiom of a former age. In particular, we are interested in the contents of their minds, how they verbalize and express themselves, how far they have come in the process of developing the interactive and expressive modalities of human intercourse; put in other ways we might say we want to know where they are, and in what posture, on the road to becoming social beings and to achieving a level of realizable potentials. In that regard, we view children as people molded by circumstance interacting with genetic potentials. On that topic we acknowledge a *constitutionalism,* a view that rejects the extremes of environmentalism and geneticism, which reject the influence of each other. We feel that somatic elements are perhaps more neglected than others at the moment; bodies lay down thresholds which environmental influences may, if they mind their manners, cross. That is, we feel environments affect children, but only after the autonomous systems of the body have projected a responsiveness, a sensitivity to external events.

In all of these themes and views there is the matter of priorities. We express them in this volume by the relative frequency with which we have taken data in various domains. We assert the importance of social development as a dimension of behavior, of expression, of becoming a fuller person. However, in developing a map of influences on the course of early development, we assign it a lower priority than language, the life of the mind, and so have gathered—and here report—less information. However, it is our hope to convey that we see in the early years dynamic processes within little friends whose complexity is as refreshing as it is impressive.

Variables

BIOLOGICAL PREDICTORS

In this investigation of influences on child development, a total of 19 predictor variables are employed, including subscales. The variables, which are schematized in Table 3.4, were grouped as four influences: Biological, Social, Family, and Maternal. The earliest set is the group of biological variables: birthweight, biological risk, Apgar scores, and sex.

Birthweight. A large number of studies have shown that low birthweight (Drillien, 1969) and high birthweight both place children at risk for a full continuum of childhood problems from cerebral palsy to learning disorders.

Biological Risk. The writer's formulation of degree of somatic disorder at birth is biological risk. Summarized in Table 3.4, *risk* is based on four elements or combinations of them. Based on review of the literature (Colborn & Salzman, 1960; Gleiss & Holderburg, 1963; Jekel *et al.,* 1972), Apgar scores in the first 5 minutes of life were considered significant if 7 or less. Weight at birth using the WHO standard of 5.5 lb was set aside in

TABLE 3.4

RATING SYSTEM FOR BIOLOGICAL RISK AT BIRTH

Risk Degree	Apgar	B. Wt.	Delivery Age (0)	(U)	Categorical	Risk Degree
0						0
1	7	5 - 4.5 lb.	38-39	15		1
2	6	4.5 - 4	40-41	14	e.g. Congenital Anomalies, Down's Syndrome, Cerebral Palsy, etc.	2
3	5	4 - 3.5	42-43	13		3
4	4	3.5 - 3	44-45	12		4
5	3	3 lb.	45	11		5

favor of a clinically more rigorous standard. High and low age at delivery was formulated as a degree of risk, according to the literature (Drillien, 1969; Jordan, 1976b; Babson, Gorham, & Clark, 1970). In this regard recent research on maternal age from the St. Louis Baby Study (Jordan & Spaner, 1978) indicates that adolescent delivery is less of a problem than generally believed. Categorical problems, for example diagnoses of congenital disorders and neurological appraisals, were used; rating these cases was more difficult, but can best be described as conservative.

The accuracy of this last statement is to some extent an empirical matter, and we present Table 3.5 which shows the distribution of ratings. Seventy-six percent of the probands were rated at zero risk. Sixteen percent of the birth cohort received mild to moderate ratings of 1 and 2, while 8% were rated at serious risk with ratings of 3 to 5. In Table 3.5 the percentiles are given and show that ratings of 3 or more are quite serious, and describe children in the worst condition. On the other hand, Table 3.5 also shows that three-quarters of the children had a 0 rating for this parameter. From the statistical point of view the risk parameter is relatively weak; but we are talking about real children and the relatively low degree of risk is clearly welcome.

Apgar Scores. Apgar scores are descriptions of newborns' status, usually in the first 5 minutes after delivery in which a numerical value of 0, 1, or 2 is assigned to five items for a perfect score of 10. The five components of

TABLE 3.5

RATING OF BIOLOGICAL RISK

Rating	N	Cumulative Percentage	Percentile
0	766	76	38
1	110	11	82
2	46	5	89
3	43	4	94
4	17	2	97
5	25	2	99

the Apgar score are heart rate, respiratory effort, reflex irritability, muscle tone, and color. Short-term predictive power is good (Rubin, Balow, & Hara, 1975).

Sex. In recent years it has been conventional to formulate sex differences as consequences of socialization through role stereotypy. While that point of view is unexceptionable, we add the formulation in this inquiry that sex differences arise from the genetic code which guides somatic development. There are sex differences in children's performance and it seems unreasonable to set them aside (Tanner, Prader, Habich, & Ferguson-Smith, 1959). We formulate sex as a constitutional element in this predictor set, grouping it with other biological variables.

SOCIAL PREDICTORS

A concern for the influences on child development incorporates the reality that circumstances of life affect virtually all aspects of growth. Accordingly, six items of social information have been gathered at several ages, as Table 3.6 shows.

Socioeconomic Status. McGuire and White's (1955) system was used to calculate an SES score from information gathered during interviews in the obstetric wards. The McGuire and White system weighs education, occupation, and *source* of income (rather than income), and creates scores ranging from 14 for *highest* SES level to 84 for the *lowest* level.

Race. In this inquiry race is categorized as non-black or other, a system in which the ascribed status of orientals, for example, places them in the majority culture. In fact, non-blacks excluded Asians, Indians, Mexicans, and other potential ethnic groups.

Parental Information. At child age 3 fathers' occupations were identified using Hollingshead's (1957) nominal system. Mothers' years of schooling were recorded, and mothers' place of work—at home, part-time out of the home, and full-time out of the home—were recorded. At child age 5, the education of the head of the household was recorded once more, to reflect changes in the circumstances of life over the first 5 years.

TABLE 3.6

PREDICTOR SETS EXTENDED WITH INCREASING
AGE OF THE COHORT

Predictor Set	Birth	3 yrs.	4 yrs.	5 yrs.
A. Biological Predictor Set.	Birthweight Bio Risk Apgar Sex			
B. Social Predictor Set	SES Race	Pop Occupation Mom Occupation Mom Education		HoH. Education
C. Family Predictor Set	Birth Order	N Siblings Father Figure	STIM	Dwelling Type
D. Maternal Predictor Set	Marital Status Delivery Age AFI$_{68}$ Social Risk			

FAMILY PREDICTORS

Research by Kukuk, Levine, and Meyer (1978) on sources of achievement in six large cities has shown that family structure is a mediating variable; this effect was particularly evident in Cleveland and in St. Louis.

Birth Order. While less central a variable than it used to be (Zajonc, 1976) the order a child holds in the sibship is interesting information. Belmont, Wittes, and Stein (1977), for example, have shown that highest development occurred in Dutch children who are singletons.

Number of Siblings. A related variable is the number of children in the family. In this cohort the number was as high as 13, at age 3 years. As a way to convey the dynamics of crowding we recall the following report:

There are six children in this family and they have doubled up with the baby sitter who has 2 children making 11 people living in 3 rooms in a tar paper shack by the side of a railroad track in the back country of far west county. There is no electricity, no gas, no water. They cook on a camp stove, use kerosene lamps, and haul water. The mother works by day, and father at night with some day work.

The home was filthy and it was difficult to find a place to sit. There were five dogs and several cats roaming about, also some rabbits. The children were poorly clad and most had colds. (Caseworker)

Fortuntely, the average number of children with whom the study children lived at age 3 was less than three.

Father Figure. At age 3 we recorded the identity of the male figure when there was one. The categories were none, male figure, and biological father. The last category is the stereotype of family structure, but the biological father was not present in 27% of the families studied at age 3.

Dwelling Type. At age 5 we recorded the home as a separate dwelling, an apartment, or a mobile home. Only a handful of children did not live in a one-family dwelling or apartment.

STIM. Whatever the objective character of a family and its dwelling, the priority question for inquiries into development is the potential for stimulating children. With the appearance of Caldwell's (1970) STIM scale it became possible to assess the quality of home-living. Published research (Jordan, 1978a) has demonstrated that Professor Caldwell's quantified description, known as HOME, is a powerful tool for studying development.

MATERNAL PREDICTORS

The primary caregiver for young children is the mother. Accordingly, we have acquired progressively more delicate information about mothers' beliefs over a period of years.

Maternal Ideology. Ernhart and Loevinger's (1969) Family Problems Scale is psychometrically rigorous and explores maternal ideology. Existing as a questionnaire, the scale was administered orally to mothers of suspect literacy. At birth the authoritarianism scale (AFI) was administered. This scale was subsequently rescored to refine the 1965 authoritarianism measure into what we call in this monograph AFI_{68};[1] we have analyzed this variable elsewhere (Jordan, 1970).

Anxiety. Six months after delivery the Bendig (1956) version of the Taylor Anxiety Scale was administered. Obviously, administration at the time of delivery would produce heightened scores, and so administration was delayed.

Intelligence. At child age 30 months the Quick Test of Vocabulary (Ammons & Ammons, 1962) was administered as a measure of mothers' intelligence.

As a final point in the matter of predictor variables we touch on the question of directionality. Our expectation is that any given predictor variable reaching statistical significance will exert its influence in a particular direction. In the case of sex and race, for example, higher criterion scores of weight tend to be associated with males when sex is influential; in the case of race we expect that nonwhite children will tend to have lower criterion scores in the cognitive domain. The data in the reporting chapters give the directionality of specific variables when significant.

---

[1] We express our thanks to Professor Claire Ernhart.

Koplyay, Gott, and Elton (1973) have pointed out that programming can help the investigator faced with a maze of complex terms in the form of interaction regression. In their system the computer program takes the variables and maximizes the proportion of criterion variance (R^2) by assaying the contributions of various combinations of variables and polynomials. We have examined the comparability of multiple linear regression and interaction regression, using a subset of the data of this inquiry from a developmental span of several years. From that methodological inquiry we concluded that interaction regression copes with the range of hypothetical forms of variables, and also yields results on positive and negative outcomes comparable to those one might obtain by use of multiple regression (Jordan, 1978a). In that inquiry there were five predictors plus the criterion from just under 200 boys and girls. While there has been speculation on the comparability of multiple and interaction regression, this study may be the only empirical examination of the matter to date.

TABLE 3-7

CRITERION MEASURES AT TEN LIFE AGES

Child Age	Physical (a) Height	(b) Weight	Intellectual	Linguistic	Somatic	Social	Motor
					DOMAINS OF DEVELOPMENT		
6 Months	Height	Weight			Ad Hoc Scale		
12 Months	"	"					
24 Months	"	"	PAR *Intellectual* PAR *Information* PAR *Ideation* PAR *Creativity*	VLDS		PAR *Responsibility*	
30 Months	"	"		*Ammons' FRPVT*			
36 Months	"	"	PPVT (A)	PAR *Communication*	PAR *Physical*		PAR *Ambulation* PAR *Manipulation*
42 Months	"	"	PPVT (A)	PAR *Communication*	PAR *Physical*		PAR *Ambulation* PAR *Manipulation*
48 Months	"	"	Preschool Inventory Boehm T. of Concepts	P.I. *Assoc. Vocab.*		P.I. *Personal Social Responsiveness*	Copy Forms
54 Months	"	"	Preschool Inventory Boehm T. of Concepts	P.I. *Assoc. Vocab.*		P.I. *Personal Social Responsiveness*	Copy Forms
60 Months	"	"	WPPSI *Vocabulary*	ITPA *Audit. Assoc.*			
66 Months	"	"	WPPSI *Vocabulary*	ITPA *Audit. Assoc.*			

CRITERIA

In this inquiry 46 criteria of development were gathered from ages 6 to 60 months. The variables are grouped in six domains (see Table 3.7).

Physical Variables. Height to one-quarter inch and weight to one-quarter pound were gathered by standardized procedures, using calibrated instruments, and supervised by a staff nurse. At birth and 6 months recumbent length was used.

Intellectual Criteria. The following measures of intellectual development were employed. At 2 years, four subscores of the Preschool Attainment Record (Doll, 1958) were employed. Through an interview technique, we went to great pains to turn test items into direct measures of child performance whenever possible. At age 3 the Peabody Picture Vocabulary Test (A) was employed. At 4 we gave Caldwell's Preschool Inventory and Boehm's Test of Basic Concepts. At age 5 we employed the *Vocabulary* subtest of Wechsler's Primary and Preschool Scale of Intelligence.

Linguistic Criteria. At age 2 the linguistic criterion of development was Mecham's (1958) Verbal Language Development Scale. A second scale was the Ammons and Ammons' (1958) Full Range Picture Vocabulary Test. At age 3 we administered the *Communication* subtest of the Preschool Attainment Record. At 4 years we used the *Associative Vocabulary* of the Preschool Inventory, and at age 4 we administered the *Auditory Association* subtest of the Illinois Test of Psycholinguistic Abilities.

Somatic Criteria. At 6 months the writer's Ad Hoc Scale of Development was used to conduct structured interviews with mothers. The *Physical* subtest of the Preschool Attainment Record was used at age 3.

Social Criteria. As with the somatic criteria this is a brief set. The *Responsibility* domain of the Preschool Attainment Record was used at age 2, and the *Personal Social Responsiveness* scale of the Preschool Inventory was administered at age 4 years.

Motoric Criteria. The *Ambulation* and *Manipulation* components of the Preschool Attainment Record were operationalized as much as possible, for example the child was asked to hop, at age 3. At age 4 a measure of fine rather than gross motor skill was employed, which was the Copy Forms test developed by Graham, Berman, and Ernhart (1960).

As another observation we call attention to the mean scores given in subsequent chapters for the criterion variables. In virtually all cases observed means are at or close to normative means. This has the effect of validating the general application of results obtained on developmental tests from the cohort. We mean, however, for this to be a report on the metropolitan St. Louis cohort only; and while conventional means suggest generalizing to groups conforming to norms, we mention them here solely to indicate that the cohort was similar to other groups of children in performance at specific ages.

Deliberately missing from the data set are variables whose gathering would have been a source of anxiety for children. For example, we have taken no blood samples, and have confined physical measures to noninvasive weighing and measuring. In a group of children we obtained a hair sample to check for levels of lead poisoning.

Not all data have been taken and some have been given. For example, we have distributed lists of clinics providing free inoculations against childhood disease. This has been done on two grounds. First, the time is passed when the population passively acquiesces to "scientific" requests. Second, ethical considerations require that even nonintrusive research provide a quid pro quo in the form of a social service. Over the years we have continued to supply case studies at parents' authorization to pediatricians and to school psychologists. This *data-giving* aspect of programmatic research is important if a project is to be a responsible element in the world of childhood.

Gathering and Processing Data

The basic unit of study has been the individual study child (proband) delivered in one of five St. Louis metropolitan hospitals. The five hospitals were selected with the goal of identifying a cohort representative of the population in the metropolitan area. On the basis of advice from experts, four area hospitals were chosen. At the time the cohort was founded, the hospitals provided service to inner-city black, inner-city white, and suburban white and black middle-class families. Because few of the latter group were appearing in the obstetric units, it was decided to find a fifth hospital where middle-class black families seemed more identifiable. Negotiations to use this last, fifth, hospital went so slowly, due to the intellectual pretensions of key administrators, that this strategy became operational quite late in the 4-month period for case identification. As a result the number of middle-class black children is less than we had originally hoped for.

The actual process of casetaking was structured in order to facilitate subsequent data taking. A span of 4 months, December–March, was used to generate a proband at perinatal risk plus a control, allowing for representation by social class and race. The specification by month has meant that subsequent data taking has been structured to provide a target population by month, week, and day. Alternatives in prospective longitudinal studies have been used. In the case of the studies by J. W. B. Douglas and associates, all 5362 newborns in England, Wales, and Scotland in 1 *week* in March 1946 were studied (Douglas, 1967, 1976). Another British study, the National Child Development Study, also chose one week in March, but the year was 1958 (Fogelman, 1976). Our use of 4 to 5 months has avoided the implicit problem of taking anniversary data in an unnecessarily concentrated span (i.e., around a particular week). December–March was selected since it would place all children, nominally, in the same year of schooling, and would pose no reciprocal hazard to timing visits for testing, except during Christmas and New Years. These dates are obviously manageable by making appointments ahead of time. The spacing permitted recruitment of a permanent staff of caseworkers who, during the time span of this corpus of data, took data for 4 to 5 months, twice a year. This schedule provided permanent employment for caseworkers, secretaries, and others. The schedule has provided time within any calendar year after the first year for training examiners, vacations, and the realities of programmatic, as opposed to project, research. In the latter group of contingencies we include visits from funding agencies.

As a procedural note we report that the probands do not constitute a "captive" population; the individual families have no common bond and do not, to the best of our knowledge, know any other family. This contrasts with the situation in which subjects for longitudinal study attend the same school, endure the same prison, or share an interest in an activity. That state of affairs results in the advantages of group testing once subjects have attained a requisite degree of maturity, but also carries the hazards of self-consciousness through group identity. This element can lead to a more than passive role in research, and provides political hazards for applied field research in volatile segments of an urban community.

As a second procedural note, we report that all testing has been carried out by examiners matched with children by race, and occasionally by sex. In addition, caseworkers have seen the same child annually, creating a sustained relationship with the family. On the basis of that expanding relationship, it became possible to obtain test data from mothers and to obtain sensitive information without destroying future cooperation. Once more we point to the difference between project research ("grab the data and run") and programmatic inquiry in which the dynamics of any single interview increase the probability of future cooperation, or destroy it. At the time of writing we have taken data from the cohort for 12 years. In some instances the families mail unsolicited materials on the children. The value of this, of course, is that we can fill out the rest of a child's life beyond a photograph.

Since there have been deaths, we have shared sorrows as well as joys with the families:

It started out to be a happy summer vacation. It ended in disaster. The parents, Mary Ann and her younger brother visited first with grandparents in Minnesota and then finished their vacation in St. Louis with Mrs. B's parents. I visited them at the grandparents' home and tested Mary Ann; she was a very wise, precocious child of 5, and scored 61 out of a possible 64 on the Caldwell.

I wished them a pleasant journey home to California. When it came time to contact the family again we learned that Mary Ann was killed in an automobile accident the day after I was there! (Caseworker)

It should be noted that data taking has not been without its risks. The investigator has had to insist that caseworkers not enter some housing units due to risk to life and limb.

Billy's home is the most hostile. One sibling was literally beaten up the stairs by the man of the house because he was playing on the sidewalk by the house. The man was most rude to me and was humiliating to the mother. (Caseworker)

Procedures for taking data have started with reviewing the salience of domains of development to the age of the cohort in an approaching testing period. As the later chapters will show, we have data in several domains, and the domains vary with the age of the children. The only constant domain of measurement has been weight and height.

After selection of domains and test procedures within them, the next step has been training examiners. Simultaneously, addresses have been validated and some families have been traced. There is a literature on this topic (Crider, Willits, & Bealer, 1972), but it can be reduced to saying that persistence pays off, and few people can really disappear. With assignment of family data, but not development data that might distort perceptions of test performance, caseworkers made appointments. In the earliest years such dates were on the birthday, but this became impractical when children were old enough to get excited, and a leeway of a few days has been tolerated.

In the matter of tests and measurements we have gone to great pains to be exact. Examiners were trained to high consistency in administration; in some instances all scoring was done by a supervisor, who checked all cases. In the matter of physical development, we have checked weight to one-quarter pound, using calibrated instruments, and have standardized all other measuring procedures.

Once gathered and checked, data were recorded on 80-column sheets that were checked before punch cards were cut. The final form of data recording has been a cumulative data tape, with disk and card backups. All original files have been shredded under university supervision. Since data are recorded by a complex file number and stored out-of-town, it is not surprising that there have been no problems of security. Were access to data gained, which would include circumventing a password, one would merely obtain from the computer a string of several hundred numerals for each of 1000 files indistinguishable, numerically, one from the other.

Future longitudinal investigations should be able to process data with greater efficiency. Use of optical scanning sheets permits economical recording of quantified information and also facilitates transfer to storage in an economic style. In addition, certain kinds of data can be taken automatically and transmitted by electronic devices. In the Nymegen longitudinal study, Prahl-Anderson, Pollman, Raaben, and Peters (1972) reported techniques of automated anthropometry, as they described it. Distances, weight, circumferences, and other measurements are taken by electronic devices attached to standard instruments. The resulting measurements are then fed by wire into devices leading to punch cards and, ultimately, to a tape. In work by John *et al.* (1977) on EEG readings, the process goes one step further. Brain wave readings of 2 minutes' duration have been fed by long lines to a computer 50 miles away. There they are processed and the 2-minute sample is stretched and analyzed. The output includes a schematic localization of the site in the brain of faulty EEGs. There is no hand-processing stage between attaching electrodes in one place and inspecting a printout in another.

In the matter of completeness of data for any single child, one tends to think of the problem of noncooperators or nonresponders. We observe that the more interesting group, as we write at child age 12 years, is the set of people providing complete data at all ages. In this regard, we have another expression of the view that social class does not distinguish people who are cooperative and noncooperative. At the time of writing we have just deciphered some notes offered by a barely literate mother. Her interest in child development persists, and she has been immensely helpful over the years.

A strategy we have deliberately chosen to set aside is provision of missing data through regressing or interpolating techniques. While this leads to a sample size which is less than one might hope for, it respects the integrity of data carefully gathered by dedicated people over many years.

With regard to the data stored in the computer, we also keep there the data analytic systems that we have modified to provide additional analyses. In the main, the reports we produce use either a program providing multiple linear regression or one providing interaction regression analyses. By means of suitable programming, we call up the data set of complete information on the variables of interest. We then call up multivariate program with specification of how the data are to be treated and analyzed.

Data Subsets

It is relatively easy to oversimplify the problem of sample size and variation in cohort research. Viewed closely the topic has several interesting aspects. A sample of any size may be used to form subgroups; that is variables $A, \ldots, K$ may be gathered on some subjects (Group 1), but variables $D, \ldots, N$ may be gathered on another group (Group 2). In this design, *three* groups may be identified, because there are subjects in Groups 1 and 2 who share the common variable set $F, \ldots, J$, As Figure 3.2 indicates. It follows, then, that in programmatic—as opposed to project—longitudinal study, the matter of fluctuation in the size of the initial cohort is not particularly relevant. What is important is the size of data sets, configurations of hypothesis-relevant variables. The data subsets themselves are ephemeral and coalesce around a particular hypothesis of theoretical interest. Accordingly, we refine the topic of cohort shrinkage into that of the quantity of time-data relevant to a particular hypothesis.

However, this last statement itself requires a refinement. It does not follow that it is the fate of all samples to shrink, decreasing as a function of passage of time or the number of data-taking contacts. Of these two, the number of contacts is perhaps the more dynamic, as contact at any given time-point increases or decreases the probability of future responsiveness. This is really a procedural question containing the uncertainty of whether a proband is feeling receptive at a given moment, whether the data taker is socially sensitive, and whether the data taken are emotionally neutral, negatively, or positively charged.

We may illustrate these points with data from the St. Louis Baby Study, data we will present in detail in later chapters. The subset, *Biological Predictors + height* contains only predictors taken in the perinatal period. The Ns by child at age 6 months, 1 year, . . . ,5 years are 637, 536, 688, 722, 781, and 744. In the case of the data set *Social Predictors + language,* the Ns at age 2 to 5 years are 714, 514, 464, and 475. In the case of the first data set the number of cases tends to rise, and in the case of the second it tends to

Group	Variables	N
1	A . . . . K	50
2	D . . . . N	50
3	F . . . . J	70

Figure 3.2. Data sets and subsets.

fall; this phenomenon is not unrelated to acquisition of the predictor variables all through the study period, as a glance at Table 3.6 will recall. There data sets require various combinations of variables, and the larger the requisite set the fewer the cases having relevant data at all time points. We see that commonly held views of the inevitability of sample shrinkage may be too gross a view of the matter and too negative an expectation.

Data Analysis

A decade of reports from the St. Louis Baby Study has conformed to the proposition that regression analysis is a particularly suitable model for studying developmental data. In particular, we have found that multiple linear regression is suitable, because it explicitly facilitates regression analysis using dichotomous and continuous data (McNeil, Kelley, & McNeil, 1975), and also because it acts as a general data-analytic system, to use the phrase employed by Cohen (1968). In regression analysis the investigator's attention is unremittingly focused on the proportion of criterion variance accounted for, although F-tests and probability levels explain the role of single variables. In the case of studies employing data from young children as the criteria, it is common for regression models employing several predictor variables to explain a modicum of criterion variance. Accordingly, studies of young children face an inordinate requirement for variance. However, there still remains the questions to be studied within the data analytic system. In addition, there is the question of how to handle hypothetical interactions when the number of predictor variables is lengthy, and when interactions are hypothetically complex. Still another question is that of nonlinearity of regression, and of course both topics can be combined to explore the possibility of interactions in which one or more variables is quadratic or a higher order polynomial. This last possibility has been reduced to a level of parsimony by the work of Joossens and Brems-Heyns (1975) in Belgium, Goldstein and Johnson (1978) in Great Britain, and Rowe et al. (1976) and Epstein and Epstein (1978) in the United States.

ERROR

We turn now to the relationship between statistical treatment and the topic of hypothesized outcomes. In particular, all statistically based analyses deal with probabilities rather than certainties in outcomes. Regression analyses tend to emphasize accounting for criterion variance, and accept residual, unexplained variance as a likely outcome. Caution leads investigators to approach findings in the mode of avoiding error rather than approximating the truth of a situation. This program of inquiries is no different in that regard, and we are conscious of two types of error.

A *Type I* error occurs when we falsely conclude that the conventional hypothesis of no (null) difference should be rejected. This leads us to place faith in spurious findings. In order to examine the statistical possibilities of the data, we have insisted on a high subject–variable ratio as basis for attributing empirical, as opposed to statistical, significance. While developmental data are analyzed in order to make the best probabilistic statement about the real world, methodological considerations—statistics—have an interest for career investigators. In the world of empirical–statistical inquiry, we recognize a second error of probability which we attempt to avoid.

A *Type II* error occurs when there are real findings, but we reject them as insignificant. The probability of this error is the reciprocal, as it were, of the Type I error. As we avoid a Type I error by insisting on high statistical significance, we also run the risk of ignoring findings which are true, but at a level of statistical probability below the level needed to avoid Type I error. Large samples help with the Type II error, but there are obvious limits to the size of data sets existing in the real world.

In the case of longitudinal study carried out prospectively on real children, studied one-by-one under varying degrees of accessibility and cooperation, conscientious investigators strive for the largest number of cases and hold expectations of significance at high statistical levels. Conscious of the logical–inferential presumptions of multivariate analyses, investigators then apply statistical techniques thoughtfully. In the enterprise of prospective longitudinal study, the uniqueness of data sets covering substantial spans of development provides perspective and balance on the application of hypothesis and inference to rare data. On the one hand the integrity of data sets gathered prospectively dictates equal care in analysis; for example one uses multivariate techniques as opposed to techniques which lump data into broad categories. On the other hand, the integrity of the corpus of data has a superordinate value which, when buttressed by conservatism in statistical interpretation, leads to confident attempts at analysis and description.

MULTIPLE LINEAR REGRESSION

With the advent of modern computers, a technological innovation whose import can only be underestimated, regression techniques acquired new practicality. Bottenberg and Ward (1963) originally developed a working program; there has since flowed an entire corpus of works on this flexible analytic technique, and we cite in particular McNeil, Kelly, and McNeil (1975). In multiple linear regression, a regression equation, or model, composed of a number of rationally selected variables is developed in order to predict a criterion, such as height at a particular age. The equation accounts for some proportion of the variance of the criterion measure; this equation containing all the variables one wishes to use to explain the criterion is called the *full* model. A second model is then constructed which is reduced, or *restricted,* by omitting a variable of theoretical interest. For example, given a full model of sex, race, and height at four previous ages, one might develop several restricted models, each of which deleted one or several of the variables. Each restricted model also accounts for variance of the criterion. Comparing the proportion of variance (R^2_{full}) of the full model with the proportion of variance of a restricted model ($R^2_{restricted}$) allows us to test statistically the effect of omitting the variable of interest.[2] The technique permits use of both continuous data such as ages and discrete data such as sex; it also allows investigators to create synthetic variables such as "5-year-old males" (versus all others). When appropriate, nonlinear and interaction terms can be synthesized.

As a final element in this chapter's account of procedures, we report the method for describing and discussing the original data of this investigation. We will present data representing six criterion sets, and four predictor sets from birth to age 5 years in the next six chapters. The volume of data requires that it be reported by domain, and with extension of the predictor set across the developmental span of interest. In the discussion presented in Chapter 10, the organization shifts from a prospective–sequential scheme to temporal cross-sections in which the comparative value of the predictor sets is assayed.

---

[2]A more technical expression of this key concept follows: In multiple linear regression (McNeil, Kelley, & McNeil, 1975), a regression equation is developed in order to predict a criterion. A critical element is deleted or collapsed, the resulting equation is designated as an alternate model, and an F-value is computed for the loss of predictive efficiency traceable to the altered vector. The basic model may be illustrated as $Y = a_0u = a_1x_1 + a_2x_2 \cdots a_nx_n = e$, where Y = a criterion of continuous or discrete data, u = a unit vector which when multiplied by the weight a_0 yields the regression constant, $a_1, a_2 \cdots a_n$ = partial regression weights arrived at by multiple linear regression techniques and calculated to minimize the error sums of squares of prediction (Σe^2), $x_1x_2 \cdots x_n$ = variables in continuous or discrete form, and e = error in predicting a criterion.

Motor Development

4

Introduction

In assessing the motoric domain of child development, we examine an aspect of growth which is relatively unconsidered. That is, it is less obvious in its relevance than language or intellectual processes. Nevertheless, there is every reason to consider the domain. Little children run and jump, and they use crayons; they hop and skip, and engage in muscle activities, large and small. Such activities are as much the business of childhood as the skills which foreshadow degrees of competence in middle childhood's later series of school tasks. In the criterion series which this chapter probes, large muscle skills are examined first, and then fine muscle skills, such as copying designs. Drawing these designs depends on visual memory and tracking, and on the use of a pencil held finely between fingers and thumb to reproduce on paper what eye and brain have perceived. In making a case for the motor domain, we regret the relative absence of programming for motor development in the young. American society in the nineteenth century had enormous respect for motor activity, a sensibility which has degenerated in the twentieth century into mere physical character overshadowed by athletics. To return to the nineteenth-century orientation is to revive a concern for aesthetic development; for it was in that spirit that the *Turnverein* and other societies approved physical development.

In considering this domain of child growth, we note the virtual absence of "music and movement" from contemporary programming for children. And yet, rhythm and grace are attainable in children's lives quite apart from dance training, and the sports rites of adolescent culture.

Our exploration of this domain is not without its applied aspects. Developmental delay in this domain suggests remediation. Also, a more complete grasp of the influences on development can help us program activities. In the case of the finest motor skills we look for order and pattern in an area which will yield readiness—or the lack of it—for writing and drawing. These two activities, practical on the one hand and aesthetic on the other, provide twin themes which flow through children's lives.

Motor Development

In the case of motor development, inquiry deals with a relatively straightforward and self-evident domain of behavior. Developmentally, it has the additional advantage of providing continuity with the period prior to birth. It consists of continued elaboration and refinement of the muscular activities of the growing child.

In the case of the years from birth to age 5 the unfolding of motor activities translates them into skills as children deal with elements in their culture. Thus, the primitive grasping reflex at birth progressively evolves into the classroom skill of handling a pencil. In the preschool years it will have been refined into handling buttons, and in adolescence may be transferred into skill at typing.

Motor development is a topic which relates to the basic science of biology. Many authorities see antecedents to preschool motor behavior in the dynamics of movement of the embryo and fetus. From the continuity of movement in both pre- and postnatal phases they create, as in the case of Gesell, some quite broad principles. To Gesell *Developmental Direction* summarized the observation that infants control their heads before their feet. *Interweaving* meant that a spurt in one area lead to a pause or regression in another. By *Functional Asymmetry* Gesell described the process of using one side of the body, rather than both, when effecting an act such as reaching. *Fluctuation* in such levels of performance he felt natural, and the whole sequence a part of the normal process of increasing effectiveness he summarized as *Maturation*. For example, in the matter of locomotion Gesell has described a sequence as follows:

  9 months—creeping
 12 months—walking with help
 18 months—walks without falling
  2 years—runs

3 years—stands on one foot
4 years—skips on one foot
5 years—skips on two feet

Under cultural conditions the levels of motor skill reached by people tend to be differentiated. For example, boys exceed girls in matters of strength and coordination of gross movement. On the other hand, girls tend to exceed boys in manual dexterity. Anastasi (1958) concluded that women's norms on standardized tests of dexterity showed uniformly higher levels of performance than those shown by men.

Of course, motor development does not take place in isolation from other processes. In particular, we are coming to appreciate the connection between motor activities and perceptual processes. Grasping by young children presupposes several things; first it requires that children know where objects are, and also that they know where *they* are. In the case of this last element, there is an entire complex built around where children think their bodies are in space, and in relation to the object they wish to grasp. It is increasingly evident that self-perceptions, including the image of one's body perceived from within, are intricately connected with how well we move our bodies, for example, reach for a toy. Moving our bodies becomes an exercise in complex movement, and it presumes we are capable of accurate appraisal of ourselves and the objects we manipulate.

Fortunately, maturation occurs quickly in children, and they are capable of sophisticated motor acts by age 3 or 4. We have slowly learned to adjust our expectations of children's performance to the reality of maturation in general, and to the specific stage reached by a given child. We recognize that reading, for example, is a complex act in which the eyes make a fine horizontal sweep which is followed by narrowly spaced parallel sweeps. Writing becomes opposition of finger and thumb plus stereoptic vision as a monitor, at least.

In the case of handicapped children one recognizes that their disabilities, when analytically formulated, consist of a number of elements. In many children the discrimination of left–right is delayed. Once we identify such a deficiency we can work on it, and so alleviate specific disabilities in children.

There has been a trend in recent years to develop tests and checklists to assess infant performance. At the other extreme, the Brazelton infant assessment scheme gives a picture of related motoric activities at a very early age. Related to this is the normative picture of motor skills developed by, for example, Cratty (1967, 1969). In his work we have useful suggestions for how we can improve performance in children. Understanding which influences affect performance, we feel, is a necessary condition.

Hypotheses

Our major hypothesis flows from the nature of the criterion series of motor tasks and the relevance of the four predictor sets. Motor development is operationally defined as scores on the test criteria at 3 and 4 years of age. At 3 years the criteria are attainments reported when a familiar figure, the caseworker, interviewed the mother and filled out the schedule of the Pre-school Attainment Record (PAR). However, we point out that verbal report from an informed third party was not the entire datum. In addition case-workers inquired into PAR items such as "Follows Leader," "Hops Around," or "Skips," by asking the study child to join in the act. In other words, this criterion was part report and part performance. Presumably, the report portion was improved by witnessing—indeed joining in—the demonstration portion. At age 4 these gross motor tasks were replaced by the precise psychomotor performance of copying designs. These tasks have a clear biological substratum, and competence is very much a matter of opportunity interacting with readiness. The latter, however, predominates in young children; for this reason we hypothesized that the Biological predictor series would exert greatest influence, that is, account for the greatest proportion of criterion variance (R^2). In a negative sense we are also led to this hypothesis; that is, one would reasonably hypothesize that birthweight, biological risk, and Apgar score, if pathological, would express themselves through lowered motor performance.

In subordinate but complementary fashion we return to the matter of "opportunity" touched on in the preceding paragraph. The training this concept predicates seems very much a matter of what caregivers will let children do. Independence training for children and adventurism expressed in motor activity are known to be influenced by maternal values. Freund and Elardo (1978) have shown that maternal behaviors influence child behaviors to a significant degree. For this reason we hypothesize that the second greatest influence, that is, the second largest R^2 values, will be derived from maternal traits.

To a still more subordinate degree the criterion series will be influenced (R^2) by the Social predictor series as a formulation of culture, we hypothesize. In last place we hypothesize a minimal role, comparatively speaking, for the demographic descriptors in the Family predictor set.

Measures

In this chapter we present information on child attainment in the criterion domain of *Motor Development*. This, the smallest domain, contains three criterion measures each given to two groups of children. At 36 and 42 months the *Ambulation* score of the Preschool Attainment Record (Doll, 1966) was gathered by interviewing mothers. At the same ages a second PAR subtest, *Manipulation,* was used. At ages 48 and 54 months a much more precise measure of motor development was employed. The Copy Forms test developed by Graham, Berman, and Ernhart (1960) is a task in which subjects reproduce from memory, with paper and pencil, a series of line drawings. The scoring of performance on this subtle measure of visual perception and motor expression was supervised by one of the test's authors, Dr. Claire Ernhart, who also trained the test administrators.

As with criteria in other domains the goal is to relate four sets of predictors to the criteria of development. As was shown in Table 3.6, the first predictor set is the *(a)* Biological series composed of birthweight, biological risk, Apgar score, and sex. This series of elements has the common factor of being gathered at the time of delivery. This first predictor set is complemented by three others, *(b)* Social series, *(c)* Family series, and *(d)* Maternal series. For each predictor series we report the character of the data subsets by SES level, race, and sex, even when these variables are not used in the predictor series.

Results

(A) BIOLOGICAL SERIES

The first motoric criterion is the *Manipulation* score on the Preschool Attainment Record at child ages 36 and 42 months. There was requisite information on five variables on 727 3-year-olds. The PAR *Manipulation* score consists of maternal reports of performance when removing covers from candy, gum, and other objects, taking simple objects apart and together, flinging objects with arm, hand, and wrist with a fair degree of accuracy in direction and distance, as well as catching them. Drawing squares, blowing one's nose, and tying shoes are upper-level skills in this domain.

There were 370 cases at 36 months with requisite data on predictor and criterion variables. Fifty-three percent of the children were males and 57% were white. The mean SES score of 55 (See Table 4.1), which is average for the data set, describes a family whose father at the time of delivery of the proband was a 24-year-old construction worker. He had a high school diploma and earned $156 a week in the late 1960s.

As a data set the 36 month criterion group is generally normal, although the range of developmental measures is quite wide. For example, the

TABLE 4.1

DESCRIPTION OF THE SUBJECTS: *BIOLOGICAL* SERIES AND THREE-YEAR PAR *MANIPULATION* AND *AMBULATION*,

AND FOUR-YEAR COPY FORMS

Variable	36 Mos. (N=370)		42 Mos. (N=357)		48 Mos. (N=294)		54 Mos. (N=361)	
	$\bar{M}$ %	σ	$\bar{M}$ %	σ	$\bar{M}$ %	σ	$\bar{M}$ %	σ
Sex (% M)	53		52		51		52	
Race (% W)	57		57		63		63	
SES	55.78	16.11	55.33	14.81	54.79	15.85	53.75	14.85
Birth Weight (lb.)	7.10	1.25	6.96	1.27	7.11	1.19	6.95	1.29
Bio Risk	.39	.91	.61	1.27	.36	.88	.62	1.29
Apgar	9.02	.93	8.57	1.62	9.00	1.20	8.49	1.66
PAR *Manipulation*	7.76	.94	8.43	1.04				
PAR *Ambulation*	9.75	2.08	11.11	1.82				
Copy Forms					28.02	13.74	36.37	12.91

smallest baby weighed less than 3 lb at delivery. The highest degree of biological risk was present—a rating of 5—and the lowest Apgar, a 10-point scale, was 2.

The results of the multiple regression analysis begin with Table 4.2. For the criterion 36 month PAR *Ambulation*, we see that no predictor out of the four was a significant source of variance. The R^2 value of the four-variable model was not significantly different from zero, $R^2 = .01$, $p = .23$.

In the case of the 36 month PAR *Manipulation* group, which was slightly smaller than the 36 month group ($N = 357$), a similarly insignificant regression model was produced. The R^2 of this model, $R^2 = .002$, was statistically insignificant, and none of the four predictors accounted for significant proportions of criterion variance.

The third criterion in Table 4.2, also from the Preschool Attainment Record, is the *Ambulation* score at 42 months from 357 3½-year-old boys and girls. At 42 months, as Table 4.1 shows, the sex ratio was approximately even, with 52% of the children being boys. Multiple regression analysis of the *Ambulation* score at 42 months was productive; one variable in the four-term Biological predictor set, birthweight, was a significant predictor. Also, the R^2 value of the four predictor model was statistically significant ($R^2 = .03$, $p = .003$).

At 42 months, as Table 4.2 shows, no variable emerged as a significant predictor of PAR *Manipulation* scores, in a statistically insignificant regression model, $R^2 = .006$, $p = .65$.

The third motoric criterion was the Graham *et al.* (1960) Copy Forms test at age 4 years. In this comparatively fine criterion in the motor domain, 18 forms are presented to be copied in pencil by the child. Data on all four predictors plus the criterion are given in Table 4.1 for 651 4-year-old boys and girls. Evenly divided by sex, there were complete data sets for 294 children at 48 months, for a larger group of 361 at 54 months. The proportion of white children at age 4 rose slightly to 63%.

In Table 4.2 we see a comparatively robust regression model of Apgar scores, biological risk, birthweight, and sex. The model explains 12% of the criterion variance, and is highly significant ($p < .00001$). A second point of departure is the increased relevance of the predictor series to the criteria. When birthweight was deleted from full Model 1, forming restricted Model 2, the comparative predictive power dropped by almost one-half, to $R^2 = .07$. Comparison of the two models' predictive power was statistically significant ($F = 16.49$, $p = .00006$). Apgar scores deleted to form Model 3 created a significant drop in proportion of variance for the restricted model to $R^2 = .08$ ($F = 13.22$, $p = .00003$). Sex was next, with a drop in R^2 to .09. Higher scores in girls were produced by a negative weight for boys.

TABLE 4.2

MULTIPLE LINEAR REGRESSION ANALYSIS OF BIOLOGICAL INFLUENCES ON MOTOR ATTAINMENT

Variable	Models Compared	36 Mos. (N=370) PAR *Ambulation* R^2	F	P	36 Mos. (N=370) PAR *Manipulation* R^2	F	P	42 Mos. (N=357) PAR *Ambulation* R^2	F	P
Birth Weight	Full Model 1	.01		.23*	.002		.90*	.03		.003*
	Model 2	.01	.23	.62	.006	.83	.36	.01	7.47	.006
				.26*			.90*			.11*
Biological Risk	Full Model 1	.01		.23*	.002		.90*	.03		.003*
	Model 3	.008	1.05	.30	.02	.006	.93	.03	.05	.81
				.67*			.95*			.02*
Apgar	Full Model 1	.01		.23*	.002		.90*	.03		.003*
	Model 4	.01	.52	.46	.002	.08	.77	.02	3.50	.08
				.29*			.80*			.01*
Sex (M)	Full Model 1	.01		.23*	.002		.90	.03		.003*
	Model 5	.005	2.14	.14	.002	.00	1.00	.03	.10	.74
				.83*			.95			.02*

	42 Mos. (N=357) PAR Manipulation			48 Mos. (N=294) Copy Forms			54 Mos. (N=361) Copy Forms		
	R^2	F	P	R^2	F	P	R^2	F	P
Birth Weight									
Full Model 1	.006		.65*	.12		.00001*	.06		.00005*
Model 2	.004	.94	.33	.07	16.49	.00006	.02	12.85	.0003
			.67*			.00005*			.01*
Biological Risk									
Full Model 1	.006		.65*	.12		.00001*	.06		.00005*
Model 3	.004	.75	.38	.11	3.37	.06	.05	1.93	.16
			.88*			.00001*			.0009*
Apgar									
Full Model 1	.006		.65*	.12		.00001*	.06		.00005*
Model 4	.06	.28	.59	.08	13.22	.0003	.04	6.68	.01
			.53*			.00001*			.001*
Sex (M)									
Full Model 1	.006		.65*	.12		.00001*	.06		.00005*
Model 5	.06	.05	.82	.09	10.97	.001	.05	3.10	.07
			.78			.00004*			.001*

*Significance of the difference from zero.

59

At 54 months, as Table 4.2 shows, the four-term regression model was far less robust, but still statistically significant when scores from 361 children were analyzed ($R^2 = .06$, $p = .00005$). Once more birthweight produced the greatest effect when the model created by deleting it was compared with the full model ($F = 12.85$, $p = .0003$). The other significant influence was the Apgar score, whose absence in restricted Model 4 significantly lowered the R^2 value from .06 to .04 ($F = 6.68$, $p = .01$).

(B) SOCIAL SERIES

This series, shown with the other predictor sets in Table 3.6, consists of perinatal data on socioeconomic status (SES) and race, and occupational data on parents, plus maternal education, at child age 3 years. Two variables in Table 3.6, dwelling type (trailer, apartment, or house) and STIM home description at 5 years are not used in the analyses reported here, since they were measured after the criteria gathered last in this series, at age 4 years.

In Table 4.3 are details of the data set on 514 3-year-old boys and girls for whom full predictor information and data on two criteria are available. The proportion of males was 50% at 36 months, and 53% at 42 months. It is useful to note that Table 4.3 shows a higher proportion of black children at 42 months, as well as a larger group of children.

Paternal occupation in Table 4.3 is similar for both study groups of children, although the 42-month level is slightly higher. This predictor is the Hollingshead (1957) two-factor description. Mothers' employment (whole, part, or none) by distribution is similar for both groups of children, although more mothers in the half-year group work out of the home full-time.

In the case of maternal education, a variable of great importance for child development, we report the levels by percentages. It is appropriate to give this variable due attention. First, we have found this to be an important variable for child development in analyses reported elsewhere (Jordan, 1978b). Second, the particular range of levels of schooling is an important index of the entire sample of children. In longitudinal data sets the level of maternal education has tended to be truncated, with practically all mothers being well educated. The mothers of the 1966 cohort cover the entire spectrum of schooling. In particular, the data subsets in this report contain mothers with comparatively little schooling. Census Bureau data relevant to the cohort, that is, Missouri women 25 years of age or older, averaged 11.8 years of schooling, with a slightly higher level in the St. Louis SMSA. The figures on maternal education in Table 4.3 conform to that generalization. However, Table 4.3 shows the presence of mothers with less than a high school education; some of them, typically 5–8%, had only 8 years of schooling. The presence of women with little education balances the average for

TABLE 4.3

DESCRIPTION OF THE SUBJECTS: SOCIAL SERIES AND THREE-YEAR PAR *MANIPULATION* AND *AMBULATION*, AND FOUR-YEAR COPY FORMS

Variable	36 Mos.			42 Mos.			48 Mos.			54 Mos.		
	$\bar{M}$	%	σ	$\bar{M}$	%	σ	$\bar{M}$	%	σ	$\bar{M}$	%	σ
		(N=201)			(N=313)			(N=170)			(N=280)	
Sex (% M)		50			53			52			53	
Race (% W)		94			65			97			69	
SES	48.29		15.29	53.91		14.85	48.24		14.78	52.81		14.63
Pop's Occupation	40.49		17.82	46.08		18.52	40.65		17.16	44.69		18.26
Mom's Employment %												
– *Full–time*		18			24			18			24	
– *Part–time*		11			5			11			5	
– *At Home*		72			71			72			71	
Mom's Education												
– *Elementary*		5			8			5			6	
– *Part H.S.*		16			24			18			23	
– *H.S.*		48			42			46			43	
– *Part College*		22			17			22			18	
– *College*		9			9			9			10	
PAR *Manipulation*	7.70		.87	8.49		1.07						
PAR *Ambulation*	9.26		1.66	10.95		1.81						

TABLE 4.4

MULTIPLE LINEAR REGRESSION ANALYSIS OF SOCIAL INFLUENCES ON MOTOR ATTAINMENT

Variable	Models Compared	36 Mos. (N=201) PAR *Ambulation*			36 Mos. (N=201) PAR *Manipulation*			42 Mos. (N=313) PAR *Ambulation*		
		R^2	F	P	R^2	F	P	R^2	F	P
SES	Full Model 1	.08		.004*	.07		.01*	.34		<.00001*
	Model 2	.07	1.98	.16	.06	1.68	.19	.13	98.98	<.00001
				.004*			.01*			<.00001*
Race (B)	Full Model 1	.08		.004*	.07		.01*	.34		<.00001*
	Model 3	.08	.38	.53	.07	.08	.77	.34	.97	.32
				.002*			.005*			<.00001*
Paternal Occupation	Full Model 1	.08		.004*	.07		.01*	.34		<.00001*
	Model 4	.08	.01	.89	.05	3.91	.04	.34	.06	.79
				.001*			.02*			<.00001*
Maternal	Full Model 1	.08		.004*	.07		.01*	.34		<.00001*
	Model 5	.04	9.27	.002	.07	.22	.63	.31	13.43	.0002
				.08			.005*			<.00001*
Maternal Education	Full Model 1	.08		.004*	.07		.01*	.34		<.00001*
	Model 6	.07	1.19	.27	.07	.56	.45	.34	.00	1.00
				.002*			.006*			<.00001*

	42 Mos. (N=313) PAR Manipulation			48 Mos. (N=170) Copy Forms			54 Mos. (N=280) Copy Forms		
	R^2	F	P	R^2	F	P	R^2	F	P
SES Full Model 1	.10		<.00001*	.09		.001*	.21		<.00001*
		17.60	.00004		10.48	.001		9.79	.001
Model 2	.05		.002*	.04		.04*	.19		<.00001*
Race (B) Full Model 1	.10		<.00001*	.09		.001*	.21		<.00001*
		9.73	.001		6.16	.01		2.37	.12
Model 3	.07		.00007*	.06		.006*	.21		<.00001*
Paternal Occupation Full Model 1	.10		<.00001*	.09		.001*	.21		<.00001*
		.23	.63		.80	.37		.89	.34
Model 4	.10		<.00001*	.09		.0006	.21		<.00001
Maternal Occupation Full Model 1	.10		<.00001*	.09		.001*	.21		<.00001*
		8.24	.004		9.00	.003		3.50	.06
Model 5	.07		<.00001*	.05		.02*	.20		<.00001*
Maternal Education Full Model 1	.10		<.00001*	.09		.001*	.21		<.00001*
		.29	.58		.82	.36		3.71	.05
Model 6	.10		<.00001*	.09		.0006*	.20		<.00001*

*Significance of the difference from zero.

63

all, and counterbalances the highly educated. Our final note on maternal schooling applies to subsequent chapters. Generally speaking, the levels of maternal schooling will be in balance in both birthday and half-year study groups; levels will also be stable at the several child ages from 6 to 66 months.

In Table 4.4 we see the influence of the social series on 201 PAR *Manipulation* scores at 36 months through a five-factor model of SES, race, paternal occupation, maternal place of work, and maternal education. Only the question of whether or not mothers engaged in work outside the home was significant ($F = 9.27$, $p = .002$), dropping the R^2 of the model from .08 to .04, a reduction of 50%. Working in the home is associated with higher PAR *Ambulation* scores.

The second 36 month criterion, PAR *Ambulation*, was also analyzed using the same set of children's data. In this analysis the full model of all relevant variables explained 8% of the variance, and was statistically significant at the .01 level. Only paternal occupation affected the criterion, dropping the R^2 from .07 to .05 ($F = 3.91$, $p = .04$).

At 42 months data were assembled on 313 children. The racial composition includes black children in the proportion of one-third. Paternal occupational score is slightly higher than at 36 months, as we saw in Table 4.1. Maternal place of work is essentially comparable in both birthday and half-year groups, with more mothers in the half-year group working full-time; this increase of 6% in the incidence of full-time working mothers can be related to the *lower* SES level evident in the higher perinatal McGuire and White SES scores.

In Table 4.4 we see that the five-term regression model created a statistically significant model with a comparatively high R^2 of .34 ($p < .00001$). From multiple linear regression analysis we see that the perinatal SES score explained almost two-thirds of the variance ($F = 98.98$, $p < .00001$), followed by mothers' scope of work outside home, to a far lesser extent ($F = 13.43$, $p = .002$).

In a model whose R^2 value is more like those observed at 36 months, ($R^2 = .10$, $p < .00001$), Table 4.4 shows the role of the five putative influences on 42 month PAR *Manipulation* scores. SES contributed .05 of the full model's account of variance ($F = 17.60$, $p = .00004$). Maternal occupation contributed 3% of the variance, as did race. In the case of the latter, the regression weight associated with race—black—was positive, indicating higher PAR scores in black 3½-year-olds. Maternal site of work, equal in statistical significance, had a negative association when outside the home.

Finally, we report the results of applying the Social predictor set to the Copy Forms scores at 48 and 54 months. Predictor and criterion information were available as a complete set for 450 4-year-olds. The 48 month group was the smaller, with 170 subjects, as Table 4.3 indicates. With the exception of paternal occupation and race predictors, the 48 month and 54 month data sets were similar.

In Table 4.4 we see the picture of antecedents to fine visual-motor development at 48 months produced by a five-factor multiple regression model. Once more, the perinatal SES score is the prime source of variance, reducing the highly significant full model of $R^2 = .09$, to .04 in Model 2 ($F = 10.48$, $p = .001$). Maternal site of work is next most influential, accounting for 4% of the variance ($F = 9.00$, $p = .003$). Race is next, reducing the full model R^2 by one-third, to the .06 of restricted Model 3. In this case, the weight associated with being black is negative, lower the score on this *fine* motor task.

In the analysis of the 54 month data set from just under 300 children at age $4\frac{1}{2}$ years, the impact of perinatal SES score is still evident, if somewhat more muted. When Model 2 omitting perinatal SES score is compared with the full five-predictor model, the R^2 drops from .21 to .19 ($F = 9.79$, $p = .001$). No other variable influenced Copy Forms criterion scores at child age $4\frac{1}{2}$ years.

(C) FAMILY SERIES

Relevant data were assembled from 630 3-year-olds. In the Family series, data on birth order are complemented by information on the number of brothers and sisters, and the identity of the father figure. Alternatives within this variable are that the biological father may be present, there may be a father figure, or there may be neither. In the data set the biological father was present in most homes, and the number of children without a father or father figure was a high 11–21%, as Table 4.5 indicates. Most children were about third in the sibship. The proportion of the sexes from 36 to 54 months was consistent, the racial composition was similar, and the perinatal SES level was virtually identical.

In Table 4.6 we see a regression model of 36 month PAR *Ambulation* scores using the Family series of four predictors. In this regression model the R^2 value is .01 ($p = .17$).

In the case of the second 3-year score to which the social predictor set was applied, PAR *Manipulation,* the only variable of significance was the father figure variable ($F = 3.96$, $p = .04$), which dropped the originally low full model R^2 to the statistical equivalent of oblivion—in this instance to $R^2 = .007$.

The same two motoric criteria were repeated on the half-year group of children; that is, those tested in the summer months. The data set is slightly larger at 42 months, but does not differ in the values of the variables used

TABLE 4.5

DESCRIPTION OF THE SUBJECTS: *FAMILY* SERIES AND THREE-YEAR PAR *AMBULATION*, AND FOUR-YEAR COPY FORMS

Variable	36 Mos. (N=312)			42 Mos. (N=318)			48 Mos. (N=223)			54 Mos. (N=269)		
	M̄	%	σ	M̄	%	σ	M̄	%	σ	M̄	%	σ
Sex (% M)		52			52			53			52	
Race (% W)		60			57			67			60	
SES	55.01		16.39	55.44		14.69	52.90		16.12	54.82		14.35
Birth Order	3.22		2.38	3.14		2.01	3.03		2.19	3.12		1.96
N Siblings	2.76		2.24	2.72		1.92	2.59		2.03	2.69		1.85
Father Figure %												
- *Father*		72			73			78			74	
- *Father Figure*		14			6			11			7	
- *None*		14			21			11			19	
STIM										32.57		5.82
Dwelling										2.64		.48
PAR *Manipulation*	7.61		.91	8.42		1.03						
PAR *Ambulation*	9.61		2.05	11.05		1.84						
Copy Forms							28.61		14.26	35.33		13.01

for the analyses, as Table 4.5 shows. At 42 months the three variables from the Family set, not yet including the STIM score and type of dwelling, were applied to PAR *Ambulation* scores ($N = 317$) in a model whose R^2 value was .12 ($p < .00001$). The sole predictor variable accounting for variance was the variable describing the father figure. Its absence in regression Model number 4 dropped the value of the R^2 from .12 to .08 ($F = 34.75$, $p < .00001$). In the case of the second 42-month motor criterion, PAR *Manipulation,* the R^2 generated by the full model was a miniscule .005 ($p = .57$). None of the predictors were significant.

At age 4 years the data set was drawn from the records of just under 500 children ($N = 492$). The criterion Copy Forms test yielded an R^2 of .17 $p < .00001$). In this analysis the number of siblings was significant ($F = 18.14$, $p = .00003$), and the model R^2 was .10. The variable describing the father figure was equally useful and also provided 7% of the theoretical variance ($F = 18.14$, $p = .00003$). Birth order was also significant, explaining 5 of the 17% in the full model ($F = 11.85$, $p = .0006$). The regression weights associated with the number of siblings and the nonfather were negative.

In the case of 54-month Copy Form analyses the full model grew by incorporating two additional variables. The first was the type of dwelling in which the child lived, and virtually all children lived in one-family dwellings and apartments. The second variable introduced was the STIM, a description of the stimulation value of the home environment developed by Professor Caldwell (1970). This variable and its role illustrates the vicissitudes of longitudinal methodology, for in this analysis, as in others, the STIM proves useful. The vicissitudes consist of not being able to use the scale sooner, since it was not available until child age 4, plus the sense of what might have been yielded had it been possible to incorporate the measure into the baseline data set at delivery. On the other hand "better late than never," is a pragmatic position and we adopt it with thanks to Professor Caldwell for her generosity in this as in other matters.

Turning to the analysis of 54-month Copy Forms we report in Table 4.6 that the STIM score explained half the .26 variance of the full model ($F = 48.10$, $p < .00001$), while the other variables within the same regression context were statistically insignificant.

(D) MATERNAL SERIES

The final predictor set applied to the motoric domain is the series of Maternal traits shown in Table 4.7.

There we see a four-predictor model composed of data gathered perinatally. As a matter of procedure, relevant maternal traits were also acquired at subsequent child testing ages. At 6 months the Bendig version of

TABLE 4.6

MULTIPLE LINEAR REGRESSION ANALYSIS OF FAMILY INFLUENCES ON MOTOR ATTAINMENT

Variable	Models Compared	36 Mos. (N=312) PAR *Ambulation* R^2	F	P	36 Mos. (N=312) PAR *Manipulation* R^2	F	P	42 Mos. (N=318) PAR *Ambulation* R^2	F	P
Birth Order	Full Model 1	.01		.17*	.01		.10*	.12		<.00001*
			.82	.36		.002	.99		.45	.50
	Model 2	.01		.12*	.01		.04*	.12		<.00001*
N Siblings	Full Model 1	.01		.17*	.01		.10*	.12		<.00001*
			1.12	.29		.30	.57		.003	.95
	Model 3	.01		.14*	.01		.05*	.12		<.00001*
Father Figure	Full Model 1	.01		.17*	.01		.10*	.12		<.00001*
			2.83	.09		3.96	.04		34.75	<.00001*
	Model 4	.006		.34*	.007		.33*	.02		.01*

		42 Mos. (N=318) PAR *Manipulation*			48 Mos. (N=223) Copy Forms			54 Mos. (N=269) Copy Forms		
		R^2	F	P	R^2	F	P	R^2	F	P
Birth Order	Full Model 1	.005		.57*	.17		.00001*	.26		<.00001*
			.02	.87		11.85	.0006		.44	.50
	Model 2	.005		.37*	.12		.00001*	.26		<.00001*
N Siblings	Full Model 1	.005		.57*	.17		.00001*	.26		<.00001*
			.06	.80		17.83	.0004		1.07	.30
	Model 3	.006		.38*	.10		.00001*	.26		<.00001*
Father Figure	Full Model 1	.005		.57*	.17		.00001*	.26		<.00001*
			1.96	.16		18.14	.00003		1.98	.16
	Model 4	.005		.99*	.10		.00001*	.25		<.00001*
STIM	Full Model 1						.00001*	.26		<.00001*
									48.10	<.00001*
	Model 5							.13		<.00001*
Dwelling	Full Model 1						.00001*	.26		<.00001*
									2.51	.11
	Model 6							.26		<.00001*

*Significance of the difference from zero.

69

the Taylor Anxiety Scale was administered. The entire data set of 52 criteria was analyzed using the four-predictor set in Table 4.7, plus the anxiety score as a fifth element. Its presence was statistically insignificant for the six criterion domains, and it also reduced the number of cases available for statistical analysis. For these reasons the anxiety score was deleted from the predictor set, and this chapter and the others report use of the four-predictor set given in Table 4.7. Similarly at child age 3 years, four subscales of Ernhart and Loevinger's Family Problems Scale (FPS), *Conventional Social Role, Denial of Hostility, Basic Distrust,* and *Moralistic Control* were also gathered. These, too, had the effect of reducing the number of cases in data sets. Reduction of sizes of samples increases the probability of a Type II error of design. For that reason, the predictor set was confined to the four maternal traits gathered at the time of delivery: marital status, age, Authoritarian Family Ideology (AFI_{68}), and social risk. In the case of this last predictor, a special word of explanation is called for. This 0–5 score is actually a representation of the five bottom deciles of the McGuire and White three-factor score. Its use in this form attempts to recognize the role of mothers as mediators and transmitters of family subcultures. Risk increases as SES decile falls below the average of the birth cohort. The 0–5 rating is used, rather than the 14–84 rating scheme of roughly 70 points, in order to modulate the role of this powerful variable, and to prevent it from swamping the hypothetical value of the other three predictors.

Results of applying the four-predictor Maternal series to the six motoric criteria at ages 3 and 4 years are given in Table 4.8. Applied to 629 3-year-olds, scores from the Preschool Attainment Record, the four-element predictor series showed significant results for only the 36 month *Ambulation* criterion. The AFI_{68} score was highly significant ($F = 9.01$, $p = .002$), and marital status at the time of the probands' delivery reached the .03 level of statistical significance. In both cases the relationship is that being married and being low in authoritarianism is associated with higher criterion scores for the children. No predictors affected the 36 month PAR *Manipulation* scores.

At 42 months the same variables, AFI_{68} and marital status, were associated with PAR *Ambulation* scores. Given the similarity of the Ns for the PAR *Ambulation* groups, any other result would be unlikely. Lest this seem too facile a comment, we note the greater size of the PAR *Ambulation* R^2 at 42 months. In the case of the 42 month PAR *Manipulation* score, age of the mothers at delivery was statistically significant ($F = 4.75$, $p = .02$).

Copy Forms scores and data on the predictors were available for almost 600 4-year-olds ($N = 579$). At 48 months we see in Table 4.8 that the AFI_{68} and social risk variables gave useful accounts of criterion variance in a

TABLE 4.7

DESCRIPTION OF THE SUBJECTS: *MATERNAL* SERIES AND THREE-YEAR PAR *AMBULATION*,

PAR *MANIPULATION*, AND FOUR-YEAR COPY FORMS

Variable	*36 Mos.* (N=312)			*42 Mos.* (N=317)			*48 Mos.* (N=256)			*54 Mos.* (N=323)		
	$\overline{M}$	%	σ	$\overline{M}$	%	σ	$\overline{M}$	%	σ	$\overline{M}$	%	σ
Sex (% M)		51			54			51			52	
Race (% W)		63			62			70			63	
SES	54.27		15.99	54.43		14.77	53.32		16.01	53.03		14.56
Marital Status (% M)												
Delivery Age	25.25		6.57	25.73		6.59	25.04		6.40	25.81		6.47
AFI 68	27.19		7.55	26.52		8.21	26.67		7.44	25.80		8.26
Social Risk	1.25		1.69	1.14		1.62	1.06		1.66	1.00		1.52
PAR *Ambulation*	9.63		2.03	11.04		1.83						
PAR *Manipulation*	7.74		.90	8.45		1.08						
Copy Forms							28.53		13.41	36.97		13.21

TABLE 4.8

MULTIPLE LINEAR REGRESSION ANALYSIS OF MATERNAL INFLUENCES ON MOTOR ATTAINMENT

Variable	Models Compared	36 Mos. PAR *Ambulation* (N=312)			36 Mos. PAR *Manipulation* (N=312)			42 Mos. PAR *Ambulation* (N=317)		
		R^2	F	P	R^2	F	P	R^2	F	P
Married	Full Model 1	.05		.002*	.01		.36*	.18		<.00001*
			4.78	.03		1.31	.25		4.40	.03
	Model 2	.03		.009*	.009		.39*	.17		<.00001*
Delivery Age	Full Model 1	.05		.002*	.01		.36*	.18		<.00001*
			.48	.48		.44	.50		1.41	.23
	Model 3	.04		.001*	.01		.27*	.18		<.00001*
AFI₆₈	Full Model 1	.05		.002*	.01		.30*	.18		<.00001*
			9.01	.002		.55	.45		24.25	<.00001
	Model 4	.02		.06*	.01		.29*	.12		.00001*
Social Risk	Full Model 1	.05		.002*	.01		.36*	.18		<.00001*
			2.05	.15		.93	.33		1.07	.30
	Model 5	.04		.002*	.01		.34*	.18		<.00001*

		42 Mos. (N=317) PAR Manipulation			48 Mos. (N=256) Copy Forms			54 Mos. (N=323) Copy Forms		
		R^2	F	P	R^2	F	P	R^2	F	P
Married	Full Model 1	.03		.03*	.16		<.00001*	.21		<.00001*
			.31	.57		1.02	.31		6.31	.01
	Model 2	.03		.01*	.16		<.00001*	.19		<.00001*
Delivery Age	Full Model 1	.03		.03*	.16		<.00001*	.21		<.00001*
			4.75	.02		.25	.61		2.15	.14
	Model 3	.01		.11*	.16		<.00001*	.20		<.00001*
AFI68	Full Model 1	.03		.03*	.16		<.00001*	.21		<.00001*
			2.20	.13		19.55	.0001		17.74	.00003
	Model 4	.02		.03	.10		.0001*	.16		<.00001*
Social Risk	Full Model 1	.03		.03*	.16		<.00001*	.21		<.00001*
			2.90	.08		4.76	.02		17.06	.00005
	Model 5	.02		.04*	.14		.00001*	.16		<.00001*

*Significance of the difference from zero.

relatively robust regression model whose $R^2 = .16$. At 54 months the same two variables prevailed, with marital status a lesser source of variance from Copy Forms scores.

Discussion

The motoric domain of child development is the smallest, and employs three measures, the *Ambulation* and *Manipulation* scores from Doll's (1959) Preschool Attainment Record, and the Graham *et al.* Copy Forms. The measures were applied over a quite narrow range of maturity in children, at 3–4 years. PAR subtests were used as performance items with the children, and they were used with mothers as a structure for interview by skilled examiners. In contrast, the Copy Forms task was administered directly, at age 4, 1 year later.

In this portion of Chapter 4 we examine the meaning of the results just presented. Beginning with the regression effects we note that the R^2 values of models were generally low. This is not surprising, since each aggregate of predictors is one-quarter of the full predictor set. Among the four models the most consistently powerful predictor, comparatively speaking, is the Social model, even when allowance is made for the R^2 value of the 42 month PAR *Ambulation* analysis. In Table 4.9 we see that the minimum R^2 value was .01, and the mean for four models was $R^2 = .01$. The Maternal model was the next most powerful, on the average, followed by the Family, and last of all, the Biological model. The trend is for the R^2 values to be higher at 4 years than at 3 years. In this regard, it is useful to recall that the span from 3 to 4 years is narrow, and that the two measures employed were quite divergent, structured interview plus performance at 3, and child performance at 4 years. However, both measures are separated from the other criteria of this investigation and are grouped together as a motoric domain. On that basis generalizations are offered.

HYPOTHESES

In considering the four models we hypothesized that the Biological model would be the best predictor. The reason for this is the salient emergence of motor activities from a neurological substratum. Readiness, in motoric terms, requires the emergence of fine muscle skills from gross performance. This is not to reject environmental influences, but to assert a logical connection between a predictor and criterion set both embedded in a common physiological source.

Once the primacy of Biological data is hazarded, for purposes of structuring inquiry, we can consider the other three, nonorganic, influences. On the basis that the intimate and sustained relationship of mother and child is

TABLE 4.9

R^2 VALUES OF MOTOR DOMAIN ANALYSES

Biological Model	Social Model	Family Model	Maternal Model	Criteria	Mean R^2
.01	.07	.01	.01	36 m. PAR *Manipulation*	.03
.006	.10	.005	.03	42 m. PAR *Manipulation*	.04
.01	.08	.01	.05	36 m. PAR *Ambulation*	.04
.03	.34	.12	.18	42 m. PAR *Ambulation*	.16
.12	.09	.17	.16	48 m. Copy Forms	.13
.06	.21	.26	.21	54 m. Copy Forms	.18
Mean R^2 .04	.15	.09	.10		.10

the greatest vector of influence, a proposition evident in hands rocking cradles and the worldwide influence which allegedly follows, we hypothesized that the second of four models in effective accounting of variance would be the Maternal variables.

Between the Family and Social influences we expect that social factors will prevail, thereby generally acknowledging the role of Social influences. Placing Family influences last postulates the limited relevance of the particular family variables for motor activities.

When the models are considered for all 24 multivariate analyses, we note that the most predictive model was the Social model of *Ambulation* at 42 months. The least powerful predictor models were the Family and Biological models of PAR *Manipulation* at 36 months, and PAR *Ambulation* at 42 months. In none of the data on models and criteria in Table 4.9 are the R^2 values consistent. The weakest models are the Biological group whose mean proportion of assigned variance is .04. Twice as useful on the average are the Family and Maternal models; the Family model is a little higher, and the Social model is three to four times more powerful than Biological model. In making this observation we note that discounting the elevation of the mean Social R^2 puts the Social, Family, and Maternal models close to each other, with the Biological model quite apart from the other three. None of four quite dissimilar models gives a very large account of motoric test scores at ages 3 and 4 years. In this regard, the motoric domain of attainment is comparable to others we have examined when children are young, and reported elsewhere.

When Table 4.9 is considered by means of the criteria the R^2 values of the rows are uneven. The most obvious break-out is the grouping of PAR scores on the one hand, with Copy Forms on the other. No trend by age 3 to 4 years, an admittedly narrow range, is permissible.

In this consideration of models we note the interesting order of the models as predictors of motoric development. Based on mean R^2 values, the column means in Table 4.5 do not support our hypothetical order of value. The weakness of the Biological model may be evaluated by asserting that it really does not tell us much about any of the six motoric criteria at ages 3 and 4. We note that in another study (Jordan, 1971), we found biological data of a relevant sort faded as a basis for understanding development by age 2 years.

Comparatively speaking, the Social model is fairly effective. After it in effectiveness (judged by mean R^2 values), come the Maternal model and the Family model. Thus, rejecting our primary hypothesis of Biological influence, we see that the remaining three influences are comparable. The slight differences in R^2, modulating the distortion of the Social model mean R^2 for the moment, do not really permit a definitive gradation of influence. The Maternal model is in third, rather than the hypothesized second place, with Family influences in the hypothesized third place.

DISCRETE INFLUENCES

From a study of child development over several years, we reasonably expect that specific variables of interest be treated, however attenuated the mathematical underpinnings. Our obligation is to give the best picture of Nature's and Society's influences. Finding as we have that the motoric domain is imprecisely grasped by even multivariate means, we still need to deal with child development as an explicable matter. On the basis of a multivariate exposition we note which variables seem influential.

In Table 4.10 we have a grouping of 24 predictor variables and the six criteria. There we see Biological, Social, Family, and Maternal variables and their relative order of magnitude in regression analyses. In the case of the Biological predictors we start by noting that not all predictors were useful. The variable biological risk is not reported at all, and sex of the child was used only once (favoring girls). In contrast, weight at birth was an influence on three motoric criteria of development when children were 3–4 years of age. In particular, this Biological predictor in the presence of three others

TABLE 4.10 PREDICTORS IN ORDER OF STATISTICAL CONTRIBUTION IN MULTIPLE REGRESSION ANALYSES TO R^2 OF FULL MODELS

CRITERION	BIOLOGICAL MODEL				SOCIAL MODEL				
	Weight	Biological Risk	Apgar	Sex (M)	SES	Race	Pop Occup.	Mom Employ.	Mom's Educat.
Child Age (Yrs.)	Birth	Birth	Birth	Birth	Birth	Birth	Three	Three	Three
36 m. PAR Manipulation					1		1		
42 m. PAR Manipulation					1	2		3	
36 m. PAR Ambulation	1				1			1	
42 m. PAR Ambulation					1			2	
48 m. Copy Forms	1		2	3	1	3		2	
54 m. Copy Forms	1		2		1				2

CRITERION	FAMILY MODEL					MATERNAL MODEL			
	Birth Order	N Siblings	Father Figure	Dwelling Type	STIM	Married	Age	AFI 68	Social Risk
Child Age (Yrs.)	Birth	3 Years	3 Years	5 Years	5 Years	Birth	Birth	Birth	Birth
36 m. PAR Manipulation								1	
42 m. PAR Manipulation					1		1	1	
36 m. PAR Ambulation						2		1	
42 m. PAR Ambulation			1			2		1	
48 m. Copy Forms	3	2							2
54 m. Copy Forms	2				1	3			2

77

was the prime influence on motoric scores. Indeed, the role is even greater, since birthweight appears as three of the six significant influences, and always as the prime influence on the fine visual-motor performance elicited by the Copy Forms test. In second place are Apgar scores, which were an influence in four instances. Finally, the sex of children was a tertiary influence at age 48 months on fine motor performance. In none of the mothers' reports of *Ambulation* and *Manipualtion* did sex differences emerge. When six differences emerged on the Copy Forms, the higher scores were those of girls.

At this point we pause in this first chapter reporting data to discuss in some detail the nature of the Apgar results. The reason is that Apgar scores, a 0–10 rating of five physiological descriptions in the first minutes of life, have two important aspects. First, the Apgar score is a statistically significant influence on several criteria at several ages. Second, the results, if not elucidated in some detail, could lead to conclusions quite the reverse of those we wish to convey.

In the analysis just reported, as in some to follow, the β weight associated with Apgar scores is negative, and the correlation between Apgar and criteria is also negative, even when the Apgar is not found significant in the multiple linear regression analysis.

At first glance we would be justified in concluding that low rather than high Apgar scores, that is, poor physiological status postpartum, are associated with high criterion measures of child attainment. On close inspection, Apgar scores are practically all above eight, a finding consistent with means of 8.57, 9.00, and 9.02 in Table 4.1. Low Apgar scores in this chapter (and occasionally in others) as opposed to high Apgars in association with the criterion, are not very low. The finding of negative rather than positive β weights with statistical significance lacks developmental and clinical significance.

The extent to which Apgars are negatively influential is a function of a given subset of data. In addition the negative relationship is replaced by a positive one in subsequent chapters. The result, as we will see from the cumulative data, is a combination of results in which low Apgar scores are seen, as here, associated with high criterion scores; at other times the more conventional relationship prevails.

In the case of the six Social variables and their influence on motoric attainment no variable was excluded as without any significance. The least frequent influence on motoric development is maternal schooling followed by paternal occupation and race. The major Social influences are clearly distinguishable as SES and maternal work site. The first is the McGuire and White perinatal social status score based on education, occupation, and source of income. The influence is less pronounced on the PAR measures, at age 36 months and more on fine motor performance at 48–54 months. A consistent pattern of secondary influence prevails for maternal employment in the home, or elsewhere. The influence of the two variables, that is, as a source of variance in regression models, on motor performance of 3- and 4-year-olds is evident.

The family domain of predictors contained up to five predictors, with the last two, STIM score and type of dwelling, being employed in analyses of the 54 month criteria, and not in analyses of criteria gathered before child age $4\frac{1}{2}$ years. All predictors except the type of dwelling influenced motoric development at one age or another. The most frequently encountered influence in this predictor set is the identity of the father figure, favoring biological fathers over substitute or no fathers.

The STIM description of home circumstances was gathered at child age $4\frac{1}{2}$ years and was incorporated into the regression model of Copy Forms scores. This peasure was of prime importance in relation to other possible influences at 54 months, as Table 4.10 indicates.

The last set of predictors consists of four Maternal variables. One of them, age at the time of delivery of the study child, was a minimal influence on motor delivery. In contrast, the AFI_{68} authoritarian–liberalism orientation to child rearing was the salient influence on four of the six motoric criteria. Marital status was a secondary influence half the time. Social risk, our formulation of the perinatal SES score by deciles below the median intended to convey the subculture of the home, was moderately influential. Its role is evident in Table 4.10 at age 4 years rather than age 3.

Ernhart and Loevinger's Authoritarian Family Ideology scale (AFI_{68}) was a comparatively substantial influence on the motoric domain, as Table 4.10 shows. Of minor influence was maternal age at delivery, which in selected instances affected scores on the Preschool Attainment Record, at age 42 months.

Having indicated the relevance of single variables within the four sets, we may now try to describe the role of the predictors in the motoric domain. In so doing it is important to recall that any single variable established its role within one of the four models, whole or part, rather than in the presence of all other 17 predictor variables concurrently, and at times in the context of regression models with low R^2 values.

It is evident that birthweight, and to some extent Apgar scores, are biological influences. Perinatal social class and mothers' work are important indices of the impact of culture on nonverbal attainment. Within the family the presence of the father is important; the stimulating value of the home should be mentioned, despite the relatively limited use of the STIM due to the reality factor of when the scale appeared. We note in passing that this is always a hazard of prospective study, and we have chosen to preserve the longitudinal, prospective integrity of the data set instead of engaging in post-diction. Finally, we note that the social orientation of mothers, and a selected aspect of maternal values, notably the FPS Authoritarian Family Ideology measure, affect the motoric domain at ages 3–4.

It is interesting to note that the motoric domain, while not greatly affected by the four predictor sets—in the sense of large accounts of variance—nonetheless is explicable in those terms. Our findings discount the role of biological data, and it is evident that social influences are comparatively powerful, and affect the motoric attainment of children.

We now consider the major question of the investigation, the relative influence by child age of the four sets of influences. At age 3, Social influences are most effective, in the sense of accounting for criterion variance, with perinatal social status score being the prime influence. At age 4, Family influences explain the largest proportion of variance, with Social and Maternal influences playing secondary roles of virtually equal significance. From those two vectors of influence we identify the presence of the biological father in the home, and the mother's degree of authoritarianism in child-rearing values as salient. In last place at both 3 and 4 years of age is the influence of perinatal Biological factors.

As a final procedural note we comment on the data set at points which refer to subsequent chapters. In the matter of the sample it is clear that there is a core of cooperative, accessible cases which is supplemented and depleted by a smaller group whose cooperation has been less stable. Our casework experience with these people indicates they are no less interested in child welfare. In some instances they have been inner-city residents who merely moved around the corner, but did so in a fashion concealing their location from prying government and social agencies. Since some such families move at intervals measured in months at the outside, and certainly not at large intervals, tracing them has been challenging. One such family moved nine times in 1 year, but always within a circumscribed area. In other instances families shuttle back and forth between the city and local small towns, although their nominal residence remains unchanged.

A second point is that we call attention to the high proportion of children who do not have the support of the biological father in the home. Up to one-quarter of the small children in this study are growing up in a nonintact family structure. While the relationship between a nominally intact family structure and child welfare is only approximate, there is every reason to think that too many children lack two parents.

Intellectual Development

5

Introduction

In this age of literacy and technology, popular conviction stresses the importance of maximizing the intellectual attainments of young children. A substantial portion of the nation's youngest children are enrolled in formal preschools, and in many cases the reason is not that mothers work, but the result of a deliberate decision to give children a head start over other boys and girls in the lifelong race for achievement and security.

In accordance with this ethic, scrutiny of the processes of intellectual growth becomes urgent, and the search for ways to bring all boys and girls to optimum levels of growth presses on. In this chapter we examine influences on intellectual development attending to seven measures of intellectual growth. For the youngest children the domain is fairly wide, including mothers' perceptions of behaviors which express creativity and play with ideas. At age 3 the criterion is recognition vocabulary. At age 4 a broad ranging inventory of accomplishments is assayed, together with mastery of verbal concepts. Finally at age 5 vocabulary is measured once more to appraise grasp of ideas, using a subtest from a comprehensive, standardized battery.

There is a methodological note to be made concerning this chapter and Chapter 6. For very good reasons, what is intellectual and what is linguistic blend. Separation into two chapters in this work has two justifications. The lesser reason is procedural—the sheer number of analyses, tables, and figures. More fundamentally important is a distinction in how tests formulate verbal tasks for children. The more dynamic uses of verbal concepts, for example, the process of using words as in the *Auditory Association* subtest of the Illinois Test of Psycholinguistic Abilities, is presented in the next chapter. In this chapter, knowledge of words in isolation is presented. The Peabody Picture Vocabulary Test (PPVT), for example, is used in this chapter rather than the next because it is construed, as Nelson (1977) put it, as a measure of exposure to majority culture and concepts. Keeping in mind this caveat lector, we assay a brief exposition of intellectual growth in children as a preface to data on the subject.

Intellectual Development

One of the little understood benefits of techniques of infant assessment is that they show us how clever newborns are. In contrast to the historic tabula rasa of the older empiricism, we now believe that the passive plasticity of that concept ignores a major reality. It is that the newborn have a remarkably well organized set of skills for coping with reality. To internal stimuli they respond by bellowing when hungry or wet, and their assessments are recognized by all, if not always appreciated. To the external world the infant applies coping skills that are quite sophisticated. Newborns can, for example, track quite well; that is they can follow an object moving across a visual field. They can appreciate it, and they can assimilate it into their formulation of what is real.

Small children have minds and can think in purposive terms. This process is greatly advanced by acquisition of language and the corresponding power to represent both nontangible and remembered reality. With the appropriate level of words, children can take care of their needs and can enter into a full social role. The basic element of intellectual development is acquisition of a good vocabulary. The power to name common objects allows children to control their own affairs to a considerable extent. Part of the process of control is assimilation. This is the term used by Piaget to describe how concepts become a part of the content of children's minds. Within the mind one idea may elicit another, and the range of associations tell us something about creativity in the young.

As with all aspects of development, circumstances affect intellectual growth. Some homes are teaching homes in which parents consciously facilitate development by informal stimulation, and by adoption of an attitude that growth can be accelerated through constructive selection of TV programs and books. Equally, the structure of the family, its size, and its relative affluence affect children, although we may have a better grasp of what inhibits mental growth than of what advances it. We know that homes have a culture and are in fact a mini-culture. The level of education of parents and their values vary from one home to another. In one home there are two parents; in another there is only one. All of these elements create unique configurations for children and influence growth.

In the case of intellectual attainment it has been fashionable, probably to an excessive degree in recent decades, to see the limits of attainment as the direct consequence of circumstances. This point of view, the super-environmentalist view, largely ignores the inner assimilating self of childhood. At a constitutional level there is a capacity to assimilate, which is one aspect of the complexity of mental life. Interacting with the self-concept and with the perception of the world as a supportive or dangerous place, for example, the capacity to absorb and integrate within the ego permeates all aspects of life.

Our interest in intellectual development as data in this chapter uses standardized measures of concepts. It does not, for example, include Piagetian measures, but not for lack of interest. Such measures were tried as a part of the testing program for each child. They were, however, set aside after some experience, and were excluded from the data set. The reason was essentially that they failed to hold up as standardized tasks in many instances. That is, the attractive simplicity of the tasks plus the evident success with them reported by others did not prevail in this inquiry. Tasks of conservation, for example, were accepted by children but in ambiguous ways. When presented in prescribed manners to children, the tasks seemed at times to mean more than one thing to children, and so were deleted with reluctance.

On the other hand, the data set reported has seemed unambiguous in meaning to children. While heavily verbal at all ages, we note for the reader's information our use of nonverbal tests at later stages of child study ages beyond the age range of this report (Jordan, 1976b, p. 301). The value of the verbal element in the *Intellectual* domain is evident in its relevance to the major task of the years which follow the span of this study. That is, 6-year-olds and older boys and girls have as their major developmental task the process of education. A largely verbal process, attending school presumes verbal intellectual skills and also consists of adding still more verbal skills to children's repertoires.

Hypotheses

As in the previous chapter our hypotheses consist of relative degrees of influence of the predictor sets on the criteria; that is, the degree of influence is expressed by the proportion of criterion variance accounted for.

The intellectual development of children emerges from a range of influences of which the most fundamental, we hypothesize, is the impact of the mother when children are young. Beginning with feeding and toileting, mothers engage in acts which have influence beyond the immediate pragmatic task. In the key nurturing contexts, we postulate, mothers convey approval for exploratory behavior, or suppress it; they may convey that infant and toddler behavior is an imposition on the autonomy of mothers, and so inhibit it for maternal advantage. In another domain mothers may, or may not, stimulate language development and playfulness with ideas. Some mothers may tolerate or welcome sustained use of toys, while others may find them a constant threat to neatness. This, we hypothesize, constitutes a fundamental vector of influence.

We hypothesize the Social predictor set as very close in influence to the Maternal predictors. That is, we hypothesize a role almost as great for the economic and cultural context of child development. The Social class of a family determines parents' values to a great extent. In particular, parents' education and occupation structure role expectations for children. Kahl (1953), for example, has shown that the sons of "common-man" fathers perceived little or no explicit pressure toward entering the professions.

Very close in influence we see the role of Family traits, the circumstances of the home. This domain conveys much of the physical context, the kind of home, the space available, density of people, and the placement of the proband in the family pecking order as a consequence of birth order.

Finally, we hypothesize that the Biological measures, taken at birth, will have extinguished, for the most part, across the developmental span of interest. In a previous study (Jordan, 1971) we have seen that biological influences tend to extinguish by age 2, and that cultural influences subsequently explain whatever measurable degree of influence we can identify.

Measures

In this chapter, unlike its predecessor, criterion measures begin 2 years after birth, and continue to age 5 years. While the data set on each child included some inquiry into cognitive attainment at age 1, the topic was scanned by means of items in the Ad Hoc Scale of Development (Jordan, 1967a). That instrument emphasizes other aspects of development, and the proportion of items dealing with cognitive development at age 12 months is not large. Such appraisals were not without interest at the time but were precluded by immaturity of the subjects and the scarcity of instruments at the time. At age 2 years, however, the probability of children exhibiting language behaviors is high, and nonperformance is less likely to be a false indicator of significantly delayed development. Even so, there are implicit problems such as the inconsistency of performance in young children simply because they are very young, and the related problem of psychometric reliability and its effects on analyses of data. Two-year-olds are pretty sociable, and especially so around their birthdays (a period chosen for family visits); but the appearance of a stranger who expects one to play games—but then takes them away—can inhibit all kinds of child behavior. With these considerations in mind we chose to interview mothers asking questions about children's routine performances. The trade-off in this approach is that experienced interviewers usually have seen the mother on several previous occasions can get valid information by indirect means. In contrast there is a substantial chance of no information obtained by direct means when Tiffy does not choose to perform for reasons which are opaque, but probably sensible to a 2-year-old. Anyone who has recently attempted transactions with 2-year-olds will recall the omnipotence of their word "No," and the fateful confusion of adults' plans that delicious word evokes.

At age 2 years, data on intellectual attainment were obtained by using Doll's Preschool Attainment Record (1966). The PAR permits an experienced interviewer to appraise children's attainments in three domains—Physical, Social, and Intellectual. There are eight specific age scales which, when added to the total scores for each domain, sum to 11 scores. The PAR is much like the Vineland Social Maturity Scale in format, and the sheer range of behaviors appraised in the eight age scales is useful. In the case of the Intellectual domain the PAR presents three age scales with items grouped by 6-month levels. In this investigation however, PAR data in all chapters are raw scores from the scales, and represent some child performances.

The first PAR Intellectual scale is called *Information*. At the lowest levels this is a matter of children recognizing their playthings and play contexts as familiar, and progresses to a sense of "ownership or priority interest in people, property, things [Doll, 1966, p. 29]." Sex role awareness and personal name are also assessed. Beyond that level, awareness of names of common objects is considered. The second Intellectual scale is *Ideation*. This starts with assertiveness of personal preferences, and progresses through use of gestures as well as words to express ideas. Evaluation of things through concepts of quantity and size come next. PAR *Creativity* at its lower levels assesses interest and curiosity, and is followed by modifying one's situation by investigating, by moving objects, and by manipulating them. Finally, all three scores are summed to provide a fourth, *Intellectual*, score for the entire domain.

Obviously, one moves in child study to direct measure of performance as soon as it is practical. In the domain treated by this chapter direct measurement arose at age 3 with the opportunity to use the PPVT. In this test a series of pictures is presented and the child is asked to point to an object named by the examiner. Norms start at child age 2 years and 3 months (2:3), and Dunn (1965) reports reliability coefficients of .75 and .81 at 36 and 42 months of age.

At age 4 years two measures are applied. The first was Boehm's (1967) Test of Basic Concepts. In this direct measure of attainment a series of line-drawings is presented, together with a question such as, "Look at the doors. Show me the door which is *widest*." A rather different, more comprehensive measure is Caldwell's Preschool Inventory (1970). Explicitly not an "intelligence test," the scale was developed to assess "what the child brought to the educational experience [a set of attainments] to some extent correlated with performance on intelligence tests ... [Caldwell, 1970, p. 4]." The Preschool Inventory results analyzed in this chapter consist of the total raw score obtained by summing scores on four subtests, *Personal–Social–Responsiveness, Associative Vocabulary, Concept–Numerical,* and *Concept–Sensory.* A reliability coefficient of .98 is reported for the scale. The children's scores are reported in this chapter because the Preschool Inventory samples what children know, the context of their minds, their intellects. While conventional intelligence tests might have been employed, it seemed more logical to use a measure more directly related to the major developmental task of the next several years of life, going to school. School performance, or rather sensitivity to it, was one of the bases for developing the Preschool Inventory, and so the scale was used at age 4 years.

Finally, a classic vocabulary scale from a major test of intelligence was employed at age 5 years. The *Vocabulary* scale of the Wechsler (1967) Preschool and Primary Scale of Intelligence (WPPSI) was employed. This measure of word meaning asks children, for example, "Shoe .... What is a shoe?" As a procedural note it is interesting to report that the research team discussed WPPSI *Vocabulary* scoring decisions from the responses of 800 5-year-old children. The consequence was considerable refinement of scoring within Wechsler's propositions and assembly of a detailed scoring guide.[1] Wechsler reports a reliability coefficient for *Vocabulary* of .82, and a correlation with the full scale score of .64 for 1200 children.

In total, the eight scores from seven tests in the Intellectual domain are varied. By child age they progress from indirect to direct measurement or performance. By task they vary from response to pictorial and vocal stimuli to requests for items of general knowledge. Finally, they range from subtest scales to complete scales.

---

[1]Available from the author.

As in the previous chapter, the first predictive model applied to these criteria will be Biological, consisting of four perinatal variables. Next comes the Social predictor set which is six variables gathered in the first 5 years of life. The Family predictors are five, and they spread over the developmental span of interest. Finally, the Maternal is composed of five traits plus a sixth which is a set of measures of childrearing values, for a total of nine predictors. The predictor set in each instance grows with the passage of time and variables are added so that both the predictor set and the criterion set express the prospective acquisition of data. This approach is not without its drawbacks from the point of view of drawing conclusions. On the other hand, a Draconian reduction of predictive data to a common baseline would throw away data and extinguish the developmental theme as we have watched the children grow—and indeed continue to do.

Results

(A) BIOLOGICAL SERIES

A data set was assembled on the subjects at 24 months of age; that is, the perinatal predictor set and the four scores from the Preschool Attainment Record. The number of cases providing complete data was almost 700 ($N = 696$). The predictor variables were birthweight, biological risk, Apgar scores, and sex. The PAR criterion scores were the *Information, Ideation,* and *Creativity* scores of the Intellectual domain; the sum of the three subtests provided a fourth, *Intellectual,* score for the entire domain. Although Table 5.1 shows four PAR criterion scores, there is only one data set for all subjects at age 2. We see in Table 5.1 that the sexes are balanced 53 to 47%, and that the proportion black toddlers was 40%. In terms of socioeconomic level, a typical score of 54 represents the family of an electrician with a little college work earning a decent income. Birthweights were good, averaging 7.00 lb, and the mean degree of biological risk at birth was slight. While this variable may lead to attenuated results, given a theoretical range for 0–5, the practical significance is more salutary. That is, the children represented by the mean score of .49, while occasionally at substantial risk, were generally healthy. The children of this report are real youngsters and their health is an element in the real world. Longitudinal investigations code and evaluate their findings in numbers, but the data are gathered by individual case study, and indeed are still being gathered, as this passage is being written, on real children.

The first 2-year criterion to which the Biological predictor series was applied is the PAR *Information* score; the multiple linear regression analysis

SERIES AND TWO-YEAR PAR *INTELLECTUAL* MEASURES, THREE-YEAR PPVT (A), FOUR-YEAR

Variable	24 Mos.			36 Mos.		
	$\overline{M}$	%	σ	$\overline{M}$	%	σ
	(N=696)			(N=354)		
Sex (% M)		53			53	
Race (% W)		61			63	
SES	53.98		15.95	55.35		16.18
Birthweight (lb.)	7.06		1.26	7.09		1.24
BioRisk	.49		1.09	.39		.92
Apgar	8.72		1.46	9.01		1.22
PAR *Intellectual*	18.01		3.69			
PAR *Information*	6.41		1.76			
PAR *Ideation*	5.41		2.84			
PAR *Creativity*	6.22		1.48			
PPVT (A)				24.94		10.59
Preschool Inventory						
Boehm Test of Concepts						

	54 Mos.			54 Mos.		
	$\overline{M}$	%	σ	$\overline{M}$	%	σ
	(N=376)			(N=310)		
Sex (% M)		51			50	
Race (% W)		62			55	
SES	54.12		14.85	55.85		14.55
Birthweight (lb.)	6.88		1.28	6.93		1.30
BioRisk	.63		1.25	.62		1.25
Apgar	8.51		1.64	8.55		1.66
Preschool Inventory	41.72		11.36			
Boehm Test of Concepts				16.72		4.77
WPPSI *Vocabulary*						

PRESCHOOL INVENTORY AND BOEHM CONCEPTS, AND FIVE-YEAR WPPSI *VOCABULARY* SCORES

42 Mos.			*48 Mos.*			*48 Mos.*		
$\bar{M}$	%	σ	$\bar{M}$	%	σ	$\bar{M}$	%	σ
(N=351)			(N=396)			(N=397)		
	52			52			51	
	58			54			54	
55.31		14.86	56.19		16.26	55.96		16.33
6.96		1.28	7.09		1.21	7.10		1.22
.58		1.24	.34		.82	.35		.84
8.56		1.61	9.07		1.13	9.06		1.15
29.96		12.68						
			13.99		4.75			
						32.98		11.70

60 Mos.			*66 Mos.*		
$\bar{M}$	%	σ	$\bar{M}$	%	σ
(N=394)			(N=366)		
	53			52	
	55			62	
55.96		16.22	54.07		14.70
7.09		1.23	6.92		1.25
.38		.88	.58		1.21
9.04		1.19	8.56		1.58
14.01		5.12	16.25		5.12

for this and other criteria analyzed using the Biological series is presented in Table 5.2. There we see that the full model of four predictors, birthweight, biological risk, Apgar, and sex, created an explanation for 2% of the PAR *Information* variance ($R^2 = .02$). The Apgar scoring of five aspects of physiological condition in the first minutes after delivery, when omitted in regression Model 4, dropped the R^2 to .01 and was negatively significant ($p = .002$), that is, comparatively low Apgars correlated with high criterion scores. Significant at a lower level was the sex of the child ($F = 6.86$, $p = .009$), favoring higher performance in girls. In the case of PAR *Ideation* scores perinatal Apgar ratings were negatively significant (low Apgars correlated with high criterion scores) predictors ($F = 6.85$, $p = .009$). Two elements in the Biological predictor series influenced PAR *Creativity* scores. They were Apgar scores ($F = 5.56$, $p = .01$) and birthweight ($F = 5.05$, $p = .02$). For the sum of all three of these PAR criteria, given in Table 5.2 as the PAR *Intellectual* domain score, biological risk ($F = 5.73$, $p = .01$) and Apgar scores ($F = 4.42$, $p = .03$) were significant sources of criterion variance. As with other analyses of predictors, the significance of any given predictor is strictly a consequence of the set of predictors with which it is compared. Clearly a predictor is an independent source of variance, but our analyses are best thought of as comparative.

At 3 years results from administering the Peabody Picture Vocabulary Test (PPVT), form A, were combined with the predictor set for just over 700 children. At 36 months there were 354 ($N = 354$) children in the data set of predictors and criteria.

In descriptive traits the 3-year-olds are much like those providing the 2-year data set. The mean scores and percentages fluctuate as particular study children are added and subtracted from the core study population.

In Table 5.2 we see that the Apgar score (negatively significant) was the greatest comparative influence in a model whose R^2 value was triple that of the preceding PAR criteria, but explained only 6% of the variance ($R^2 = .06$). For the 36 months PPVT (A) criterion Apgar scores (negatively significant) were the prime influence. Deletion in the form of regression Model 4 dropped the R^2 from .06 to .01 ($F = 18.14$, $p = .00003$) a highly significant result. A far lesser influence was evident in the statistically significant contribution of the biological risk scores ($F = 4.07$, $p = .04$), which declined as criterion scores rose. At 42 months the Apgar scores (negatively significant) remained the prime source of variance ($F = 6.89$, $p = .005$), followed by birthweight ($F = 6.06$, $p = .01$).

At 4 years the intellectual criterion series includes Boehm's Test of Basic Concepts and Caldwell's Preschool Inventory. For both measures the data sets are substantial. The requisite five pieces of information for the Boehm concepts analysis were available for 700 4-year-olds ($N = 707$), and there were

772 in the Preschool Inventory data set. In the case of data sets at 4 and 5 years, we point out that that continuity in the traits of the data sets can be estimated in two ways. First, any age group by year can be compared as a whole with preceding or following year groups. Second, any given group can be compared with its preceding birthday or half-year group for the same study period. The latter comparison is more precise and, as Table 5.1 records, indicates minor fluctuations in traits such as race, sex, and SES level.

Boehm Concepts scores at 48 months are influenced to some extent by three predictors. In order, the predictors are Apgar scores, biological risk, and sex—the latter favoring females. The Apgar variable (negatively significant) explained .04 of the full model's $R^2 = .06$ ($F = 13.71$, $p = .0002$) followed by sex and risk. At 54 months the Boehm R^2 was .02, and only birthweight achieved statistical significance ($F = 3.85$, $p = .04$).

Preschool Inventory scores at 48 months yielded an $R^2 = .09$. All four predictors played some role, with the Apgar scores (negatively significant) being most influential and accounting for .05 of the full model's R^2. Biological risk and birthweight were next, and were influential in the expected direction. Sex, favoring girls, was the least significant influence, as Table 5.2 shows, explaining .01 of the .09 R^2 value. At 54 months the data set provided a lower R^2 through the full model ($R^2 = .03$); the prime source of variance was birthweight ($F = 5.69$, $p = .01$) favoring higher rather than lower weights, followed by negatively significant Apgar scores ($F = 4.35$, $p = .03$).

The 5-year data set was composed of predictor and criterion scores from 760 boys and girls. Once more there is no substantial change in the traits of the study set summarized in Table 5.1. More specifically, the two data sets at 5 years resemble closely their antecedent sets at previous ages. Interestingly, both birthday and half-year groups resemble each other more in R^2 size at 60 and at 66 months than at previous ages. At 60 months the R^2 of .03 is dropped to virtually nothing by omission of the Apgar scores (negatively significant) in restricted regression Model 4 ($F = 9.78$, $p = .001$). Biological risk provides the other significant influence ($F = 6.50$, $p = .01$). At 66 months only the Apgar score is a significant source of variance from the WPPSI *Vocabulary* scores ($F = 5.52$, $p = .01$). As in the previous instances we have noted as *negative significance,* we report low Apgars associated with the criterion, within the limits of the regression model, its R^2 value, and a narrow distribution of high scores.

(B) SOCIAL SERIES

The variables of the Social predictor series are SES, race, father's occupation, mother's education and outside work, and education of the head of the household. The number of these variables in any given regression model

TABLE 5.2: MULTIPLE LINEAR REGRESSION ANALYSIS OF

Variable	Models Compared	24 Mos. (N=696) PAR *Information*			24 Mos. (N=696) PAR *Ideation*		
		R^2	F	P	R^2	F	P
Birth Weight	Full Model 1	.02		.0006*	.01		.01*
			1.10	.27		.97	.32
	Model 2	.02		.001*	.01		.01*
Biological Risk	Full Model 1	.02		.0006*	.01		.01*
			4.86	.02		2.80	.09
	Model 3	.01		.03*	.01		.15*
Apgar	Full Model 1	.02		.0006*	.01		.01*
			9.01	.002		6.85	.009
	Model 4	.01		.04*	.005		.25*
Sex (M)	Full Model 1	.02		.006*	.01		.01*
			6.86	.009		2.94	.08
	Model 5	.01		.06*	.01		.15*

Variable	Models Compared	48 Mos. (N=396) Boehm Concepts T.			48 Mos. (N=397) Preschool Inventory		
		R^2	F	P	R^2	F	P
Birth Weight	Full Model 1	.06		.00002*	.09		.00001*
			2.51	.11		7.84	.005
	Model 2	.05		.00007*	.07		.00001*
Biological Risk	Full Model 1	.06		.00002*	.09		.00001*
			6.54	.01		8.09	.004
	Model 3	.04		.0003*	.07		.00001*
Apgar	Full Model 1	.06		.00002*	.09		.00001*
			13.71	.0002		23.07	.00001
	Model 4	.02		.01*	.04		.0005*
Sex (M)	Full Model 1	.06		.00002*	.09		.00001*
			5.32	.02		6.44	.01
	Model 5	.04		.001*	.08		.00001*

*Significance of the difference from zero.

BIOLOGICAL INFLUENCES ON INTELLECTUAL ATTAINMENT

24 Mos. (N=696) PAR *Creativity*			24 Mos. (N=696) PAR *Intellectual*			36 Mos. (N=354) PPVT (A)			42 Mos. (N=351) PPVT (A)		
R^2	F	P	R^2	F	P	R^2	F	P	R^2	F	P
.02		.002*	.01		.04*	.06		.00003*	.04		.0007
	5.05	.02		.23	.63		3.14	.07		6.06	.01
.01		.02*	.01		.04*	.05		.0001*	.03		.01*
.02		.002*	.01		.04*	.06		.00003*	.04		.0007
	.02	.87		5.73	.01		4.07	.04		3.13	.07
.02		.01*	.003		.79*	.05		.001*	.03		.01*
.02		.002*	.01		.04*	.06		.00003*	.04		.0007
	5.56	.01		4.42	.03		18.14	.00003		6.89	.009
.01		.03*	.005		.29*	.01		.12*	.02		.01*
.02		.002*	.01		.04*	.06		.00003*	.04		.0007
	1.78	.18		1.81	.17		1.23	.26		.12	.72
.01		.02*	.009		.27*	.06		.0005*	.04		.0005

54 Mos. (N=375) Boehm Concepts T.			54 Mos. (N=376) Preschool Inventory			60 Mos. (N=394) WPPSI *Vocabulary*			66 Mos. (N=366) WPPSI *Vocabulary*		
R^2	F	P	R^2	F	P	R^2	F	P	R^2	F	P
.02		.04*	.03		.004*	.03		.004*	.02		.01*
	3.89	.04		5.69	.01		.35	.55		1.88	.17
.01		.74*	.01		.06*	.03		.005*	.02		.03*
.02		.04*	.03		.004*	.03		.004*	.02		.01*
	1.84	.17		2.17	.14		6.50	.01		.54	.46
.01		.28*	.02		.05*	.01		.24*	.02		.07*
.02		.04*	.03		.004*	.03		.004*	.02		.01*
	1.77	.18		4.35	.03		9.78	.001		5.52	.01
.01		.09*	.02		.03*	.00*		.32*	.01		.16*
.02		.04*	.03		.004*	.03		.004*	.02		.01*
	.61	.43		2.57	.10		.007	.93		.15	.47
.01		.18*	.03		.10*	.03		.02*	.02		.07*

is determined by the availability of particular criterion and predictor mea-sures at any given series of data points in development. In the Social series are two variables which appear merely as descriptors in other models, race and SES.

In the case of the four intellectual domain scores from the 2-year Pre-school Attainment Record there were salient variables from just under 700 toddlers ($N = 696$). The only substantial change is the drop in the propor-tion of black youngsters in the birthday series at 3, 4, and 5 years of age. This drop is correlated with the slight elevation, about one-third of a stan-dard deviation, of the McGuire and White SES scores. The reader will recall that higher SES values mean a *lower* social level, of course. The correlation between SES and race in the PAR data set is a highly significant $r = .58$ (p <.00001). The second correlate is a rise in the proportion of mothers work-ing full-time outside the home by about one-half, to approximately 25%. These and other items of information are recorded in Table 5.3.

The first set of Social variables applied to the four PAR scores consisted of SES and race, both of which provided statistically useful accounts of PAR *Information* variance with a full model, explaining 5% of the variance. Of the two the more important variable of influence, as Table 5.4 shows, was perinatal SES ($F = 10.97$, $p = .001$); it was, however, followed fairly closely by race ($F = .23$, $p = .007$). Low scores were related to being black and lower class. Neither SES nor race influenced PAR *Ideation* scores, in a very weak regression model. In the case of PAR *Creativity,* race is the more significant influence with higher scores in white children ($F = 94.79$, $p = .00001$). SES is the second influence, as the drop in R^2 from .12 to .11 indicates ($F = 10.07$, p <.001). In the sum of the three scores, presented as PAR *Intellectual* domain scores, SES gives the larger account of criterion variance dropping the R^2 values of the full regression model from $R^2 = .02$ to .002 when deleted in Model 3. Race was also significant ($F = 7.89$, $p = .005$). Higher scores were associated with non-lower-class white chidren.

At 3 years PPVT (A) scores and predictor information represented just over 500 boys and girls ($N = 504$). At this age the predictor series incorpo-rated the occupation of father figures, mother's site of work, and mother's level of schooling. As Table 5.4 shows, R^2 values of regression models rose substantially. At 36 months race did not account for criterion variance. The years of schooling of mothers, a more analytic social variable, was the most important source of variance accounting for .04 in a full model whose $R^2 = .13$ ($F = 9.29$, $p = .002$). Of minimal statistical influence was SES, explaining 1% of the variance ($F = 3.66$, $p = .05$). PPVT scores were higher when mother's education and socioeconomic status were higher. At 42 months SES was the greatest of three influences in a model explaining 38% of the variance of PPVT (A) scores. When deleted, in regression Model

2, SES dropped the R^2 from .38 to .31, about one-quarter of the variance ($F = 36.49$, $p < .00001$). Of mutually comparable, but lesser influence were maternal education ($F = 9.79$, $p = .001$), and the occupational level of fathers ($F = 9.49$, $p = .002$), which when high was related to high PPVT scores.

At 4 years the data set for Boehm Concepts scores and the five predictor variables represented about 500 children ($N = 480$). In the birthday data set the R^2 of .19 was accounted for by three variables of modest influence. SES contributed .03 ($F = 6.25$, $p = .01$), maternal education contributed .02 ($F = 4.62$, $p = .03$), and race explained .02 ($F = 3.65$, $p = .05$). The same three variables prevailed in the 54 month data set, and in the same order. SES was the largest source of variance ($F = 7.19$, $p = .007$), followed by maternal education ($F = 5.48$, $p = .01$), and race ($F = 4.79$, $p = .02$).

The second intellectual criterion at 4 years, the Preschool Inventory, combined data from 4-year-olds virtually identical with the 3-year-olds ($N = 482$). SES was the prime influence ($F = 5.74$, $p = .01$), followed by maternal education ($F = 4.09$, $p = .04$), and race ($F = 3.97$, $p = .04$). At 54 months maternal education was the prime source of variance in a robust model whose $R^2 = .24$ equaled that in the birthday group. When maternal education was deleted from the full model, in Model 6, the R^2 dropped to .21 ($F = 13.00$, $p = .0003$). Less dramatic was the role of maternal site of work ($F = 6.98$, $p = .008$) and race ($F = 6.46$, $p = .01$).

A group of similar size provided data from the predictor variables and WPPSI *Vocabulary* ($N = 478$). In the birthday (60 months) group the full model $R^2 = .10$. When maternal education was deleted, in Model 6, the R^2 dropped by one-half, to $R^2 = .05$ ($F = 9.37$, $p = .002$). No other variable was significant. In the half-year group the R^2 was much larger, $R^2 = .19$. Only maternal employment was influential, and then to a slight degree, dropping the R^2 from .19 to .18 ($F = 3.63$, $p = .05$). In both cases higher child scores were associated with mother's not working and better education.

(C) FAMILY SERIES

The Family series of predictors and PAR *Intellectual* scores come from the 311 children. The study group's traits are listed in Table 5.5 and are similar to other such groups. At age 24 months birth order is the sole predictor. The regression analysis consisted of testing the significance of the one-predictor model against a model of zero information. In the case of PAR *Information* the $R^2 = .04$ was significantly different from zero ($F = 12.91$, $p = .0003$). For PAR *Ideation* the R^2 was .02 ($F = 5.88$, $p = .01$). For PAR *Creativity* the R^2 also was .02 ($F = 7.13$, $p = .007$). Finally, for the entire PAR *Intellectual* domain the R^2 was .04 ($F = 14.91$,

TABLE 5.3

DESCRIPTION OF THE SUBJECTS: SOCIAL SERIES AND TWO-YEAR PAR *INTELLECTUAL* MEASURES, THREE-YEAR PPVT (A), FOUR-YEAR PRESCHOOL INVENTORY AND BOEHM CONCEPTS, AND FIVE-YEAR WPPSI *VOCABULARY* SCORES

Variable	24 Mos. (N=718)			36 Mos. (N=196)			42 Mos. (N=308)			48 Mos. (N=193)			48 Mos. (N=192)		
	$\bar{X}$	%	σ	$\bar{X}$	%	σ	$\bar{X}$	%	σ	$\bar{X}$	%	σ	$\bar{X}$	%	σ
Sex (% M)		53			51			53			50			50	
Race (% W)		61			94			65			94			94	
SES	54.06		15.86	48.04		15.29	53.89		14.91	48.05		15.24	48.19		15.24
Paternal Occup.				40.09		17.72	46.11		18.54	40.08		17.89	40.28		17.89
Maternal Employm.															
- *Full-time*					18			25			17			17	
- *Part-time*					11			4			11			11	
- *Home*					72			71			72			72	
Maternal Education															
- *Elementary*					5			8			5			5	
- *Part H.S.*					16			24			16			17	
- *H.S.*					48			43			47			47	
- *Part College*					21			16			22			22	
- *College*					8			8			10			9	
PAR *Intellectual*	18.03		3.69												
PAR *Information*	16.41		1.76												
PAR *Ideation*	5.41		2.81												
PAR *Creativity*	6.23		1.49												
PPVT (A)				27.32		11.14	31.17		12.85						
Preschool Inventory										35.92		10.73			
Boehm Test of Concepts													15.26		4.63

Variable	54 Mos. (N=289) $\bar{X}$	%	σ	54 Mos. (N=288) $\bar{X}$	%	σ	60 Mos. (N=195) $\bar{X}$	%	σ	66 Mos. (N=283) $\bar{X}$	%	σ
Sex (% M)		53			53			50			53	
Race (% W)		66			66			93			68	
SES	53.20		14.72	53.26		14.72	48.24		15.19	53.12		14.76
Paternal Occup.	45.28		18.49	45.32		18.50	40.37		17.88	45.00		18.48
Maternal Employm.												
– Full-time		24			24			17			25	
– Part-time		5			5			11			5	
– Home		71			71			72			70	
Maternal Education												
– Elementary		6			6			5			6	
– Part H.S.		24			24			17			24	
– H.S.		43			43			47			43	
– Part College		17			17			22			17	
– College		9			9			9			10	
Head of H. Education												
– To 9th Grade								22			31	
– H.S.								34			33	
– Part College								20			14	
– College								24			22	
Preschool Inventory	41.63		11.75									
Boehm Test of Concepts				17.26		4.64						
WPPSI Vocabulary							14.60		5.15	16.20		5.04

TABLE 5.4: MULTIPLE LINEAR REGRESSION ANALYSIS

Variable	Models Compared	24 Mos. (N=718) PAR *Information*			24 Mos. (N=718) PAR *Ideation*		
		R^2	F	P	R^2	F	P
SES	Full Model 1	.05		<.00001*	.007		.06*
			10.97	.001		.03	.85
	Model 2	.04		<.00001*	.007		.02*
Race (B)	Full Model 1	.05		<.00001*	.007		.06
			7.23	.007		3.15	.07
	Model 3	.04		<.00001*	.003		.13
Paternal Occup.	Full Model 1						
	Model 4						
Maternal Employm.	Full Model 1						
	Model 5						
Maternal Education	Full Model 1						
	Model 6						

Variable	Models Compared	48 Mos. (N=192) Boehm Concepts T.			48 Mos. (N=193) Preschool Inventory		
		R^2	F	P	R^2	F	P
SES	Full Model 1	.19		<.00001*	.24		<.00001*
			6.25	.01		5.74	.01
	Model 2	.16		<.00001*	.22		<.00001*
Race (B)	Full Model 1	.19		<.00001*	.24		<.00001*
			3.65	.05		3.97	.04
	Model 3	.17		<.00001*	.22		<.00001*
Paternal Occup.	Full Model 1	.19		<.00001*	.24		<.00001*
			.00	.94		1.11	.29
	Model 4	.19		<.00001*	.24		<.00001*
Maternal Employm.	Full Model 1	.19		<.00001*	.24		<.00001*
			2.28	.13		.27	.59
	Model 5	.18		<.00001*	.24		<.00001*
Maternal Education	Full Model 1	.19		<.00001*	.24		<.00001*
			4.62	.03		4.09	.04
	Model 6	.17		<.00001*	.22		<.00001*
Head of Househ. Education	Full Model 1						
	Model 7						

*Significance of the difference from zero.

24 Mos. (N=718) PAR *Creativity*			24 Mos. (N=718) PAR *Intellectual*			36 Mos. (N=196) PPVT (A)			42 Mos. (N=308) PPVT (A)		
R^2	F	P	R^2	F	P	R^2	F	P	R^2	F	P
.12		.00001*	.02		.00009*	.13		.00002*	.38		<.00001*
	10.07	.001		18.91	.00002		3.66	.05		36.49	<.00001*
.11		.00001*	.001		.72*	.12		.00004*	.31		<.00001*
.12		.00001*	.02		.00009*	.13		.00002*	.38		<.00001*
	94.79	.00001		7.89	.005		2.01	.15		.03	.84
.01		.004*	.01		.0009*	.13		.00002*	.38		<.00001*
						.13		.00002*	.38		<.00001*
							.86	.35		9.49	.002
						.13		.00001*	.36		<.00001*
						.13		.00002*	.38		<.00001*
							.03	.84		.18	.66
						.13		.00001*	.38		<.00001*
						.13		.00002*	.38		<.00001*
							9.29	.002		9.79	.001
						.09		.00005*	.36		<.00001*

54 Mos. (N=288) Boehm Concepts T.			54 Mos. (N=289) Preschool Inventory			60 Mos. (N=195) WPPSI *Vocabulary*			66 Mos. (N=283) WPPSI *Vocabulary*		
R^2	F	P	R^2	F	P	R^2	F	P	R^2	F	P
.22		<.00001*	.24		<.00001*	.10		.0009*	.19		<.00001*
	7.19	.007		.40	.52		.46	.49		.72	.39
.20		<.00001*	.24		<.00001*	.10		.001*	.19		<.00001*
.22		<.00001*	.24		<.00001*	.10		.0009*	.19		<.00001*
	4.79	.02		6.46	.01		.02	.88		2.65	.10
.21		<.00001*	.23		<.00001*	.10		.009*	.19		<.00001*
.22		<.00001*	.24		<.00001*	.10		.0009*	.19		<.00001*
	.10	.74		.12	.72		.13	.71		.02	.88
.22		<.00001*	.24		<.00001*	.10		.001*	.19		<.00001*
.22		<.00001*	.24		<.00001*	.10		.0009*	.19		<.00001*
	3.32	.06		6.98	.008		2.36	.12		3.63	.05
.21		<.00001*	.23		<.00001*	.09		.002	.18		<.00001*
.22		<.00001*	.24		<.00001*	.10		.0009*	.19		<.00001*
	5.48	.01		13.00	.0003		9.37	.002		1.17	.27
.21		<.00001*	.21		<.00001*	.05		.04*	.19		<.00001*
						.10		.0009*	.19		<.00001*
							.00	1.00		2.34	.12
						.10		.0009*	.19		<.00001*

TABLE 5.5

DESCRIPTION OF THE SUBJECTS: FAMILY SERIES AND TWO-YEAR PAR INTELLECTUAL MEASURES, THREE-YEAR PPVT (A), FOUR-YEAR PRESCHOOL INVENTORY AND BOEHM CONCEPTS, AND FIVE-YEAR WPPSI VOCABULARY SCORES

Variable	24 Mos. (N=311)			36 Mos. (N=300)			42 Mos. (N=313)			48 Mos. (N=284)			48 Mos. (N=294)		
	$\bar{X}$	%	σ	$\bar{X}$	%	σ	$\bar{X}$	%	σ	$\bar{X}$	%	σ	$\bar{X}$	%	σ
Sex (% M)		54			52			52			52			52	
Race (% W)		62			60			67			61			60	
SES	54.05		16.39	54.65		16.45	55.43		14.74	54.45		16.29	54.80		16.41
Birth Order	2.88		2.30	3.21		2.36	3.13		2.02	3.22		2.38	3.25		2.39
N Siblings				2.75		2.20	2.71		1.91	2.75		2.22	2.78		2.32
Father Figure															
– *Father*					76			73			77			76	
– *F. Figure*					12			6			12			11	
– *None*					12			20			11			13	
STIM										33.31		5.45			
Dwelling															
– *House*											70				
– *Apartment*											30				
– *Trailer*															
PAR *Intellectual*	18.20		3.54												
PAR *Information*	6.55		1.73												
PAR *Ideation*	5.33		1.57												
PAR *Creativity*	6.26		1.43												
PPVT (A)				24.59		10.62	29.23		11.95						
Preschool Inventory										33.37		11.63			
Boehm Test of Concepts													14.01		4.90

	54 Mos. (N=278)			54 Mos. (N=277)			60 Mos. (N=288)			66 Mos. (N=264)		
	$\bar{X}$	%	σ	$\bar{X}$	%	σ	$\bar{X}$	%	σ	$\bar{X}$	%	σ
Sex (% M)		51			51			52			52	
Race (% W)		59			59			62			60	
SES	55.15		14.39	55.21		14.37	54.52		16.29	54.71		14.33
Birth Order	3.12		1.96	3.11		1.96	3.22		2.37	3.07		1.91
N. Siblings	2.69		1.85	2.69		1.85	2.75		2.21	2.65		1.81
Father Figure												
- *Father*		73			73			77			74	
- *F. Figure*		7			7			11			7	
- *None*		20			20			12			19	
STIM	32.26		6.23				33.25		5.54	32.54		6.03
Dwelling												
- *House*		65						70			67	
- *Apartment*		34						29			33	
- *Trailer*		.40						.30				
Preschool Inventory	40.83		11.40	16.87		4.62						
Boehm Test of Concepts							13.84		5.04			
WPPSI *Vocabulary*										15.80		5.03

101

$p = .0001$). Higher PAR scores were associated with lower bith order. In this regard it is interesting to note that birth order ran as high as thirteenth in the data set.

At 36 and 42 months the predictor set incorporated the number of siblings and identity of the father figure if one was present. For the variable set there were just over 600 cases ($N = 613$) with requisite predictor and PPVT (A) criterion data. In the case of the added predictors the mean number of brothers and sisters was 2.7, and one out of four children did not have the biological father as the head of the household. Multiple linear regression analyses of the two PPVT data sets are given in Table 5.6. At 36 months father figure was the variable of interest accounting for half the R^2 value of .08 ($F = 14.16$, $p = .0002$). At 42 months the same result obtained, but at a still higher level of statistical significance ($F = 26.78$, $p < .00001$). Higher performance on the PPVT was associated with the presence of the biological father.

The 4-year Boehm Concepts data set represented nearly 600 boys and girls ($N = 571$). We point to a difference in the predictor sets at the two ages studied. In the case of the half-year group the predictor set incorporated two more variables, the STIM description of the home and the type of dwelling. In the case of the latter virtually no children lived in trailers, and the proportion of single family dwellings to apartments was two to one. In the case of the 48 month Boehm Concepts scores, the only variable accounting for a statistically significant proportion of criterion variance was the variable, father figure ($F = 20.40$, $p = .00001$). Higher Concepts scores were associated with the presence of the biological father in the home. In the 54 month data set, one of the additional predictor variables was extremely significant; the STIM score accounted for .21 of the .30 R^2 value of the full regression model 1 ($F = 82.88$, $p < .00001$). Within the five-factor regression model, the role of the father figure variable was virtually nonexistent.

In the case of the 4-year Preschool Inventory scores from nearly 600 children ($N = 573$), all three variables were influential at 48 months. Father figure was the important variable, as with the other 48 month criterion. Father figure explained .08 of the full model's $R^2 = .16$ ($F = 22.69$, $p < .00001$). The influence of the number of siblings was the next most significant influence ($F = 14.28$, $p = .0001$), with birth order contributing 2% of the variance ($F = 8.50$, $p = .003$). At 54 months, the STIM variable performed in a fashion similar to that we have just reported for the Boehm score. STIM explained .18 of the 26% of variance in the full five-variable model ($F = 66.16$, $p < .00001$). No other variable was influential.

Finally, we present the results of applying the Family model of five predictors to the 5-year *Vocabulary* scores from the Wechsler Preschool and Primary Scale of Intelligence using just under 300 children ($N = 288$). At

TABLE 5.6

MULTIPLE LINEAR REGRESSION ANALYSIS OF FAMILY INFLUENCES ON INTELLECTUAL ATTAINMENT

Variable	Models Compared	36 Mos. (N=300) PPVT (A)			42 Mos. (N=313) PPVT (A)			48 Mos. (N=295) Preschool Inventory			48 Mos. (N=294) Boehm Concepts T.		
		R^2	F	p	R^2	F	p	R^2	F	p	R^2	F	p
Birth Order	Full Model 1	.08		<.00001*	.12		<.00001*	.16		<.00001*	.09		<.00001*
	Model 2	.08	.39	.52	.12	.43	.51	.14	8.50	.003	.09	.49	.48
N Siblings	Full Model 1	.08		<.00001*	.12		<.00001*	.16		<.00001*	.09		<.00001*
	Model 3	.08	2.10	.14	.11	2.62	.10	.12	74.28	.0001	.08	.09	.18
Father Figure	Full Model 1	.08		<.00001*	.12		<.00001*	.16		<.00001*	.09		<.00001*
	Model 4	.04	14.16	.0002	.04	26.78	.0007*	.08	27.69	<.00001*	.03	20.40	.00001

Variable	Models Compared	54 Mos. (N=278) Preschool Inventory			54 Mos. (N=277) Boehm Concepts T.			60 Mos. (N=288) WPPSI *Vocabulary*			66 Mos. (N=264) WPPSI *Vocabulary*		
		R^2	F	p	R^2	F	p	R^2	F	p	R^2	F	p
Birth Order	Full Model 1	.26		<.00001*	.30		<.00001*	.26		<.00001*	.12		<.00001*
	Model 2	.26	.02	.87	.30	.13	.71	.26	.00	1.00	.11	1.57	.21
N Siblings	Full Model 1	.26		<.00001*	.30		<.00001*	.26		<.00001*	.12		<.00001*
	Model 3	.26	.0003	.98	.30	.00	1.00	.26	.41	.51	.12	.11	.73
Father Figure	Full Model 1	.26		<.00001*	.30		<.00001*	.26		<.00001*	.12		<.00001*
	Model 4	.26	.00	1.00	.30	.01	.88	.26	.15	.68	.12	.89	.34
STIM	Full Model 1	.26		<.00001*	.30		<.00001*	.26		<.00001*	.12		<.00001*
	Model 5	.08	66.16	.00008*	.09	82.88	.00002*	.11	60.31	<.00001*	.08	11.44	.0008
Dwelling	Full Model 1	.26		<.00001*	.30		<.00001*	.26		<.00001*	.12		<.00001*
	Model 6	.26	.76	.38	.30	.64	.42	.26	.01	.91	.11	3.76	.05

*Significance of the difference from zero.

60 months only the STIM variable was useful; it accounted, however, for .60 of the variance in the full model's $R^2 = .26$ ($F = 60.31$, $p < .00001$). At 66 months the STIM variable remained most powerful in the full model whose $R^2 = .12$. The STIM accounted for one-third of the variance ($F = 11.44$, $p = .0008$). A second variable, dwelling type, explained 1% of the variance and just attained statistical, if not developmental, significance ($F = 3.76$, $p = .05$). Higher criterion scores were associated with single family dwellings.

(D) MATERNAL SERIES

The last predictor series applied to the intellectual domain of development was the set of four maternal traits gathered at delivery of the proband: marital status, age, AFI_{68} (authoritarian–liberalism), and social risk. This last, it will be recalled, is based on a 0–5 score for the lowest five deciles of the perinatal SES score. The proportion of black children is higher in this subset of variables than in the other three. Most mothers were married, and the mean AFI_{68} scores were typical of those we have reported elsewhere (Jordan, 1970). Social risk was modest for the whole sample, representing an SES level just a little below average. As a final note on the information summarized in Table 5.7, we point out that the predictor series of four maternal traits is identical for all 10 multivariate analyses at nine ages.

We present first the multiple regression analysis of PAR scores at 24 months from just over 600 children ($N = 618$) (see Table 5.8). Within the four predictor model of PAR *Information,* the prime source of variance was AFI_{68} ($F = 8.63$, $p = .003$); higher child performance was associated with lower authoritarianism scores. Social risk, intended to convey the ambience for child rearing, was almost equally influential, negatively ($F = 6.19$, $p = .01$). The correlation within the data set for these two variables is $r = .17$ ($p < .0001$). In the case of PAR *Ideation,* the R^2 of the full model of four maternal traits was influenced by two of the variables to an almost identical degree. Delivery age was slightly more influential than social risk, but the level of statistical probability for drop in R^2 from .01 to .008 and .009 was an identical $p = .03$. Higher child performance was associated with lower maternal ages and lesser degrees of social risk at delivery. In the case of PAR *Creativity* scores only marital status was influential, dropping the full model R^2 when deleted, in Model 2, from .04 to .03 ($F = 9.59$, $p = .002$). Higher child scores were associated with being unmarried ($r = .18$, $p < .0001$) also with lower SES levels ($r = .08$, $p = .05$); being unmarried at delivery is highly correlated with lower SES level. The sum of the three PAR subtests yield the fourth *Intellectual* domain score. Interestingly, strong influences waned in the composite score. Delivery age was an influence ($F = 4.18$, $p = .04$), as was social risk ($F = 4.10$, $p = .04$), which was also present in two of the three subtests, *Ideation* and

Information. In both instances the less desirable traits, being unmarried and of lower socioeconomic status, were associated with lower child performance.

PPVT (A) scores for over 600 3-year-olds ($N = 612$) and the four maternal traits may be reported next. At 36 months AFI_{68} scores were most influential, explaining about one-third of the full model's $R^2 = .17$ ($F = 18.35$, $p = .00003$). Slightly less influential, explaining 3% of the variance, was social risk ($F = 10.03$, $p = .001$). the same two variables in the same order of magnitude accounted for variance in the model of 42 month PPVT scores. In a slightly more robust regression model, $R^2 = .23$, maternal authoritarianism in child rearing beliefs explained about one-quarter of the variance ($F = 21.74$, $p = .00001$). Social risk accounted for 4% of the variance ($F = 16.52$, $p = .00006$). The direction of the influence of these two variables was the same as at 36 months on the PPVT criterion. That is, higher child performance on the test was associated with lower scores on the AFI_{68} scale, and being at minimal or zero risk for lower social class membership.

At 4 years there were over 600 boys and girls ($N = 670$) providing all four pieces of predictive data plus the criterion scores from Boehm's Test of Basic Concepts. At 48 months the prime influence in the birthday group was AFI_{68} ($F = 27.34$, $p < .00001$); it was followed by social risk ($F = 7.49$, $p = .006$). In the first instance AFI_{68} provided .07 of the full regression model R^2 of .16, and social risk contributed .02. In a slightly more powerful model of Boehm Concepts scores $R^2 = .18$, at 54 months AFI_{68} provided .05 of the R^2 value ($F = 20.16$, $p = .00001$), and social risk provided .04 of the variance ($F = 14.23$, $p = .0001$). It is interesting to see the consistency of the direction of influence of the two variables on PPVT scores in both 4-year study groups, as in the 3-year data.

Next we present the multiple linear regression analysis of 4-year Preschool Inventory scores using four maternal traits as the predictor set. The regression models of the birthday and half-year subgroups had R^2 values of .20 and .18, respectively. Within the former, the AFI_{68} score dropped the R^2 when deleted, in regression model 4, to .14 ($F = 76.53$, $p < .00001$), while social risk was almost as influential, as Table 5.8 indicates ($F = 21.93$, $p < .00001$). In the 54 month data set the same two variables were influential, but with the slight difference of degree of influence reversed. In the multiple regression analysis of 54 month Preschool Inventory total scores, social risk contributed .05 of the R^2 value of .18 ($F = 18.32$, $p = .00002$), while authoritarian family ideology contributed .04 ($F = 18.32$, $p = .00002$). The direction of the influences remains consistently negative at this age.

Finally we report the results of applying the four maternal traits to WPPSI *Vocabulary* scores from 664 children. Beginning with the 60 month data set, we report that social risk accounted for 4% of the *Vocabulary*

TABLE 5.7: DESCRIPTION OF THE
TWO-YEAR PAR INTELLECTUAL MEASURES, THREE-YEAR PPVT (A), FOUR-YEAR PRESCHOOL

Variable	*24 Mos.* $\bar{M}$	%	σ	*36 Mos.* $\bar{M}$	%	σ
	(N=618)			(N=300)		
Sex (% M)		53			52	
Race (% W)		65			64	
SES	53.15		15.75	53.97		16.12
Married		88			88	
Delivery Age	25.67		6.54	25.36		6.56
AFI$_{68}$	26.15		8.05	27.07		7.58
Social Risk	1.10		1.63	1.23		1.68
PAR *Intellectual*	17.94		3.69			
PAR *Information*	6.40		1.79			
PAR *Ideation*	5.52		3.17			
PAR *Creativity*	6.14		1.43			
PPVT (A)				25.61		10.70
Preschool Inventory						
Boehm Test of Concepts						

	54 Mos. $\bar{M}$	%	σ	*54 Mos.* $\bar{M}$	%	σ
	(N=334)			(N=333)		
Sex (% M)		53			53	
Race (% W)		66			66	
SES	53.34		14.87	53.39		14.86
Married		88			88	
Delivery Age	25.77		6.52	25.72		6.47
AFI$_{68}$	25.85		8.30	25.90		8.26
Social Risk	1.05		1.56	1.06		1.56
Preschool Inventory	42.15		11.21			
Boehm Test of Concepts				17.34		4.52
WPPSI *Vocabulary*						

SUBJECTS: MATERNAL SERIES AND

INVENTORY AND BOEHM CONCEPTS, AND FIVE-YEAR WPPSI VOCABULARY SCORES

	42 Mos.			48 Mos.			48 Mos.	
$\overline{M}$	%	σ	$\overline{M}$	%	σ	$\overline{M}$	%	σ
	(N=312)			(N=338)			(N=338)	
	53			51			51	
	62			60			60	
54.41		14.82	54.43		16.33	54.56		16.22
	87			86			86	
25.52		6.42	25.09		6.54	25.09		6.55
26.63		8.21	27.57		7.44	27.61		7.46
1.14		1.62	1.29		1.43	1.29		1.73
30.77		12.54						
			33.71		11.39			
						14.20		4.65

	60 Mos.			66 Mos.	
$\overline{M}$	%	σ	$\overline{M}$	%	σ
	(N=338)			(N=326)	
	51			53	
	61			66	
54.43		16.17	53.24		14.59
	86			88	
25.04		6.45	25.82		6.56
27.57		7.38	25.87		8.20
1.28		1.72	.99		1.51
14.25		5.12	16.47		5.09

TABLE 5.8: MULTIPLE LINEAR REGRESSION ANALYSIS OF

Variable	Models Compared	24 Mos. (N=618) PAR *Information*			24 Mos. (N=618) PAR *Ideation*		
		R^2	F	P	R^2	F	P
Married	Full Model 1	.04		.00001*	.01		.04*
			.27	.59		.44	.50
	Model 2	.04		<.00001*	.01		.02*
Delivery Age	Full Model 1	.04		.00001*	.01		.04*
			2.66	.10		4.72	.03
	Model 3	.04		.00001*	.008		.15*
AFI$_{68}$	Full Model 1	.04		.00001*	.01		.04*
			8.63	.003		.02	.88
	Model 4	.08		.0002*	.01		.01*
Social Risk	Full Model 1	.04		.00001*	.01		.04*
			6.19	.01		4.34	.03
	Model 5	.03		.00007*	.009		.13*

		48 Mos. (N=337) Boehm Concepts T.			48 Mos. (N=338) Preschool Inventory		
		R^2	F	P	R^2	F	P
Married	Full Model 1	.16		<.00001*	.20		<.00001*
			.63	.42		.03	.84
	Model 2	.15		<.00001*	.20		<.00001*
Delivery Age	Full Model 1	.16		<.00001*	.20		<.00001*
			3.13	.07		1.79	.18
	Model 3	.15		<.00001*	.20		<.00001*
AFI$_{68}$	Full Model 1	.16		<.00001*	.20		<.00001*
			27.34	<.00001		26.53	<.00001
	Model 4	.09		<.00001*	.14		<.00001*
Social Risk	Full Model 1	.16		<.00001*	.20		<.00001*
			7.49	.006		21.93	<.00001
	Model 5	.14		<.00001*	.15		<.00001*

*Significance of the difference from zero.

ATERNAL INFLUENCES ON INTELLECTUAL ATTAINMENT

24 Mos. (N=618) PAR Creativity			24 Mos. (N=618) PAR Intellectual			36 Mos. (N=300) PPVT (A)			42 Mos. (N=312) PPVT (A)		
R^2	F	P	R^2	F	P	R^2	F	P	R^2	F	P
.04		.00002*	.01		.03*	.17		<.00001*	.23		<.00001*
	19.59	.002		.32	.56		3.30	.07		1.77	.18
.03		.0005*	.01		.02*	.16		<.00001*	.23		<.00001*
.04		.00002	.01		.03*	.17		<.00001*	.23		<.00001*
	1.56	.21		4.18	.04		2.20	.13		.31	.57
.04		.00001	.009		.11	.17		<.00001*	.23		<.00001*
.04		.00002	.01		.03*	.17		<.00001*	.23		<.00001*
	2.24	.13		.98	.32		18.35	.00003		21.74	.00001
.04		.00002	.01		.02*	.12		<.00001*	.18		<.00001*
.04		.00002	.01		.03*	.17		<.00001*	.23		<.00001*
	.005	.94		4.10	.04		10.03	.001		16.52	.00006
.04		.00001	.009		.11*	.14		<.00001*	.19		<.00001*

54 Mos. (N=333) Boehm Concepts T.			54 Mos. (N=334) Preschool Inventory			60 Mos. (N=338) WPPSI Vocabulary			66 Mos. (N=326) WPPSI Vocabulary		
R^2	F	P	R^2	F	P	R^2	F	P	R^2	F	P
.18		<.00001*	.18		<.00001*	.13		<.00001*	.12		<.00001*
	.90	.34		.78	.37		3.21	.07		.004	.94
.18		<.00001*	.18		<.00001*	.12		<.00001*	.12		<.00001*
.18		<.00001*	.18		<.00001*	.13		<.00001*	.12		<.00001*
	.51	.47		.32	.56		5.54	.02		.22	.63
.18		<.00001*	.18		<.00001*	.12		<.00001*	.12		<.00001*
.18		<.00001*	.18		<.00001*	.13		<.00001*	.12		<.00001*
	20.16	.00001		16.19	.00007		6.92	.008		6.65	.01
.13		<.00001*	.14		<.00001*	.11		<.00001*	.10		<.00001*
.18		<.00001*	.18		<.00001*	.13		<.00001*	.12		<.00001*
	14.23	.0001		18.32	.00002		15.27	.0001		17.83	.00003
.14		<.00001*	.13		<.00001*	.09		<.00001*	.07		.00001*

criterion variance in a model explaining 13% ($F = 15.27$, $p = .0001$). Explaining 2% of the variance was AFI_{68} ($F = 6.99$, $p = .008$); in addition, delivery age accounted for 1% of the variance ($F = 5.54$, $p = .02$). At 66 months social risk was influential, accounting for 5% of the variance in a model explaining 12% ($F = 17.83$, $p = .00003$). The second influential variable was AFI_{68} ($F = 6.65$, $p = .01$).

Discussion

MODELS

As a brief summary of the materials to be discussed, we recall that four regression models containing 19 predictors in total were applied in multiple regression analyses to 12 criteria in the *Intellectual* domain. The criterion measures were first taken at 24 months and the data at that age were maternal perceptions of child attainment. In subsequent years the criterion measures use direct child performance examined individually by a tester matched by race. The later measures were subtests of standardized scales or standardized tests at ages 3–5 years.

Regression analyses emphasize the basic value of a predictor set when it is used to assess a criterion by assigning its variance. In Table 5.9 we see the mean R^2 values—proportion of variance—of four predictor models applied to 12 criteria. The individual R^2 values are given, as are the mean R^2 for criteria. The range of R^2 values in the table is from $R^2 = .01$ to $R^2 = .38$. The regression models present various aggregates of predictors associated with the developmental stage at which both predictors and criterion variables were gathered. The lowest R^2 values occur at youngest ages when the predictor series were the least elaborate. Yet mere brevity of the predictor series is an insufficient explanation; two of the models, the Biological and Maternal series, consist of perinatal data, and so were complete when applied in the first model. All things considered, the R^2 values of the four models of 12 criteria in Table 5.9 are not very powerful. They explain at best one-third of the criterion variance; on the average they explain far less, the grand mean R^2 being .14.

Considering the entire developmental span covered by the 12 *Intellectual* criteria, the best predictive set is the Social model. Ranging up from $R^2 = .02$ this model generated the highest R^2 value, .38, and the mean value was $R^2 = .15$. On the average, less effective was the Maternal model with a mean $R^2 = .12$. In third place was the model composed of Family data, in which the mean $R^2 = .09$. The least effective model was the Biological predictor set which has a mean $R^2 = .03$; the highest R^2 among the Biological models was .09. Two predictive models, Social and Maternal

TABLE 5.9

R^2 VALUES OF INTELLECTUAL DOMAIN ANALYSES

				CRITERIA	Mean R^2
Biological Model	Social Model	Family Model	Maternal Model		
.01	.02	.04	.01	24 M. PAR *Intellectual*	.02
.02	.05	.04	.04	24 M. PAR *Information*	.04
.01	.007	.01	.01	24 M. PAR *Ideation*	.01
.02	.12	.02	.04	24 M. PAR *Creativity*	.05
.06	.13	.08	.17	36 M. PPVT (A)	.11
.04	.38	.12	.23	42 M. PPVT (A)	.19
.06	.24	.16	..20	48 M. Preschool Inventory	.16
.09	.19	.09	.16	48 M. Boehm Test of Concepts	.16
.03	.24	.26	.18	54 M. Preschool Inventory	.18
.02	.22	.30	.18	54 M. Boehm Test of Concepts	.18
.03	.10	.26	.13	60 M. WPPSI *Vocabulary*	.13
.02	.19	.12	.12	66 M. *Vocabulary*	.11
Mean .03	.15	.09	.12		.11

variables, were fairly similar in predictive power and were much better than the Biological model. The predictive value of the models tends to peak at age 3–4, and declines subsequently. The least predictive criteria in Table 5.9 are clearly those at age 2 years. The most predictable criteria, that is, those with the highest R^2 values, are those at child ages 42–54 months.

HYPOTHESES

Our hypothesis of comparative effects of the models was given earlier in this chapter. Briefly, it postulated that the most predicting models in terms of R^2 value across the development span of interest would be in the order of first, the Maternal predictor set, followed closely by the Social predictors, and the Family model. At a lesser level of predictor value, well below the first three, would be the Biological model. Table 5.9 gives R^2 values of the four models of 12 predictors from 24 to 66 months of age. None of the models account for half of the criterion variance; the highest R^2 value, .38 at 42 months (PPVT), is in the predictor set hypothesized as second most influential. The mean R^2 value of the hypothetically prime Maternal model is .11, and it is second highest. The predictor set hypothesized as third in influence, that is, providing an account of criterion variance, was the Family set, and its relative influence was confirmed. The hypothesized role of least influential predictor set was confirmed for the Biological model. With a mean $R^2 = .03$, this set of four perinatal predictors gave consistently low accounts of criterion variance, except at age 3–4 years. At virtually all other ages and for virtually all criteria the Biological model R^2 values are the lowest. Accordingly, we see that the hypothesized primary influences on *Intellectual* attainment, that is, Maternal influences, were not supported. The hypothetically lesser influence of Social data was greatest in the sense of the mean R^2 generated by regression models.

DISCRETE INFLUENCES

Our goal of examining the influence of four domains of variables also permits examination of particular variables. Within the four predictor domain are 19 predictor variables gathered at child ages from the moment of delivery, for example, the Apgar score, to age 66 months. In the case of the Biological and Maternal models, all variables are perinatal. Of the four variables of weight, biological risk, Apgar, and sex, the least useful in the sense of being identified in the regression analyses as a source of variance was the sex of the children. It appears in Table 5.10, but only as a relatively low order source of variance, and does not appear at all for the last three criteria. It seems appropriate to comment, however, that the effect may be due to selection of items which expressly suppress sex differences in standardized tests. In contrast, the Apgar score is much more commonly associated with the 12 *Intellectual* criteria, and is the prime source of variance in 7 of 11 analyses. We note, however, that low rather than high Apgars are associated with high criterion scores, an anomalous finding. The next influence in terms of overall contribution is birthweight, which tends to be either the prime or secondary source of variance. A minor degree of influence is associated with biological risk, which (as Table 5.10 shows) while only once the prime source of criterion variance for the 12 *Intellectual* criteria, was a secondary or tertiary influence about half the time. In considering these observations it is salutary to keep in mind that they are made solely within the context of the set of four variables; accordingly, when speaking of the primary role of a predictor, we ascribe its influence to its relative position within the given set of variables. Change the variable set and the role of a given variable will rise, fall, or disappear as a way to account for the variance.

In the case of the six variables grouped as Social predictors, we recall that a role for any predictor other than SES or race is not possible until the fifth test criterion was gathered at age 3 years. This is because only SES and race were available until information on parents was gathered at 3 years. On the other hand, from 36 months on the role of the earliest predictor is appraised when later predictors were incorporated into the predictive model. In the right hand side of Table 5.10 we see the comparative influence of SES and race at age 2 years. Race—ethnic identity—of the children studied is the greater influence in mothers' reports of their children's development through the Preschool Attainment Record. However, when the occupation of mother and father plus maternal education were incorporated at 36 months, the influence of race declined. Obviously, there is a high correlation between SES and the three parental variables, and these more discrete variables become salient. Much the same phenomenon is evident when the variable of education of the head of the household is incorporated at age 5.

Considering the Social predictor set across the developmental span from 24 months to 66 months, the substantial role of the perinatal SES score is evident. Even when the predictor set includes all six Social variables, the McGuire and White SES score calculated at birth is a source of criterion variance. Race, formulated here as ethnic group and hence not in the Biological group as a predictor, plays some role when not competing with other variables in the first half of the predictors in Table 5.10. Once the predictor set became complex, the race of the subjects disappeared as an influence. The level of education of the mother is an important influence as a prime or subordinate source of criterion variance in several instances. Whether or not mothers work outside the home is not very important for intellectual test scores, comparatively speaking. The occupation of the father is a persistent but minor influence. In the case of the education of the head of the household, typically the biological father, we regret this variable was not gathered sooner. In making this observation we note that, as a part of data-processing, it could have been incorporated into analyses of even the 6-month data. However, that tactic would have vitiated the time-specific and prospective nature of the array of predictor variables. The observation also illustrates that having employed a prospective technique of data taking, one must be prepared to cope with the wisdom of hindsight at a later date.

The Family set of predictors starts with birth order, adds the number of siblings and specification of the father figure at age 3, and ends with a description of the home through the type of dwelling and the STIM score at ages 4–5 years. From the data summarized in Table 5.10, it is evident that the

TABLE 5.10

PREDICTORS IN ORDER OF STATISTICAL CONTRIBUTION IN MULTIPLE REGRESSION ANALYSES TO R^2 OF FULL MODELS

CRITERION	BIOLOGICAL MODEL				SES	Race	SOCIAL MODEL			
Child Age (Yrs.)	Weight	Biological Risk	Apgar	Sex (M)			Pop's Occup.	Mom's Employ.	Mom's Educat.	Head of Househ. Educat.
	Birth	*Birth*	*Birth*	*Birth*	*Birth*	*Birth*	*Three*	*Three*	*Five*	*Five*
24 M. PAR *Intellectual*		1	2	2	2	1				
24 M. PAR *Information*		3	2	1	2	1				1
24 M. PAR *Ideation*			1							
24 M. PAR *Creativity*	2		1		1	2				2
36 M. PPVT (A)		2	1		2					
42 M. PPVT (A)	2		1		1		3			
48 M. Preschool Inventory	2	3	1	4	1	3				2
48 M. Boehm Test of Concepts		2	1	3	1	3				2
54 M. Preschool Inventory	1		2			3		2		2
54 M. Boehm Test of Concepts	1				1	3				1
60 M. WPPSI *Vocabulary*		2	1							2
66 M. *Vocabulary*			1					1		1

114

	FAMILY MODEL						MATERNAL MODEL			
	Birth Order	N Siblings	Father Figure	Dwelling Type	STIM		Married	Age	AFI_{68}	Social Risk
	Birth	3 Years	3 Years	5 Years	5 Years		Birth	Birth	Birth	Birth
24 M. PAR *Intellectual*	1*									2
24 M. PAR *Information*	1*								1	
24 M. PAR *Ideation*	1*							1		2
24 M. PAR *Creativity*	1*						1	2		
36 M. PPVT (A)			1						1	2
42 M. PPVT (A)			1						1	2
48 M. Preschool Inventory	3	2	1						1	2
48 M. Boehm Test of Concepts			1						1	2
54 M. Preschool Inventory					1				2	1
54 M. Boehm Test of Concepts					1				1	2
60 M. WPPSI *Vocabulary*					1			2	3	1
66 M. WPPSI *Vocabulary*									2	1

*1=Sole Predictor.

115

type of residence occupied by children (house, apartment, or trailer) is not very useful information. In addition we recall that virtually no children lived in trailer homes, and about one-third lived in apartments. The nature of the father figure has some significance at child ages 3 and 4, but then disappears. The number of brothers and sisters play a minor but steady role in several analyses. Birth order effects are evident up to age 4, even when appraised in the presence of other variables.

The most interesting element is the role of the STIM scores gathered once at age 54 months: In the last four Family analyses listed in Table 5.10, we see that the STIM score is the prime source of variance. What is interesting about this finding of influence in all possible predictor sets is that in virtually all instances, no other Family variables were found to account for the criterion variance in addition to the STIM score. As with the Social variable of education of the head of the household, one would have liked to use STIM scores as baseline data. However, the scale was not in existence at the time the cohort was formed, but was added to the data set at the first opportunity.

In the case of the maternal model, all four variables were perinatal-marital status, delivery age, authoritarianism score (AFI_{68}), and social risk. The effect of this, in contrast to birth order for example, was to apply a substantial predictor set to even the 2-year criteria. The least useful Maternal predictors were marital status and age at delivery of the proband, and these two maternal traits tended to have little relevance to the *Intellectual* domain. In contrast, authoritarian child rearing orientation—or the lack of it—was consistently the prime or the secondary source of criterion variance across the entire developmental span. The fourth perinatal measure, social risk, was of secondary influence at age 2 and 3 years but subsequently extended its increasing influence as an important source of variance to age 66 months.

In summarizing the relative merits of the 19 predictors, we note in passing the size of the accounts of variance (R^2) given in Table 5.10. We also note the time dependence of the regression models that is expressed by the number of predictors in the regression models at specific child ages. Within the regression models and their explicit constitution and predictive power, the Apgar score is a useful if peculiar predictor, followed by birthweight. Among the Social predictors, perinatal SES and the level of maternal education are important. Within the Family predictors the STIM score is most interesting, and at some distance so is the identity of the father figure. From the Maternal domain social risk, meaning the SES subcultural structure the mother represents, and authoritarianism are influential.

Language Development

6

Introduction

Thought encompasses many styles of manipulating reality; at one extreme is the challenge to solve a geometric puzzle by viewing lines and angles in new ways, a process in which imagery and the ability to go beyond the given visual image predominate. Rather different is the process of thought in which the ear is the important modality. Sounds and words can be refined into abstractions, and the product set forth by children can be language in a receptive or expressive mode (Jordan, 1976b).

For the most part people agree that language is the critical aspect of mental growth in young children. For youngsters adept at using abstractions and words, the preschool years flow into those of middle childhood and its developmental tasks. Centered in schooling, these challenges rely on language in reading, writing, speaking, and in comprehending. For those whose progress in language is inadequate in the early years, the subsequent phases of life are difficult for all but those lucky enough to receive special help for extended periods of time.

In this chapter we examine influences on language attainment. The domain is not absolutely different from that which precedes it; intellectual development, as we styled the domain examined in the preceding chapter, is itself often linguistic, if not exclusively so. In consequence, the datum of this chapter may be thought of as distinct from that of the preceding chapter. However, there is only a distinction, rather than a difference, from the domain of intellectual development presented in the previous chapter, and the topic of linguistic attainment in this chapter. The distinction applies more to those aspects in the preceding chapter with a broad range of mental processes, ranging from use of ideas and knowledge of concepts to grasp of vocabulary. In the domain analyzed in this chapter, emphasis is on use of words as process. Understandably, there are times when the distinction is not robust, because knowledge of words and syntax, and their use in the purposeful activity we call language, become very close. When taken together both domains express the richness of mental life in children. Indeed, it is this sharing of skills in development which leads us to make a mere distinction, rather than present data in Chapters 5 and 6, however continuous, as if they were quite different. A further note of compatibility is that the language datum to be presented is virtually identical in developmental span to the intellectual measures. The child measures grouped as linguistic start at child age 24 months. In both cases, however, parents are informants. This is a reality element in research strategy since obtaining data in language from all subjects directly at age 24 months is not likely.

The writer is conscious of certain arbitrariness in dividing the 13 tests of these two sections into *Intellectual* and *Linguistic*. While arbitrary, the division is not irrational. Thus, at age 5, WPPSI *Vocabulary* means knowing word meanings, but ITPA *Auditory Association* means using meanings purposefully. At an earlier age, 2 years, the PAR inquires into exploratory behavior and curiosity, while Mecham's (1958) Verbal Language Development Scale (VLDS) asks about use of the word "another," and whether toilet needs are expressed in words. Nevertheless, we feel obliged to assert a sense of continuity between the criterion measures of Chapter 6, and those of the preceding chapter.

Language Development

Few topics are as fascinating as the emergence of language in man. Through the process people develop much of their essential normality. Those whose language development is arrested, for example by deafness, are robbed of an enriching quality in life. Those more fortunate acquire a key to a fuller life and to the social interaction on which so much of life's business depends.

Our understanding of how children acquire language is not great, and the reasons are not hard to understand. Language has two aspects, one external, the other internal. In the case of the external we know what children say, and by sampling across ages we can develop a picture of the sequence of stages. For example, we can record samples of oral activity at intervals of 3 months and identify the development sequence in the early years. Virtually any standard text on child development will provide an account of sequential levels of children's language. These descriptive accounts tell us the size of children's *vocabulary* and the stages of articulation. They may go further and describe the kinds of words in the vocabulary—its *lexical* variety. That is, the frequency and proportion of nouns, verbs, adjectives, and so forth.

However, there is a parallel, internal track. It is the process by which a sentient but exceedingly immature member of the species responds to sounds through a complex neurophysiological process. At one end of the process is the ear, and at the other end is the brain. Information from brain injuries tells us that the cortex is the site of language activity. To Mowrer (1958) the process is built on fun, food, and friendly companionship. Babies hear sounds, and recall them (reminiscence) because of their association with feeding and social relations. The biggest problem, of course, is how the infant's brain assimilates noises and sorts them out. It seems not unreasonable to postulate that this is species-specific behavior, a tendancy much like that in other creatures to build nests, or to engage in grooming; it is a capacity to manipulate within the infant linguistic stimuli from the world. Accordingly, the inner child has a central nervous system wired to elaborate auditory signals through memory and play.

In recent years we have begun to see more complex aspects of language placed under scrutiny. Work by Menyuk (1969), Crystal, Fletcher, and Gorman (1976), Carrow (1974), Lee (1974), and Snyder-McLean and McLean (1978), has looked at the process by which the syntax of language is generated. We are beginning to learn a little about how words are put together. For example, Joe can comprehend with equal clarity a statement in the active voice, *Tiffy kicked the ball,* and also get a comparable understanding from the statement, *The ball was kicked by Tiffy.* However, this work has far to go and is not yet analyzable on a broad scale.

At intermediate levels of complexity are accounts of language development in terms of abstraction and use. In the case of the former, we can identify maturity in young children by the level of abstraction in words and frequency they have attained in vocabulary. In use of abstraction human beings do remarkable things. A child may talk about someone who is not present, or about the possibility of going out to play. Also, the child may move back and forward in time. Yesterday and tomorrow may be impossible to convey to children, but they eventually assimilate them as concepts.

Still another approach is to consider language as a process reflecting psychological and linguistic components jointly. In that formulation we note that some meanings are elicited very easily by association from children. We say "A daddy is big," and quite small children can supply the missing word when we go on to say, "A baby is _____." In the psycholinguistic approach we recognize that language has passive and active directions, since children comprehend and also speak. We also recognize that language may be connected to signals arriving through the senses; that is, we know that language as an inner process of the children's minds can be reached by sending messages through vision, or through hearing. Obviously, this process can be reversed and observable child performance involving thought in language can go in one modality and out another. Thus, a school child can read out loud, and a skilled secretary can write shorthand or type from a recording device.

Finally, we note that study of language excludes asking children how they talk, for as with adults the mind does not know its own knowing. Accordingly, with young children we may be forced to ask an informed person about how a small child uses language. While this is inferior to asking the child, it is superior to receiving a blank stare from a 2-year-old. Indeed, even a fluent 3-year-old may be quieted by the inhibiting presence of a strange lady, or be cast into pensive silence by the visitor's beard.

Despite the difficulties, study of language in children is rewarding. In this chapter we attempt to assess a variety of influences on a range of language elements, doing so by means of relatively well standardized procedures at ages 2–5 years.

Hypotheses

We start this statement of research hypotheses by offering several propositions about language development based on many years of clinical and research interest in the topic. First, we note that language is the major tool of acculturation, the process by which one becomes someone in society. That is, we acquire values and roles through exposure to language. Some strata of society and, indeed some societies, value languages more than others. Some levels of society consider language in children evidence of the success or failure of child rearing. Bernstein (1960) has pointed out that middle-class people value language and develop a capacity to elaborate syntax in their children, while lower class people are also less word centered, and tend to inculcate in their young stereotype in idiom-restriction rather than linguistic innovation. The tendency to do either one of these, as well as the parents' attitudes toward linguistic training of the young (or the lack of it) are themselves effects of the parents' cultural setting. As a consequence, we hypothesize for this inquiry that the Social model of predictor variables will explain more variance in the language measures from 24 to 66 months than any of the other three predictor sets. The Social series consists of elements which are marker variables for the social ambience within which language emerges.

However, there needs to be greater specification of language development. Accordingly, we note that much of language training is exposure to people speaking, and this means members of the family. For this reason we hypothesize that the second most important influence in this investigation will be the Family predictor series. It includes for example the sheer number of people who will be talking, and the structure of the family group, size, and father figure.

In all of these contexts there is the figure of the mother, the prime caregiver when children are small. We hypothesize that she will be an influence, but less so in her individual traits than the cumulative effect of her own cultural context (e.g., the social risk predictor and her family as major socializing influences). For this reason we hypothesize the Maternal model is the third influence on language attainment; after the Social and Family predictor variables.

There is at this point only one predictor set left; it is the Biological model. While not without a strong conviction about constitutional bases of language growth (i.e., an innate disposition toward language by virtue of the way the genetic code shapes the central nervous system), we find that the Biological series contains little or nothing touching on that formulation. We hypothesize a weak, minimal role for the Biological series of predictors in this investigation of growth in language.

Measures

This chapter examines stages of growth in language from age 2 to age 5 years. There are five criteria, the first of which is the Verbal Language Development Scale developed by Mecham (1958). This scale is an extension of the communication portion of the Vineland Social Maturity Scale. The scale, according to the author, has a split-half reliability of .98. It yields a "language age" normatively, although in the case of this study, raw scores were the actual form of the criterion. As with the Preschool Attainment Record employed in the preceding chapter, an informant rather than the child provides the datum. The pros and cons remain the same; the indirect acquisition of information offsets the possibility of nonresponse at age 2 years to direct inquiry, plus there is the added value of using the views of the child's caregiver, usually the biological mother.

A second test at 2 years is a direct measure of language attainment, the Full Range Picture Vocabulary Test (FRPVT), developed by Ammons and

Ammons (1958), and widely accepted because of its applicability and validity. The scale assesses people's ability to produce a verbal response to a picture stimulus. It has the interesting attribute of applicability to the old, and, as in the case of this study, to the very young. Granted the risk of nonexistent data from the most immature at our study age of 30 months the scale differs from the Mecham by using the child as the source of data, rather than an informant. Even so, the risk of nonresponse needs to be weighed against informed views of a caregiver. Obviously, one shifts to direct measures as soon as the risk of nonresponse seems worth taking.

At age 3 years the views on language attainment in probands of informed caregivers were elicited once more. At this age the *Communication* section of Doll's PAR scale was employed once more.

At age 4 years the *Associative Vocabulary* scale of Caldwell's (1970) Preschool Inventory was given to each child. In this subtest the examiner asks questions designed to demonstrate awareness of the connotation of a word by an action or association to qualities of the underlying verbal concept. There are 12 such items in the revised version of the Preschool Inventory.

The last language measure was the *Auditory Association* subtest of Kirk and McCarthy's (1968) Illinois Test of Psycholinguistic Abilities, known for convenience as the ITPA. The examiner says, "grass is green," and the child is expected to reply that sugar is "white."

In considering this criterion series it is appropriate to note the nature of the linguistic measures, which constitute the elements, whether gathered directly or indirectly. In most uses the datum consist of words, items in children's lexicons in the case of the measures using direct responses of children. The domain does not employ measures of syntax, for example those of Crystal, Fletcher, and Gorman (1976), or of skill in generation of language in the sense used by Chomsky (1957) and by Menyuk (1969). Neither does one find the lexical ratios, for example Type-to-Token (TTR), which we have discussed elsewhere (Jordan, 1976b). However, in that work we presented results from the corpus of data drawn on here in the form of articulation and auditory discrimination scores at an age beyond the scope of this work, 6 years. Nonetheless, there are merits in the present series and its application to the years up to age 5. For example, the ITPA *Auditory Association* subtest has been identified by Bereiter and Engelmann (1966) as particularly useful in educational planning for young children. Equally, single word vocabulary, elicited by presenting either the word or its picture, plus the abstract level of words have a long tradition of utility in studies of development. For example, in 1914 Binet and Simon emphasized the role of oral language in their inquiry. Suffice it to say we are conscious of the range and richness of language as a dimension of child development, and report case data at four ages, 2–5 years, employing five measures applicable to young children.

Once more we apply four models to the criterion series. The Biological predictor set of four elements from the perinatal period is followed by the Social series composed of six items identified at ages from birth to 5 years. The Family series of predictors contains five items from birth to 5 years. The Maternal predictor set comprises four perinatal elements. Thus 19 independent variables are grouped into four sets. As with analyses in preceding chapters, not all variables are applied to all criteria. The predictor series reflects the prospective nature of the inquiry and grows, as does the criterion series, with the development of the children year by year.

Results

(A) BIOLOGICAL SERIES

At age 24 months data on the four predictor variables plus the criterion Verbal Language Development Scale (Mecham, 1958) are available on nearly 700 children ($N = 692$). This criterion, an extension of the Vineland Social Maturity Scale, obtains a picture of language attainment from the principal caregiver by interview. Items in the scale at the relevant age range ask, for example, if the child talks in short sentences, names common pictures, uses plurals, and verbalizes toilet needs. One very bright child whose attainments have been striking through his first full decade of life at the time of writing, was able to recite numbers into the thirties, print simple words, and name coins. At the opposite extreme were a few children still operating, effectively, at the level of infants. As a group, however, at age 2 years the mean level by norm was 2.3 years. Given the normal distribution of SES scores, our use of 700 children may be considered self-norming for all practical purposes. In the VLDS data set the sexes and races are about evenly divided, and other traits given in Table 6.1 are consistent with those in other chapters. In this regard we note that the 30 month FRPVT data set contains both fewest cases and fewest black children. The reason is that the process of data taking at age 2½ years was quite reduced by the procedural difficulties that affect any long-term enterprise at one time or another.

Turning to the multiple regression analyses, which are summarized in Table 6.2, we consider the influence of Biological variables on early language. At 24 months, three of the four predictors were influential in the regression model. Sex was the chief influence. Higher scores were found in girls ($F = 19.50$, $p = .00001$), and deletion of this variable in regression

TABLE 6.1

DESCRIPTION OF THE SUBJECTS: BIOLOGICAL SERIES AND TWO-YEAR VERBAL LANGUAGE DEVELOPMENT SCALE AND FULL RANGE PICTURE VOCABULARY SCALE, THREE-YEAR PAR *COMMUNICATION*, FOUR-YEAR P.I. *ASSOCIATIVE VOCABULARY*, AND FIVE-YEAR ITPA *AUDITORY ASSOCIATION*

Variable	24 Mos. (N=692)		30 Mos. (N=216)		36 Mos. (N=370)		42 Mos. (N=357)	
	$\bar{X}$ / %	σ	$\bar{X}$ / %	σ	$\bar{X}$ / %	σ	$\bar{X}$ / %	σ
Sex (% M)	53		58		53		52	
Race (% W)	60		72		67		59	
SES	54.00	15.96	50.86	16.62	55.78	16.11	55.33	14.79
Birthweight	7.06	1.26	7.12	1.25	7.10	1.25	6.96	1.27
BioRisk	.49	1.09	.52	1.13	.39	.91	.61	1.27
Apgar	8.73	1.46	8.68	1.46	9.02	1.21	8.57	1.62
VLDS	19.53	4.53						
FRPVT			9.26	3.04				

Variable	48 Mos. (N=377)		54 Mos. (N=366)		60 Mos. (N=390)		66 Mos. (N=363)	
	$\bar{X}$ / %	σ	$\bar{X}$ / %	σ	$\bar{X}$ / %	σ	$\bar{X}$ / %	σ
Sex (% M)	53		52		53		52	
Race (% W)	47		68		55		63	
SES	55.32	16.37	53.96	14.87	55.72	16.11	54.07	14.72
Birthweight	7.11	1.20	6.97	1.30	7.08	1.24	6.96	1.25
BioRisk	.33	.80	.60	1.27	.35	.88	.57	1.20
Apgar	9.05	1.17	8.52	1.63	9.03	1.19	8.55	1.59
P. I. *Assoc. Vocab.*	5.53	2.84	7.31	2.77				
ITPA *Audit. Assoc.*					15.36	5.16	18.32	5.11

Model 5 dropped the R^2 from .04 to .01. Apgar scores explained 1% of the model's variance ($F = 10.31$, $p = .001$), and biological risk only a little less ($F = 9.00$, $p = .002$). In the case of the second language criterion at 2 years, the Full Range Picture Vocabulary Test, the pattern was slightly different. Biological risk accounted for .06 of the regression model's .08 ($F = 12.14$, $p = .0006$), and sex was a close influence ($F = 10.56$, $p = .001$) with higher scores for girls once more.

At 3 years the linguistic criterion was the *Communication* scale of the Preschool Attainment Record in a data set from over 700 children ($N = 727$). At 36 months, sex was the prime source of criterion variance, contributing practically all of the full model's $R^2 = .09$ ($F = 35.12$, $p < .00001$). Biological risk at birth was also influential, and contributed .02 of the variance ($F = 9.06$, $p = .002$). At 42 months the full model of four predictors explained 4% of the variance. Within that context, Apgar scores accounted for criterion variance ($F = 7.18$, $p = .007$), as did birthweight ($F = 5.11$, $p = .02$) to a lesser extent.

The data set of four Biological predictors was applied at age 4 to *Associative Vocabulary* scores from nearly 800 ($N = 743$) children who took the Preschool Inventory. In the 48 month data set, no sex effects were apparent. The major influence within the regression model explaining 5% of the variance was the Apgar score which contributed 3% ($F = 13.95$, $p = .0002$). Criterion scores were negatively correlated with Apgar scores, $r = -.14$ ($p = .01$); that is, slightly lowered physiological status at birth was associated with high language scores. Biological risk was a second influence ($F = 7.04$, $p = .008$), followed by birthweight, which just achieved statistical significance ($p = .05$). Risk scores were negatively correlated with the criterion, but not at a significant level, and birthweight was positively correlated with criterion scores at the .02 level of statistical significance. At 54 months Apgar scores were the prime influence within the four-term set which explained 3% of the variance ($F = 6.15$, $p = .01$). Birthweight reached the .02 level of probability, explaining .01 of the full regression model's .03 ($F = 5.16$, $p = .02$). Apgar's were negatively correlated with the criterion, but not at a significant level, while birthweight was positively correlated with Associative Vocabulary scores ($p = .02$).

A data set larger by 10 cases than the 4-year set was used at 5 years ($N = 753$). Apgar scores were influential in both the birthday and half-year groups. At 60 months the prime source of variance in the model whose $R^2 = .03$ was Apgar score. It explained 2% of the variance ($F = 10.03$, $p = .001$). Biological risk explained less than 1% ($F = 3.61$), but just reached the .05 level of statistical significance. At 66 months the full regression model's R^2 value was also .03. The Apgar score explained about 2 of the 3% of the full model ($F = 9.99$, $p = .01$).

TABLE 6.2

MULTIPLE LINEAR REGRESSION ANALYSIS OF BIOLOGICAL INFLUENCES ON LINGUISTIC ATTAINMENT

Variable	Models Compared	24 Mos. (N=692) VLDS			30 Mos. (N=216) FRPVT			36 Mos. (N=370) PAR *Communication*			42 Mos. (N=357) PAR *Communication*		
		R^2	F	P	R^2	F	P	R^2	F	P	R^2	F	P
Birth Weight	Full Model 1	.04		<.00001*	.08		.0004*	.09		<.00001*	.04		.0001*
			.47	.49		.70	.40		.55	.45		5.11	.02*
	Model 2	.04		<.00001*	.07		.0006*	.09		<.00001*	.02		.01*
Biological Risk	Full Model 1	.04		<.00001*	.08		.0004*	.09		<.00001*	.04		.0001*
			9.00	.002		12.14	.0006		9.06	.002		1.13	.28
	Model 3	.03		.0005*	.02		.31*	.07		.00006*	.03		.01*
Apgar	Full Model 1	.04		<.00001*	.08		.0004*	.09		<.00001*	.04		.0001*
			10.31	.001		1.36	.24		35.12	<.00001*		7.18	.007
	Model 4	.03		.05*	.07		.005	.006		.50*	.02		.03*
Sex (M)	Full Model 1	.04		<.00001*	.08		.0004*	.09		<.00001*	.04		.0001*
			19.50	.00001		10.56	.001		.35	.55		.12	.71
	Model 5	.01		.03*	.03		.005*	.09		<.00001*	.04		.009*

		48 Mos. (N=377) Preschool Inventory A-V			54 Mos. (N=366) Preschool Inventory A-V			60 Mos. (N=390) ITPA A-A			66 Mos. (N=363) ITPA A-A		
		R^2	F	P	R^2	F	P	R^2	F	P	R^2	F	P
Birth Weight	Full Model 1	.05	3.69	.00005*	.03	5.16	.005*	.03	2.22	.001*	.03	2.36	.002*
				.05			.02			.13			.12
	Model 2	.04		.0003*	.02		.05*	.03		.003*	.03		.007*
Biological Risk	Full Model 1	.05	7.04	.00005*	.03	1.34	.005*	.03	3.61	.001*	.03	3.11	.002*
				.008			.24			.05			.07
	Model 3	.04		.008*	.03		.04*	.03		.03*	.03		.04*
Apgar	Full Model 1	.05	13.95	.00005*	.03	6.15	.005*	.03	10.03	.001*	.03	9.99	.002*
				.0002			.01			.001			.01
	Model 4	.02		.03*	.01		.08*	.01		.12*	.01		.21*
Sex (M)	Full Model 1	.05	1.61	.00005*	.03	.15	.005*	.03	1.40	.001*	.03	1.79	.002*
				.20			.60			.23			.18
	Model 5	.05		.0008*	.03		.02*	.03		.01*	.03		.02*

*Significance of the difference from zero.

127

TABLE 6.3

DESCRIPTION OF THE SUBJECTS: SOCIAL SERIES AND TWO-YEAR VERBAL LANGUAGE DEVELOPMENT SCALE AND FULL RANGE PICTURE VOCABULARY SCALE, THREE-YEAR PAR *COMMUNICATION*, FOUR-YEAR P. I. *ASSOCIATIVE VOCABULARY*, AND FIVE-YEAR ITPA *AUDITORY ASSOCIATION*

Variable	24 Mos. (N=714)			30 Mos. (N=222)			36 Mos. (N=201)			42 Mos. (N=313)		
	$\bar{M}$	%	σ	$\bar{M}$	%	σ	$\bar{M}$	%	σ	$\bar{M}$	%	σ
Sex (% M)		54			58			51			53	
Race (% W)		61			72			94			65	
SES	54.07		15.87	51.20		16.57	48.29		15.25	53.91		14.85
Paternal Occup.							40.49		17.77	46.08		18.52
Maternal Employm.												
- *Full-time*								72			71	
- *Part-time*								11			5	
- *Home*								17			25	
Maternal Educ.												
- *Elementary*								5			8	
- *Part H.S.*								16			24	
- *H.S.*								48			42	
- *Part College*								22			17	
- *College*								9			9	
VLDS	19.62		5.01									
FRPVT				9.23		3.04						
PAR *Communication*							8.07		1.66	7.98		2.10

	48 Mos. (N=184)			54 Mos. (N=280)			60 Mos. (N=195)			66 Mos. (N=280)		
	x̄	%	σ	x̄	%	σ	x̄	%	σ	x̄	%	σ
Sex (% M)		50			53			50			53	
Race (% W)		94			66			94			69-	
SES	47.29	1	15.15	53.00		14.71						
Paternal Occup.	39.15		17.54	44.86		18.36						
Maternal Employm.												
- Full-time		73			71			72			70	
- Part-time		9			5			11			5	
- Home		17			24			17			25	
Maternal Education												
- Elementary		4			5			5	1			6	
- Part H.S.		15			25			17			24	
- H.S.		49			43			48			43	
- Part College		23			17			21			17	
- College		9			10			9			9	
Head of H. Educ.												
- To 9th Grade								22			31	
- H.S.								34			33	
- Part College								19			14	
- College								25			22	
P.I. Assoc. Vocab.	6.12		2.72	7.37		2.79						
ITPA Audit. Assoc.							16.28		4.75	18.57		5.11

(B) SOCIAL SERIES

We recall that the Social series consists of six variables, gathered cumulatively at birth, 3 years, and 5 years. The first analysis combined social class, as determined by the McGuire and White three-factor score, and race with the Verbal Language Development Scale at age 24 months. In a data set drawing on just over 700 children, the proportions of male and white children were 54 and 61%, respectively. The SES level conformed to the pattern in other data sets, as Table 6.3 indicates. The sole influence on VLDS scores was race–ethnic group ($F = 16.74$, $p = .00005$), with higher levels reported for white children.

At 30 months the data set incorporating the Full Range Picture Vocabulary Test was drawn from a small group of children ($N = 222$). A quite robust regression model with an $R^2 = .21$ was formed by the two predictors. Both variables were significant sources of variance: SES was the prime influence accounting for one-third of the variance ($F = 19.43$, $p = .00001$); race accounted for a smaller proportion that was statistically significant, although to a much lesser extent ($F = 6.21$, $p = .01$). The correlation between the two variables was .58, a highly significant correlation.

At 3 years the predictor set included three parental variables: the job title of the father as coded in Hollingshead's (1957) system, and the two maternal traits of education and the extent of work outside the home. The five variable model plus criterion PAR *Communication* scores were drawn from 500 3-year-olds ($N = 513$). The predictor set accounted for 10% of the variance. At 36 months, as Table 6.4 shows, SES was the prime influence, accounting for 2% of the model's variance ($F = 6.21$, $p = .01$). The level of maternal education achieved statistical significance as an influence ($F = 4.25$, $p = .04$). As one might expect, the direction of influence matched higher maternal education with higher criterion scores. At 42 months SES remained the prime influence in a regression, generating an account of 26% of the variance. SES alone explained 7 of the 26% ($F = 31.86$, $p < .00001$). However, there were other influences, and maternal schooling was almost as powerful as SES, explaining 6% of the variance. Race explained 1%, but at a statistically significant level, as Table 6.4 shows.

At 4 years the data set used the *Associative Vocabulary* score of the Preschool Inventory as the criterion, drawing on nearly 500 youngsters ($N = 464$). The full model of five predictor variables had an $R^2 = .12$. None of the predictors was a statistically significant influence. At 54 months the predictor set generated an $R^2 = .21$, and three variables were significant. The prime influence was mother's work, with higher criterion scores reported for mothers working only in the home ($F = 8.80$, $p = .003$).

Other variables influential at the .01 level of probability, accounting for 2% of the variance, were mother's education ($F = 5.63$) and race ($F = 6.71$).

A slightly larger data set ($N = 475$) was used at age 5 with the WPPSI *Vocabulary* criterion. In a model that incorporated the education of the head of the household (usually the father as in Table 6.3, but not always so), the R^2 value achieved at 60 months was .22. Only race was statistically significant ($F = 6.57$, $p = .01$). However, at 66 months the R^2 rose to .27, and several influences were identified. Chief among them was race, explaining .02 of the variance ($F = 6.04$, $p = .01$). It was followed by the education of the head of the household ($F = 5.44$, $p = .02$), and by mother's work in the home or out of it ($F = 4.22$, $p = .04$).

(C) FAMILY SERIES

Up to age 3 years the sole variable in the Family predictor aggregate is birth order. At 24 months the data were derived from 300 children ($N = 311$), and birth order accounted for 2% of the variance, a model significantly different from zero at the .004 level. However, in the case of the second linguistic criterion at child age 2 years, the Ammons' Full Range Picture Vocabulary Test, a statistically insignificant model was created by birth order.

At 3 years the predictor set was augmented by data on the number of brothers and sisters plus identity of the father figure. In an analysis of *Communication* scores from the Preschool Attainment Record, the variable of influence was the father figure variable; it accounted for .08 of the .10 of the variance ($F = 26.29$, $p < .00001$). The same variable was the sole influence at 42 months ($F = 10.41$, $p = .001$). High scores were associated with the biological father in the home.

The same three predictors were used at four years to analyze *Associative Vocabulary* scores from the Preschool Inventory. All three were significant, the prime source of variance being the identity of the father figure, which when deleted in regression model 4 dropped the R^2 from .14 to .06 ($p < .00001$). Two percent of the variance was associated with the number of siblings ($F = 7.86$, $p = .005$), and criterion scores were negatively correlated with the size of the sibship ($r = .31$, $p < .0001$). In this analysis, birth order explained 1% of the variance, but was a statistically significant influence ($F = 3.98$, $p = .04$). At 54 months the three predictors were also statistically significant, and in the same order as in the 48 month data set, as Table 6.6 shows.

At age 5 years, the Family predictor set grows to five variables with addition of the STIM score and type of dwelling as predictors of *Auditory Association* scores from the ITPA. The R^2 of the full model at 60 months

TABLE 6.4

MULTIPLE LINEAR REGRESSION ANALYSIS OF SOCIAL INFLUENCES ON LINGUISTIC ATTAINMENT

Variable	Models Compared	24 Mos. (N=714) VLDS			30 Mos. (N=222) FRPVT			36 Mos. (N=201) PAR Communication			42 Mos. (N=313) PAR Communication		
		R^2	F	P	R^2	F	P	R^2	F	P	R^2	F	P
SES	Full Model 1	.03		.00001*	.21		<.00001*	.10		.004*	.26		<.00001*
			.09	.75		19.92	.00001		6.21	.01		31.86	<.00001*
	Model 2	.03		<.00001*	.14		<.00001*	.08		.002*	.19		<.00001*
Race (B)	Full Model 1	.03		.00001*	.21		<.00001*	.10		.004*	.26		<.00001*
			16.74	.00005		6.21	.01		.01	.91		6.04	.01
	Model 3	.008		.01*	.19		<.00001*	.10		.0001*	.25		<.00001*
Paternal Occup.	Full Model 1							.10		.004*	.26		<.00001*
									.47	.49		.54	.46
	Model 4							.10		.0001*	.26		<.00001*
Maternal Employm.	Full Model 1							.10		.004*	.26		<.00001*
									1.42	.23		24.37	<.00001*
	Model 5							.10		.002*	.20		<.00001*
Maternal Educ.	Full Model 1							.10		.004*	.26		<.00001*
									4.25	.04		.69	.40
	Model 6							.08		.001*	.26		<.00001*

		48 Mos. (N=184) Preschool Inventory A-V			54 Mos. (N=280) Preschool Inventory A-V			60 Mos. (N=195) ITPA A-A			66 Mos. (N=280) ITPA A-A		
		R^2	F	P	R^2	F	P	R^2	F	P	R^2	F	P
SES	Full Model 1	.12		.0003*	.21		<.00001*	.22		<.00001*	.27		<.00001*
			.49	.48		2.41	.12		.00	1.00		2.58	.10
	Model 2	.11		.0001*	.20		<.00001*	.22		<.00001*	.26		<.00001*
Race (B)	Full Model 1	.12		.0003*	.21		<.00001*	.22		<.00001*	.27		<.00001*
			2.22	.13		6.71	.01		6.52	.01		6.04	.01
	Model 3	.10		.0003*	.19		<.00001*	.20		<.00001*	.25		<.00001*
Paternal Occup.	Full Model 1	.12		.0003*	.21		<.00001*	.22		<.00001*	.27		<.00001*
			.22	.63		.005	.92		.05	.82		2.02	.15
	Model 4	.11		.0001*	.21		<.00001*	.22		<.00001*	.26		<.00001*
Maternal Employm.	Full Model 1	.12		.0003*	.21		<.00001*	.22		<.00001*	.27		<.00001*
			.29	.58		8.80	.003		.17	.67		4.22	.04
	Model 5	.11		.0001*	.18		<.00001*	.22		<.00001*	.26		<.00001*
Maternal Educ.	Full Model 1	.12		.0002*	.21		<.00001*	.22		<.00001*	.27		<.00001*
			2.07	.15		5.63	.01		3.44	.06		1.92	.16
	Model 6	.11		.0003*	.19		<.00001*	.21		<.00001*	.27		<.00001*
Head of Househ. Education	Full Model 1							.22		<.00001*	.27		<.00001*
									.04	.83		5.44	.02
	Model 7							.22		<.00001*	.26		.00001*

*Significance of the difference from zero.

TABLE 6.5

DESCRIPTION OF THE SUBJECTS: FAMILY SERIES AND TWO-YEAR VLDS AND FRPVT, THREE-YEAR PPVT

(A) AND PAR *COMMUNICATION*, FOUR-YEAR P.I. *ASSOCIATIVE VOCABULARY*, AND FIVE-YEAR WPPSI *VOCABULARY* SCORES

Variable	24 Mos. (N=311) $\bar{X}$	%	σ	30 Mos. (N=110) $\bar{X}$	%	σ	36 Mos. (N=312) $\bar{X}$	%	σ	42 Mos. (N=318) $\bar{X}$	%	σ
Sex (% M)		54			56			51			52	
Race (% W)		62			73			60			58	
SES	54.05		16.38	51.12		16.46	55.02		16.39	55.44		14.69
Birth Order	2.91		2.33	2.90		2.42	3.22		2.38	3.14		2.01
N Siblings							2.76		2.24	2.72		1.92
Father Figure												
- *Father*								76			73	
- *F. Figure*								12			7	
- *None*								12			20	
Mecham VLDS	19.37		4.46									
Ammons FRPVT				8.99		2.64						
PAR *Communication*							7.29		1.85	7.66		2.18

	48 Mos. (N=275) X̄	%	σ	54 Mos. (N=271) X̄	%	σ	60 Mos. (N=284) X̄	%	σ	66 Mos. (N=261) X̄	%	σ
Sex (% M)		52			52			52			53	
Race (% W)		61			59			63			63	
SES	53.81		16.42	55.05		14.35	54.45		16.17	53.89		15.05
Birth Order	3.14		2.30	3.09		1.96	3.19		2.30	2.44		2.08
N Siblings	2.69		2.13	2.67		1.85	2.71		2.15	2.00		2.01
Father Figure												
– Father		77			74			76			75	
– F. Figure		11			6			12			7	
– None		12			20			12			18	
STIM				32.40		6.10	33.45		5.22	32.55		6.01
Dwelling												
– House					65			65			67	
– Apartment					35			35			33	
– Trailer												
P.I. Assoc. Vocab.	5.62		2.79	7.08		2.81						
ITPA Audit. Assoc.							15.24		4.93	17.96		4.88

TABLE 6.6

MULTIPLE LINEAR REGRESSION ANALYSIS OF FAMILY INFLUENCES ON LINGUISTIC ATTAINMENT

Variable	Models Compared	24 Mos. (N=311) VLDS R²	F	P	30 Mos. (N=110) FRPVT R²	F	P	36 Mos. (N=312) PAR *Communication* R²	F	P	42 Mos. (N=318) PAR *Communication* R²	F	P
Birth Order	Full Model 1	.02			.003			.10		$<.00001^{*}$	.05		$.0003^{*}$
			8.22	$.004^{*}$		.40	$.52^{*}$		.13	.71		2.41	.12
	Model 2							.10		$<.00001^{*}$	.04		$.0003^{*}$
N Siblings	Full Model 1							.10		$<.00001^{*}$	.05		$.0003^{*}$
									.96	.32		4.00	.04
	Model 3							.10		$<.00001^{*}$	.04		$.0006^{*}$
Father Figure	Full Model 1							.10		$<.00001^{*}$	.05		$.0003^{*}$
									26.29	$<.00001$		10.41	.001
	Model 4							.02		$<.01^{*}$	.02		$.01^{*}$

	48 Mos. (N=275) Preschool Inventory A-V			54 Mos. (N=271) Preschool Inventory A-V			60 Mos. (N=284) ITPA A-A			66 Mos. (N=264) ITPA A-A		
	R^2	F	P	R^2	F	P	R^2	F	P	R^2	F	P
Birth Order												
Full Model 1	.14		<.00001*	.16		<.00001*	.30		<.00001*	.12		<.00001*
Model 2	.13	3.99	.04 / <.00001*	.15	4.41	.03 / <.00001*	.30	.20	.65 / <.00001*	.11	1.57	.21 / <.00001*
N Siblings												
Full Model 1	.14		<.00001*	.16		<.00001*	.30		<.00001*	.12		<.00001*
Model 3	.12	7.86	.005 / <.00001*	.14	6.85	.009 / <.00001*	.30	1.45	.22 / <.00001*	.12	.11	.73 / <.00001*
Father Figure												
Full Model 1	.14		<.00001*	.16		<.00001*	.30		<.00001*	.12		<.00001*
Model 4	.06	25.39	<.00001 / .0001*	.04	38.07	<.00001 / .001*	.30	.009	.92 / <.00001*	.12	.85	.34 / <.00001*
STIM												
Full Model 1							.30		<.00001*	.12		<.00001*
Model 5							.13	67.83	<.00001 / <.00001*	.08	11.44	.008 / .0001*
Dwelling												
Full Model 1							.30		<.00001*	.12		<.00001*
Model 6							.28	7.67	.005 / <.00001*	.11	3.76	.05 / <.00001*

*Significance of the difference from zero.

was .30, a comparatively large value. Nearly two-thirds of it was due to STIM scores ($F = 67.83$, $p < .00001$); regression model 5, deleting STIM, explained only .13 of the variance, which is far less than the .30 value of the full model including STIM scores. Dwelling in a one-family house or apartment was also statistically significant, an outcome favoring high criterion scores for children living in one-family dwellings, in this data set from nearly 300 children ($N = 284$). Not surprisingly, living in a one-family home is associated with higher rather than low SES levels. At 66 months the same two variables in the same order influenced *Auditory Association* scores. STIM, however, accounted for a smaller proportion of variance, about one-third of the .12 of the full model ($F = 11.44$, $p = .008$). Type of dwelling barely achieved statistical significance and explained 1% of the variance ($F = 3.76$, $p = .05$).

(D) MATERNAL SERIES

Unlike the preceding set of predictors, all four maternal traits were present as perinatal antecedents to measures of development. The data set of criterion language measures plus marital status, age, AFI_{68}, and social risk were drawn from 600 children ($N = 616$) at age 24 months. As Table 6.7 shows, the characteristics of this data set were generally similar to those previously reported. The four-term Maternal set accounted for only 2% of the variance from the Verbal Language Development Scale. Within that model only social risk was an influence ($F = 5.34$, $p = .02$).

At 30 months the R^2 value of the model of the Ammons' FRPVT scores from 200 children ($N = 186$) was .07. The AFI_{68} measure of authoritarian values in child rearing accounted for 2% of the variance ($F = 4.58$, $p = .03$).

Just over 600 boys and girls ($N = 629$) provided scores from the predictor series and PAR *Communication* scale at age 3 years. In a model explaining 19% of the variance AFI_{68} explained 4% of the variance ($F = 15.40$, $p = .00001$), social risk accounted for 3% ($F = 11.64$, $p = .0007$), and marital status accounted for 2% ($F = 7.49$, $p = .006$). The same variables were influential at 42 months, with AFI_{68} remaining the prime source of variance and accounting for 3 of the model's 16% of criterion variance. However, marital status was the second influence, followed by social risk. In neither the birthday nor half-year data set was mothers' age at delivery influential.

At 4 years the four term predictor set of four maternal traits generated R^2 values of .13 and .17, using Preschool Inventory *Associative Vocabulary* scores as the criterion. In the 48 month birthday group, which was almost one-half of the subjects ($N = 323$), the greater influence was AFI_{68} scores, accounting for 4% of the variance ($F = 12.17$, $p = .0005$). The lesser influence was social risk, which explained 3% in model 5. The second study group, at 54 months, was slightly larger ($N = 328$) and raised the total number of 4-year-olds studied to 651. However, the influence of the two variables was in reversed order, the greater influence being social risk, which accounted for .07 of the full model's $R^2 = .17$. A substantially lesser role was played by the authoritarianism score, AFI_{68} ($F = 8.83$, $p = .003$). Higher child scores are reported for children whose mothers have lower authoritarianism scores, and are at lesser degrees of social risk.

Still higher R^2 values, the proportion of criterion variance traceable to the maternal traits, were generated in the 5 year data set. At that age, the five requisite scores were available from 658 children. The descriptive traits of these children, as with the 4 year group, were typical of those presented in earlier chapters. Consistent with the 4 year birthday (48 month) group, but using 60 month ITPA *Auditory Association* scores as the criterion, social risk gave the greater account of variance. The AFI_{68} scores accounted for .05 in the .17 R^2 value ($p = .00001$). A similar influence was executed by AFI_{68}, which also explained 5% of the variance, with a slightly lower F-value, but virtually identical statistical probability, $p = .00001$. In the 66 month, half-year study group, social risk remained influential, but at a slightly higher level; social risk accounted for 6 of the 20% of variance in the full regression model ($F = 24.44$, $p < .00001$). 4% of the variance was explained by AFI_{68} scores ($F = 16.36$, $p = .00007$).

Discussion

In the study of child development, language is in many ways the most critical topic in the minds of many people. Abstractions are caught in language, and reality can be played with in ways that are constructive. From the point of view of maturity, language can be construed as a dimension of intellect, a point we have elaborated elsewhere (Jordan, 1976b). In this section of Chapter 6, we appraise the meaning of results just presented on the influence of 19 variables in four sets on eight measures of linguistic attainment.

With the exception of height and weight, no criterion domain has a broader developmental span than language. The first measure was taken at child age 24 months and the last at 66 months. As in the preceding chapter, the earlier measures use reports of stable, frequently observed behaviors obtained when trained examiners, who were matched by race, interviewed mothers. The earliest direct measure came a little earlier in the linguistic domain, 6 months before direct measures in the intellectual domain, with administration of the Full Range Picture Vocabulary Test (Ammons & Ammons, 1962). The value of this scale, which has wide utility in a range of

TABLE 6.7

DESCRIPTION OF THE SUBJECTS: MATERNAL SERIES AND TWO-YEAR VERBAL LANGUAGE DEVELOPMENT
SCALE AND FULL RANGE PICTURE VOCABULARY SCALE, THREE-YEAR PAR *COMMUNICATION*,
FOUR-YEAR P. I. *ASSOCIATIVE VOCABULARY*, AND FIVE-YEAR ITPA *AUDITORY ASSOCIATION*

Variable	24 Mos. (N=616)			30 Mos. (N=186)			36 Mos. (N=312)			42 Mos. (N=317)		
	$\overline{M}$	%	σ	$\overline{M}$	%	σ	$\overline{M}$	%	σ	$\overline{M}$	%	σ
Sex (% M)		53			58			51			54	
Race (% W)		65			79			63			62	
SES	53.15		15.79	49.72		16.30	54.27		15.99	54.43		14.77
Marital Status (% M)		88			88			88			87	
Delivery Age	25.70		6.54	26.23		6.44	25.25		6.57	25.73		6.59
AFI68	26.19		8.03	24.68		7.78	27.19		7.55	26.52		8.21
Social Risk	1.11		1.63	.88		1.50	1.25		1.69	1.14		1.62
VLDS	19.59		4.58									
FRPVT				9.41		2.72	7.36		1.85	7.82		2.17
PAR *Communication*												

	48 Mos. (N=323)			54 Mos. (N=328)			60 Mos. (N=334)			66 Mos. (N=324)		
	$\overline{M}$	%	σ	$\overline{M}$	%	σ	$\overline{M}$	%	σ	$\overline{M}$	%	σ
Sex (% M)		50			53			52			53	
Race (% W)		60			66			61			67	
SES	53.88		16.38	53.33		14.92	54.15		16.04	53.25		14.59
Marital Status (% M)		86			88			87			88	
Delivery Age	24.87		6.35	25.74		6.48	25.02		6.36	25.79		6.50
AFI$_{68}$	27.51		7.50	25.84		8.24	27.49		7.38	25.89		8.15
Social Risk	1.23		1.71	1.05		1.57	1.23		1.69	.99		1.52
P. I. Assoc. Vocab.	5.65		2.77	7.37		2.74						
ITPA Audit. Assoc.							15.61		5.12	18.62		5.08

TABLE 6.8
MULTIPLE LINEAR REGRESSION ANALYSIS OF MATERNAL INFLUENCES ON LANGUAGE ATTAINMENT

Variable	Models Compared	24 Mos. (N=616) VLDS			30 Mos. (N=186) FRPVT			36 Mos. (N=312) PAR Communication			42 Mos. (N=317) PAR Communication		
		R^2	F	p	R^2	F	p	R^2	F	p	R^2	F	p
Marital Status	Full Model 1	.02		.002*	.07		.005*	.19		.00001*	.16		.00001*
			.09	.76		.92	.33		7.49	.006		9.18	.002
	Model 2	.02		.001*	.07		.003*	.17		.00001*	.13		.00001*
Delivery Age	Full Model 1	.02		.002*	.07		.005*	.19		.00001*	.16		.00001*
			1.57	.20		.002	.95		1.99	.15		.54	.46
	Model 3	.02		.002	.07		.002*	.18		.00001*	.16		.00001*
AFI68	Full Model 1	.02		.002*	.07		.005*	.19		.00001*	.16		.00001*
			3.17	.07		4.58	.03		15.40	.00001		11.11	.0009
	Model 4	.02		.004*	.05		.01*	.15		.00001*	.13		.00001*
Social Risk	Full Model 1	.02		.002*	.07		.005*	.19		.00001*	.16		.00001*
			5.34	.02		.85	.35		11.64	.0007		7.72	.005
	Model 5	.01		.01*	.07		.003*	.16		.00001*	.14		.00001*

		48 Mos. P.I. Assoc. Vocab. (N=323)			54 Mos. P.I. Assoc. Vocab. (N=328)			60 Mos. ITPA Assoc. Vocab. (N=334)			66 Mos. ITPA Assoc. Vocab. (N=324)		
		R^2	F	P	R^2	F	P	R^2	F	P	R^2	F	P
Marital Status	Full Model 1	.13		<.00001*	.17		<.00001*	.17		<.00001*	.20		<.00001*
	Model 2	.12	1.31	.25	.17	.02	.88	.17	.15	.69	.20	.01	.90
				<.00001*			<.00001*			<.00001*			<.00001*
Delivery Age	Full Model 1	.13		<.00001*	.17		<.00001*	.17		<.00001*	.20		<.00001*
	Model 3	.12	.48	.48	.17	.52	.46	.17	1.14	.28	.20	.05	.81
				<.00001*			<.00001*			<.00001*			<.00001*
AFI$_{68}$	Full Model 1	.13		<.00001*	.17		<.00001*	.17		<.00001*	.20		<.00001*
	Model 4	.09	12.17	.0005	.15	8.82	.003	.12	20.48	.0001	.16	16.36	.00007
				<.00001*			<.00001*			<.00001*			<.00001*
Social Risk	Full Model 1	.13		<.00001*	.17		<.00001*	.17		<.00001*	.20		<.00001*
	Model 5	.10	9.03	.002	.10	29.22	.00001	.12	21.09	.00001	.14	24.44	<.00001*
				<.00001*			<.00001*			<.00001*			<.00001*

*Significance of the difference from zero.

143

problem situations in the field of testing, is considerable. According to Kimbrell (1966), FRPVT-based IQs and revised Stanford–Binet IQs were virtually identical in a group of 63 mentally immature children. The other direct measures are subscales of comparatively recent scales for children, for instance, the Preschool Inventory, and the ITPA.

As with the preceding chapters, we begin by considering the regression models within which our statistical technique appraises the effects of specific variables. The Biological model accounted for a consistently low proportion of criterion variance; six of the eight full regression model R^2 values in Table 6.9 are .05 or below. The 30 month FRPVT and 36 month PPVT analyses explained 8 and 9% of the criterion variance at best. The picture in Table 6.9 shows that the Biological model influence dropped sharply after 36 months in the linguistic domain. In the case of the Social model, the mean R^2 value is .18, and from child age 30 months on, beginning with the FRPVT scale, does not go below .10. There is a general uniformity of influ-

TABLE 6.9

R^2 VALUES OF LINGUISTIC DOMAIN ANALYSES

Biological Model	Social Model	Family Model	Maternal Model	CRITERIA	Mean R^2
.04	.03	.02	.02	24 M. Mecham VLDS	.03
.08	.21	.003	.07	30 M. Ammons FRPVT	.09
.09	.10	.10	.19	36 M. PAR *Communication*	.12
.04	.26	.05	.16	42 M. PAR *Communication*	.13
.05	.12	.14	.13	48 M. P. I. *Assoc. Vocab.*	.11
.03	.21	.16	.17	54 M. P. I. *Assoc. Vocab.*	.14
.03	.22	.30	.17	60 M. ITPA *Audit. Assoc.*	.18
.03	.27	.12	.20	66 M. ITPA *Audit. Assoc.*	.15
ean .05	.18	.11	.14		.11

ence in the sense of accounting for criterion variance especially at ages 4 and 5 years. The Family model, perhaps because it contained both the briefest and largest predictor sets, has the widest range of R^2 values, from .003 to .30; the mean R^2 of .11 is perhaps misleading for that reason. The Maternal full regression model is also a fairly consistent predictor of criterion variance. Excepting the Biological predictor series, the trend is for R^2 values to rise across the years from birth to age 5. This is evident also when the R^2 values are analyzed criterion by criterion. Under that rubric the R^2 values from all sources, as indicated by means for rows in Table 6.9, have their lowest values at 2 years and rise to their highest values at 5 years.

When the regression models as a whole are compared, we see that the Biological model stands apart from the other three sets of predictors. The most powerful (Social) regression model is three to four times more powerful than the weakest (Biological) model, in terms of accounting for variance across the developmental span from 24–66 months.

HYPOTHESES

Our hypothesis for the comparative value of the four models emerges from research published elsewhere (Jordan, 1976a). In those inquiries social factors were found to influence heavily both verbal and nonverbal measures of attainment in young children. As a consequence, we hypothesized for this inquiry that the prime influence on language attainment would be the Social predictor set, followed closely by the Family predictor set, and the Maternal set. The Biological set seemed least relevant to this criterion set, if not to others.

The 1976 results showed that SES was a powerful influence on two linguistic criteria, and was followed by STIM scores as the prime influence on a third criterion. The outcome of this inquiry is that the most complete account of criterion variance from the linguistic domain is provided by the Social model, although it did not supply the highest single R^2. The second most substantial influence among the four was the Maternal model, followed by the Family set of predictors. In last place was the Biological predictor model, which accounted for less than one-third of the variance in the most predictive model, and only one-half of the variance of the next best predictor set. The hypothesis of a prime role played by the social class score and ethnic group at birth plus other elements described at child ages 3–5 years is upheld. However, the order of models and describing Family and Maternal influences as hypothesized in terms of mean R^2 values is reversed.

DISCRETE INFLUENCES

While the relationship of four predictor sets to the criterion is interesting, it is also possible to break the predictor sets into their components. In

TABLE 6.10

PREDICTORS IN ORDER OF STATISTICAL CONTRIBUTION IN MULTIPLE REGRESSION ANALYSES TO R^2 OF FULL MODELS

	BIOLOGICAL MODEL				CRITERION	SOCIAL MODEL					
	Weight	Biological Risk	Apgar	Sex (M)		SES	Race	Pop's Occup.	Mom's Employm.	Mom's Educat.	Head of Househ. Educat.
Child Age (Yrs.)	*Birth*	*Birth*	*Birth*	*Birth*		*Birth*	*Birth*	*Three*	*Three*	*Five*	*Five*
24 M. Mecham VLDS		.3	2	1			1				
30 M. Ammons FRPVT		1	2			1	2				
36 M. PAR *Communication*	2					1				2	
42 M. PAR *Communication*			1			1	3		2		
48 M. Preschool Inventory *A-V*	3	2	1			1					
54 M. Preschool Inventory *A-V*	2		1				2		1	3	
60 M. ITPA *Audit. Assoc.*		2	1				1				
66 M. ITPA *Audit. Assoc.*			1				1			3	2

	PREDICTORS					MATERNAL MODEL			
Child	Birth Order	N Siblings	Father Figure	Dwelling Type	STIM	Married	Age	AFI 68	Social Risk
Age (Yrs.)	Birth	3 Years	3 Years	5 Years	5 Years	Birth	Birth	Birth	Birth
24 M. Mecham VLDS	1							2	1
30 M. Ammons FRPVT			1					1	
36 M. PAR *Communication*		2	1			3		1	2
42 M. PAR *Communication*		2	1			2		1	3
48 M. Preschool Inventory A-V	3	2	1					1	2
54 M. Preschool Inventory A-V	3	2	1					2	1
60 M. ITPA *Audit. Assoc.*				2	1				
66 M. ITPA *Audit. Assoc.*				2	1			2	1

Table 6.10, we see the frequency with which the 19 predictors appear as significant elements in the regression analysis, as well as the absence of these variables. In Table 6.10 are combined the frequencies of predictors with the four predictor models. In the case of the Biological set of perinatal items, we note that all four appeared in analyses of the linguistic domain. However, there is a substantial difference in the frequency—influence—of the variables. Birthweight is of no significance before age $3\frac{1}{2}$ years, and then plays a secondary role. Biological risk is more spread across the years under study, but it plays a subordinate role. Apgar scores are influential, and especially after age 3 they play a major role. It will be recalled that we discussed the meaning of Apgar scores in the discussion portion of Chapter 4. There we pointed to the fact that Apgar scores in this population are distributed around a high mean, and low scores are only comparatively low, rather than conveying substantial numbers of Apgars low and clinically significant.

Here, as in the context of motor development, the effect is not large in terms of accounting for the variance of language test scores. Sex differences were not great; in such findings one can never be quite sure that the finding is avoidable. That is, some tests are built from items whose retention when constructing scales is based on their lack of discrimination between the sexes. A sexless test, like a culturally fair test, is quite feasible. The decision to permit sex, race, cultural, and SES effects to show is an exquisite exercise in balancing options and becomes an expression of values, not of facts, in child development. In the case of both minor and major effects in this predictor domain, we reiterate that findings are within the matrix of the given four-term predictor set, and we recall that the Biological model was the weakest of the four.

In the case of the Social model of language, Table 6.10 shows that race (i.e., ethnic group) was a steady influence across the years 2–5. SES was a briefer, early influence, but also more powerful. Paternal occupation gathered at age 3 did not materially explain test variance, but maternal employment did. Presumably by age 3 the absence of mothers for jobs outside the home, something affecting about one child in four, was perceptible. It is also an index of the economics of life at a time when a second income is felt necessary by even prudent families. Maternal level of education was not a prime influence in this data set on language attainment, an outcome we find interesting since it is not quite reconcilable with another analysis using the same variable (Jordan, 1978a). Finally, we note that the education of the head of the household, gathered fairly late in the data set but just prior to the onset of schooling, was a subordinate influence. In making these observations, we offer the reminder that the findings about each variable are within the best model of the four.

Family influences begin with one variable, birth order. Within the context of the set of data, birth order is a peripheral influence. In saying this we repeat that our birth order data were not constrained, containing up to 13 children in various sets. The number of brothers and sisters exerted a slight influence at age 3 and extinguished rapidly. Yet the identity of the father figure was of prime importance. With regret we recall from Table 6.3 that the original father was absent in about one-quarter of the children's families. Dwelling type, in fact either house or apartment, had a slight influence. This variable obviously correlates with SES level, but of course that relationship can be oversimplified. A rural, one-family shack, as we noted in Chapter 3, is no index of affluence; a luxurious apartment is hardly a state of deprivation. Finally, the STIM measure of home stimulation turned out to be a powerful influence on attainment in language. Introduced relatively late, the STIM became more influential than other variables in the Family set.

Finally, we consider the Maternal traits, all of which like the Biological set were present for the first criterion. Being married turned out to be very close to noninfluential; at best, it was secondarily important at age 3 and at no other time. The age of mother at the time of delivery was not at all influential.

In the entire birth cohort, the range of delivery ages was from 13 to 44 years. Across this span delivery age was not influential. In contrast maternal authoritarianism–liberalism in child rearing ideology was influential. We have shown elsewhere (Jordan, 1970) that this variable is very much attuned to social class level. It was an influence at virtually every age, and generally the prime influence at most ages within the explicit nature of the four-term predictor set. Social risk, meaning the degree of low social class milieu, rose in importance across the developmental span from 2 to 5 years.

In summarizing these findings we note that within the weakest regression models, the Biological series of predictors, Apgar scores were an influence on language. In the case of Social influences social class and ethnic group were powerful. Among the Family predictors the role of the father figure is least ambiguous, especially at child ages 3–4 years. Finally, the child rearing ideology of mothers, liberalism to authoritarianism, seems to be the prime maternal influence.

In listing these influences it should be born in mind that the proportion of variance explained by the four models was less than ideal. The reason was in part exclusion of much child data from the predictor series. The influence of the predictors, while frequently attenuated, is not clouded by the confounding effect of child developmental measures in a study of child development. We conclude that the linguistic attainment of small children is subject to the influence of a number of identifiable external influences.

Somatic Development

7

Introduction

Despite the limited amount of data one can take from young children at one time, and the superordinate role of linguistic and intellectual criteria, the case studies from which our data are often drawn incorporated gross physical information, here labelled *somatic* as a generic term. In this domain we have tried to evaluate the gross physical aspects of growth at two ages—6 months and 3 years. Our reason for this is an attempt to demonstrate a respect for constitutional aspects of growth. While the high water mark of environmentalism in child development was probably reached in the 1960s, it is still true that people tend to slight the fact that children have bodies and that constitutional elements are not to be overlooked in understanding how children grow. While not reported in this investigation, we have calculated body symmetry in terms of a two-by-two array of height and weight, for example, high weight + low height. Such corporal measures are generally not considered very useful when, for example, they are used as indices of nutrition. Nevertheless we remain convinced that bodies are here to stay, and that study of somatic development, how the body moves and is moved, is a topic only beginning to be appreciated. While not central to this chapter, but in order to explain an otherwise inordinate interest in this neglected topic, we note the scarcely explained matter of circadian rhythms in children—a mysterious somatic process of great theoretical interest with conceivably practical applications if better understood. According to Tanner (1978), Marshall has found that the months March–July provide the peak period for rate of growth in height. Tanner adds that blind children do not synchronize growth rate with the season, an observation with interesting implications for research and supporting our view that we still have much to learn about patterns of somatic growth.

Here we look at a relatively gross set of measures and justify their study in this chapter, avoiding the greater shortcoming of ignoring how bodies grow and how children move. The measures presented here were taken at age 6 months and at 3 years. Although data were taken in between those ages on development by means of the Ad Hoc interview instrument used first at 6 months, the items had shifted away from essentially gross somatic behaviors to discriminable items such as language, fine motor, and other topics.

Somatic Development

From conception to maturity, the stages and skills demonstrated by children reflect the fundamental refinement of the body. Growing children do so by elaboration of the subtleties of the central nervous system, the discrete organs of the body, and through the constitution which emerges from the genetic plan interacting with vectors of health and social circumstance.

During gestation the DNA code influences the shape of the ear, the density of vital brain cells, and the color of the hair. Within the uterine environment placental capacity mediates the genetic plan; noxious elements in the mother's life may determine whether the child is carried to full term, or born with congenital disorders. Normally at delivery we have a healthy infant ready to function autonomously, weighing about 7 lb like the average child in this study, and about as prepared as one can be for life in human society. That state, as Brazelton (1971) has shown us, and as explained through the work of our colleague Dr. Judy McNeil (1974),[1] is far more sophisticated than people generally realize. The neonate is capable of complex, integrated activity, largely subcortical to begin with, but increasingly an expression of a forming consciousness and voluntarism.

Perhaps the most remarkable thing is the speed with which discrete functions emerge, and subsequently evolve into subsets of functions. With

[1]As a part of the St. Louis Baby Study, but not data reported in the monograph, the development of Brazelton's infant assessment technique led to another cohort of infants, which has been reported by Dr. Judy E. McNeil (1974).

time, children reach developmental norms, and as a purpose of this chapter one comes to ask why some children are more or less competent than others. Our data do not permit examining more than a fraction of the vectors of influence, and we can but speculate about genetic components or the quality of uterine life. And yet the infant foreshadows the adolescent, the adult, so that the matter of how that adumbration arises is a fascinating question.

In this chapter we examine some relatively gross data on this neglected topic, paying attention to two time points. The first is 6 months postpartum, the second at age 3 years. The former is still in the shadow of delivery, and the second, for anyone who has not been accosted by a 3-year-old recently, is in the mainstream of early life, running, jumping, and generally having a wonderful time.

Hypotheses

As with preceding chapters, hypotheses deal with the relative influence of the four predictor sets on the criterion measures. In so far as the Biological predictor series and the criterion domain are both formulations of constitutional elements, we hypothesize that the Biological predictor set will explain a greater proportion of the criterion variance than the other predictors. Turning to the other three predictor series, we hazard that cultural expectations associated with social class level and related elements of occupation and education will be the second most influential set of vectors. For this reason we hypothesize that the Social predictor series will be the second most effective predictor group, comparatively speaking. The third hypothesis is that the specifics of mother–child interaction will, within the larger matrix of cultural factors, be determined by maternal traits. That is, mothers' influence will include expectations, inducements, and concrete acts, all of which flow from their values and from their personal configurations of attributes such as age and intelligence. Finally, we hypothesize that the least influence will be demographic aspects of life incorporated in the Family predictor series.

In offering these hypotheses we note that the length and inclusiveness of the predictor series is limited by the developmental age at which the criterion measures were applied. Thus the predictor elements are those antecedent to a criterion or concurrent with it. Tables in the chapter specify the age at which measures are taken.

Measures

There are two measures in the somatic domain. The first is the writer's Ad Hoc Development Scale (see footnote 1) developed as a response to the need to gather information from mothers on the subject of their infants' development. The particular difficulty leading to development of the Ad Hoc Scale was the lack of sophistication of some mothers, who represent in many ways one of the greater challenges to understanding child development. Poorly educated women of lower socioeconomic status are not sophisticated, and, while loving, are less able to report accurately the attainments of their children to examiners, even when matched by race and by sex. Accordingly, one of the prime attributes of the scale had to be the relative lack of ambiguity in particular child behaviors. The scale was developed by searching the literature of early development to identify salient behaviors that were also readily understood. Although the scale was also used at 12 and 18 months after birth, it is not reported in this study. At ages beyond 6 months, the observable behaviors of the scale are less matters of general bodily development and can be construed as aspects of speech, hearing, locomotion, and motor coordination. Behaviors range up to child age 30 months, according to the research literature in which they were identified (e.g., Carmichael, 1954; Griffith, 1954; Mecham, 1958; Doll, 1966). The scale at 6 months seems independent of what we call intelligence at the later age of 2 years. That is, there is an insignificant r between scores on the Ad Hoc Scale at 6 months and 24 month IQ. The 12 month Ad Hoc Scale correlates highly ($p < .001$) with the 24 month IQ (Jordan, 1967a).

At age 3 years the second measure was employed, the *Physical* domain of the Preschool Attainment Record. At age 3 the behaviors deal with climbing, jumping, hopping, throwing, and catching. In administering the test items, the examiners engaged the children in the tasks rather than relying solely on maternal report, whenever possible. For example, instead of asking if the proband could join in games involving going in a circle (e.g., Farmer in the Dell, London Bridge, and Looby Loo) the examiner, mother, and child formed a circle and played a game. Similarly, the matter of children's ability to skip was not merely left to the informant, but was gauged by holding hands with the child and skipping. For children's mastery of unwrapping, they were presented with a wrapped lollipop; for throwing a ball, examiner and child threw a ball, with appropriate regard for the surroundings.

In some respects the criterion measures can be considered quite different, if only because children at 6 months and at 3 years exhibit quite different behaviors. A more trenchant reason might be that the PAR criterion could be labelled locomotor or gross motor skill. In the sense that at both 6 months and 3 years we are dealing with nonverbal, nonintellectual skills, the two criteria share something physical–somatic and quite gross. The important things are of course the criteria themselves, presented here in separate analyses.

Results

(A) BIOLOGICAL SERIES

At 6 months the number of infants for whom the four-item predictor set and criteria were assembled was over 600 ($N = 669$). It will be recalled that the Biological series consisted of four perinatal items, so that even at criterion age 6 months all predictors were available.

As Table 7.1 shows, the sexes were evenly balanced at 6 months, and the mean birthweight for the Ad Hoc criterion group at birth was 6½ lb. In other respects the infants were in good health on the average. That is, Biological risk at delivery was low ($\overline{M} = .49$) and Apgar scores were proportionately high ($\overline{M} = 8.76$), and certainly above the level at which adverse sequelae may be anticipated.

The predictor series of four perinatal, biological elements was applied to the 6 month Ad Hoc scores. In Table 7.1 we see that the subjects had a mean criterion score of 8.18, and a standard deviation of 1.43. One predictor did not contribute to the regression analysis, sex of the child. In contrast, Apgar scores, biological risk, and birthweight gave explanations of variance in a model with an $R^2 = .02$, which was statistically highly significant. The variance assigned to the prime source Apgar scores was 1%, which was

TABLE 7.1

DESCRIPTION OF THE SUBJECTS: BIOLOGICAL SERIES AND SIX-MONTH AD HOC SCALE,

THIRTY-SIX MONTH AND FORTY-TWO MONTH PRESCHOOL ATTAINMENT RECORD *PHYSICAL* SCALE

Variable	*6 Mos.*			*36 Mos.*			*42 Mos.*		
	$\overline{M}$	%	σ	$\overline{M}$	%	σ	$\overline{M}$	%	σ
	(N=669)			(N=370)			(N=357)		
Sex (M)		51			53			52	
Race (W)		57			53			57	
SES	54.75	16.02		55.78	16.13		55.33	14.81	
Birth Weight (lb.)	6.60	1.24		6.66	1.24		6.55	1.29	
Biological Risk	.49	1.11		.39	.91		.61	1.27	
Apgar	8.76	1.49		9.01	1.21		8.57	1.61	
Ad Hoc Scale	8.15	1.43							
PAR *Physical*				17.31	2.54		19.53	3.89	

TABLE 7.2

MULTIPLE LINEAR REGRESSION ANALYSIS OF BIOLOGICAL INFLUENCES ON SOMATIC ATTAINMENT

Predictor Variable	Models Compared	6 Mos. (N=667) Ad Hoc Scale			36 Mos. (N=370) PAR *Physical*			42 Mos. (N=357) PAR *Physical*		
		R²	F	P	R²	F	P	R²	F	P
Birth Weight	Full Model 1	.02		.007*	.006		.51*	.008		.37*
			4.51	.03		.002	.96		2.06	.15
	Model 2	.01		.005*	.006		.51*	.002		.79*
Biological Risk	Full Model 1	.02		.007*	.006		.51*	.008		.37*
			6.33	.01		.65	.41		1.05	.30
	Model 3	.01		.05*	.004		.89*	.005		.84*
Apgar	Full Model 1	.02		.007*	.006		.51*	.008		.37*
			12.42	.0004		.23	.62		.01	.90
	Model 4	.007		.19*	.005		.56*	.008		.71*
Sex (M)	Full Model 1	.02		.007*	.006		.51*	.008		.37*
			2.28	.13		1.46	.22		.14	.70
	Model 5	.02		.01	.002		.97*	.008		.38*

*Significance of the difference from zero.

one-half of the assigned variance. As Apgar scores rose so did criterion scores at 6 months, a relationship we might expect but have not always seen in preceding chapters where criteria of development are from older children. As biological risk rose, Ad Hoc scores declined, and Ad Hoc scores rose with increasing birthweight.

At age 3 years data sets were generated for over 700 children ($N = 727$). The birthday and half-year groups were almost equal in size, 370 and 357 children. In neither case did application of the predictor set explain any of the PAR *Physical* scores variance.

(B) SOCIAL SERIES

It will be recalled that this predictor set has two elements antecedent to the 6-month criterion; they are race and McGuire and White SES score. The number of infants from whose these two scores plus the Ad Hoc Scale scores at 6 months were taken was almost 700 ($N = 689$). The SES score of the subjects' families was 54.79, which is virtually the mean for the entire birth cohort. The group was about half white and black, with a slight preponderance of white infants (57%).

When applied to 6 month Ad Hoc Scale, scores in a full regression model explain 6% of the variance in the perinatal SES score, and accounted for 5% ($F = 30.73$, $p = .00001$) of the PAR *Physical* scores that rose as SES level declined. With addition of the additional parental variables at age 3, as Table 7.4 shows, the sole predictor became the extent to which mothers work outside the home ($F = 6.32$, $p = .01$). The variable in question, labelled maternal employment, explained 3 of the 5% accounted for by the five-term predictor set. Criterion scores were higher when mothers worked. At age 42 months both significant predictors at 6 and 36 months provided accounts of PAR *Physical* scores. In a model explaining 8% of the variance, SES accounted for 5% ($F = 15.59$, $p = .0001$) and maternal employment explained 1% ($F = 3.73$, $p = .05$). However, unlike the birthday group results, higher criterion scores were associated with mothers working less than full-time.

(C) FAMILY SERIES

This predictor set begins with birth order, and adds the number of brothers and sisters and identity of the father figure at age 3. The study group at age 6 months consisted of data from nearly 300 babies. As a group they were of typical social status, with a slight preponderance of white infants (60%). At 6 months birth order was not related to the criterion Ad Hoc scores. At 36 months the added predictor, number of brothers and sisters, explained half of the variance of the full model ($R^2 = .02$). The F-value of the drop in R^2 in regression Model 3, due to deletion of the

TABLE 7.3

DESCRIPTION OF THE SUBJECTS: SOCIAL SERIES AND SIX-MONTH AD HOC SCALE, THIRTY-SIX MONTH AND FORTY-TWO MONTH PRESCHOOL ATTAINMENT RECORD *PHYSICAL* SCALE

Variable	6 Mos. (N=689) $\overline{M}$	%	σ	36 Mos. (N=201) $\overline{M}$	%	σ	42 Mos. (N=313) $\overline{M}$	%	σ
Sex (M)		52			51			53	
Race (W)		57			94			66	
SES	54.79		15.92	48.29		15.29	53.91		14.85
Paternal Occupation				40.49		17.82	46.08		18.52
Maternal Employment									
– *Full Time*					17			24	
– *Part Time*					11			5	
– *At Home*					72			71	
Maternal Education									
– *Elementary*					5			8	
– *Part H.S.*					16			24	
– *H.S.*					48			42	
– *Part College*					22			17	
– *College*					9			9	
Ad Hoc Scale	8.19		1.42						
PAR *Physical*				16.97		2.18	19.66		4.07

TABLE 7.4

MULTIPLE LINEAR REGRESSION ANALYSIS OF SOCIAL INFLUENCES ON SOMATIC ATTAINMENT

Predictor Variable	Models Compared	6 Mos. (N=689) Ad Hoc Scale			36 Mos. (N=201) PAR *Physical*			42 Mos. (N=313) PAR *Physical*		
		R^2	F	P	R^2	F	P	R^2	F	P
SES	Full Model 1	.06		<.00001*	.08		.004*	.08		.00005*
			30.73	<.00001*		.45	.50		15.50	.0001
	Model 2	.01		.0003*	.08		.002*	.03		.01*
Race (B)	Full Model 1	.06		<.00001*	.08		.004*	.08		.00005*
			.37	.54		.12	.72		2.36	.12
	Model 3	.06		<.00001*	.08		.002*	.07		.00005*
Paternal Occup.	Full Model 1				.08		.004*	.08		.00005*
						.86	.35		.15	.69
	Model 4				.08		.002*	.08		.00002*
Maternal Employm.	Full Model 1				.08		.004*	.08		.00005*
						6.32	.01		3.75	.05
	Model 5				.05		.02*	.07		.0001*
Maternal Educ.	Full Model 1				.08		.004*	.08		.00005*
						1.24	.26		1.14	.28
	Model 6				.07		.228*	.08		.00001*

*Significance of the difference from zero.

159

TABLE 7.5

DESCRIPTION OF THE SUBJECTS: FAMILY SERIES AND SIX-MONTH AD HOC SCALE,

THIRTY-SIX MONTH AND FORTY-TWO MONTH PRESCHOOL ATTAINMENT RECORD *PHYSICAL* SCALE

Variable	*6 Mos.*			*36 Mos.*			*42 Mos.*		
	M	%	σ	M	%	σ	M	%	σ
	(N=285)			(N=313)			(N=318)		
Sex		53			51			52	
Race		60			60			58	
SES	54.31		16.71	55.07		16.40	55.44		14.69
Birth Order	2.86		2.30	3.21		2.33	3.14		2.01
N Siblings				2.76		2.24	2.72		1.92
Father Figure									
- *Father*					73			73	
- *Father Figure*					14			7	
- *None*					13			20	
Ad Hoc Scale	8.05		1.49						
PAR *Physical*				17.29		2.51	19.69		4.04

predictor under consideration, was 3.90 ($p = .04$). As Table 7.6 shows, the R^2 value at 42 months was also .02, but just missed statistical significance. In that model the identity of the father figure was significant ($F = 6.75$, $p = .009$). Higher criterion scores were associated with the biological father.

(D) MATERIAL SERIES

In the case of the Maternal series, there are four perinatal variables present at all three criterion ages. At each age the descriptive characteristics of the subjects resemble those we have seen in other data sets based on a criterion and the predictors marital status, age, AFI_{68}, and social risk. Of the four criterion applied to 600 children at 6 months of age ($N = 592$), only one accounted for criterion variance in a model, explaining 5% of the Ad Hoc Scale variance. It was the AFI_{68} measure of degree of authoritarianism, and it accounted for 3 of the 5% ($F = 21.64$, $p < .00001$). Contrary to other relationships, higher child scores at 6 months were associated with

TABLE 7.6

MULTIPLE LINEAR REGRESSION ANALYSIS OF FAMILY INFLUENCES ON SOMATIC ATTAINMENT

Predictor Variable	Models Compared	6 Mos. (N=285) Ad Hoc Scale			36 Mos. (N=313) PAR *Physical*			42 Mos. (N=318) PAR *Physical*		
		R^2	F	P	R^2	F	P	R^2	F	P
Birth Order	Full Model 1	.004	1.28	.25*	.02	1.98	.05* .15 .06*	.02	.63	.08* .42 .04*
	Model 2				.01			.01		
N Siblings	Full Model 1				.02	3.90	.05* .04 .16*	.02	.29	.08* .59 .04*
	Model 3				.01			.02		
Father Figure	Full Model 1				.02	.00	.05* 1.00 .02*	.02	6.75	.08* .009 .04*
	Model 4				.02			.01		

*Significance of the difference from zero.

161

TABLE 7.7

DESCRIPTION OF THE SUBJECTS: MATERNAL SERIES AND SIX-MONTH AD HOC SCALE,

THIRTY-SIX MONTH AND FORTH-TWO MONTH PRESCHOOL ATTAINMENT RECORD *PHYSICAL* SCALE

Variable	6 Mos.			36 Mos.			42 Mos.		
	$\overline{M}$	%	σ	$\overline{M}$	%	σ	$\overline{M}$	%	σ
		(N=592)			(N=312)			(N=317)	
Sex (M)		52			52			54	
Race (B)		61			63			68	
SES	53.70		15.89	54.27		15.99	54.43		14.77
Marital Status (M)		87			88			88	
Delivery Age	25.29		6.55	25.25		6.57	25.73		6.59
AFI_{68}	26.43		8.11	27.19		7.55	26.52		8.21
Social Risk	1.18		1.68	1.23		1.69	1.14		1.62
Ad Hoc Scale	8.19		1.40						
PAR *Physical*				17.38		2.50	19.72		4.07

greater authoritarianism. The same variable was influential at 36 months, explaining half of the $R^2 = .04$ of the full model ($F = 7.46$, $p = .006$). It was followed by marital status, which explained 1% of the variance ($F = 4.79$, $p = .03$); higher child scores were associated with mothers being married. At 42 months the AFI_{68} variable was the sole variable reaching statistical influence. In a full model accounting for 3% of the PAR *Physical* variance, the perinatal AFI_{68} scores of mothers explained two-thirds of the variance ($F = 4.96$, $p = .02$). The relationship with child traits was that reported at 36 months, namely higher child scores associated with more authoritarianism.

Discussion

Summarizing to this point, we have so far in Chapter 7 presented data on the influence of Biological, Social, Family, and Maternal predictors on somatic criteria at ages 6 months and 3 years. At 6 months data were assembled on almost 700 ($N = 689$) children and over 700 children

TABLE 7.8

MULTIPLE LINEAR REGRESSION ANALYSIS OF MATERNAL INFLUENCES ON SOMATIC ATTAINMENT

Predictor Variable	Models Compared	6 Mos. (N=592) Ad Hoc Scale			36 Mos. (N=312) PAR *Physical*			42 Mos. (N=317) PAR *Physical*		
		R^2	F	P	R^2	F	P	R^2	F	P
Married	Full Model 1	.05		.00001*	.04		.004*	.03		.02*
			.46	.49		4.79	.03		.46	.49
	Model 2	.05		<.00001*	.03		.01*	.03		.01*
Delivery Age	Full Model 1	.05		.00001*	.04		.004*	.03		.02*
			2.97	.08		.09	.75		.68	.40
	Model 3	.05		<.00001*	.04		.001*	.03		.01*
AFI$_{68}$	Full Model 1	.05		.00001*	.04		.004*	.03		.02*
			21.64	<.00001		7.49	.006		4.96	.02
	Model 4	.02		.003*	.02		.04*	.01		.11*
Social Risk	Full Model 1	.05		<.00001*	.04		.004*	.03		.02*
			.38	.53		2.38	.12		.19	.65
	Model 5	.05		<.00001*	.04		.004*	.03		.01*

*Significance of the difference from zero.

163

($N = 740$) at age 3 years. At age 6 months the criterion was the writer's Ad Hoc Scale of Development, and at 3 years it was the *Physical* score of the Preschool Attainment Record.

Table 7.9 summarizes by row and by column the proportions of criterion variance associated with the four vectors of hypothesized influence. For the set of 12 R^2 values the range is .006 to .08; no less than three of the values are virtual zeros and two of them are associated with the Biological predictors at age 3 years. While not high, the R^2 values of the second, Social model in Table 7.9 are comparatively robust, averaging $R^2 = .07$. In the case of the Family model, one of the R^2 values is .004, whereas the other two are each .02. In the case of the Maternal model, summarized in Table 7.9, the R^2 values average .04 and they also are fairly consistent. By criterion the three measures are quite comparable, on the average.

HYPOTHESES

In assessing the hypothesized effects in light of these empirical findings, we apply both the test of size of R^2 across all three criteria plus degree of effectiveness for the three criteria, for example, the absence or presence of the zero R^2 values. By that procedure all our hypotheses are rejected. That is, the most effective model is not the Biological model; in fact it is the least predictive model of the set of four, providing zero accounts of variance in two instances, and a relatively low account in the third. Our second

TABLE 7.9

R^2 VALUES OF SOMATIC DOMAIN ANALYSES

R^2 Values				Criteria	Mean R^2
Biological Model	*Social Model*	*Family Model*	*Maternal Model*		
.02	.06	.004	.05	6 M. Ad Hoc Devpm.	.03
.006	.08	.02	.04	36 M. PAR *Physical*	.03
.008	.08	.02	.03	42 M. PAR *Physical*	.04
Mean .01	.07	.01	.04		.03

hypothesis of a secondary level of influence due to Social factors is also rejected. In fact the Social set provided comparatively fair accounts of variance for all three criteria, and was the only predictor group to do so; the set of R^2 values in Table 7.9 is .06, .08, and .08.

The third hypothesis of Maternal traits as the tertiary level of influence is not sustained by virtue of the third largest R^2 value in the set of 12. The final hypothesis of least influence for the Family model is partially accepted because the Biological model was the least effective of the four predictor sets. It needs to be reiterated that the hypotheses of comparative effect are tested within data presented in Table 7.9, a data set which in no instance suggests any given predictor set is much of an influence on the domain as a whole.

DISCRETE INFLUENCES

When the role of predictor variables presented in Table 7.10 is examined, the frequency with which any discrete variable is present and its ordinal role in the regression scheme can be seen. The salience of the Biological predictors is evident in Table 7.10. There we see that the Apgar score was useful, and that weight and biological risk were influences on somatic development at 6 months. Within the Social influences socioeconomic status was important at ages 6 and 42 months, with maternal work style a secondary influence at the latter child age. In the Family aggregate of predictors, only two variables were significant, the number of siblings and the father figure. This series is restricted to three predictor variables because dwelling type and STIM were gathered only at child ages subsequent to the last child age reported in this chapter. Among the Maternal variables, the AFI_{68} score showed its influence at all three child ages, and marital status had a supplemental value at age 3 years.

Blending these uneven findings, we hazard that Apgar scores, social class, father figure, and AFI_{68} are the four variables of prime influence from the entire (but attenuated) set. It is at age 42 months only that confidence can be placed in forming a set of substantial influences; the variables in question are father figure, SES, and AFI_{68}. However, we need to add to this consideration of specific variables a few comments on the direction of influence of variables. In the case of social class, and authoritarian child rearing attitudes, higher child development scores were associated with the theoretically less desirable condition in the predictor, that is, high authoritarian and low social status at particular ages. In the case of working mothers, the relationship between the highest level of this variable at 36 months is that children of working mothers have highest PAR *Physical* scores, while such children have lower scores at 42 months. In both cases the correlation with the criterion is significant at the .01 level. These results are irreconcilable in

TABLE 7.10

PREDICTORS IN ORDER OF STATISTICAL CONTRIBUTION IN MULTIPLE REGRESSION ANALYSES TO FULL MODEL R^2

CRITERION	BIOLOGICAL MODEL				SOCIAL MODEL					
	Weight	Biological Risk	Apgar	Sex (M)	SES	Race	Pop Occup.	Mom Employ.	Mom Educat.	Head of Househ. Educat.
Child Age (Yrs.)	Birth	Birth	Birth	Birth	Birth	Birth	Three	Three	Five	Five
6 M. Ad Hoc Devpm	3	2	1		1					
36 M. PAR Physical								1		
42 M. PAR Physical					1			2		

CRITERION	FAMILY MODEL			MATERNAL MODEL			
	Birth Order	N Siblings	Father Figure	Married	Age	AFI_{68}	Social Risk
Child Age (Yrs.)	Birth	3 Years	3 Years	Birth	Birth	Birth	Birth
6 M. Ad Hoc Devpm						1	
36 M. PAR Physical		1		2		1	
42 M. PAR Physical			1			1	

their directions while consistent in their significance. Accordingly, we offer the observation that working to some degree outside the home is statistically significant, but the practical import is contradictory in these data.

We note the absence of birth order data as important at any age. Research by Zajonc (1976; Zajonc & Marcus, 1975) suggests that in fact it is birth *interval* rather than order that explains effects of ordinal placement in a sibship. Among the Maternal characteristics, scores on the AFI_{68} measure of authoritarian family ideology were important at ages 6, 36, and 42 months.

Concluding this discussion of predictors in four aggregates on three scores in the *Somatic* domain, we note that the last test was given at age $3\frac{1}{2}$ years. This meant that a handful of predictors were not incorporated in the regression models, since they were not antecedent or concurrent. They were dwelling type, STIM score, and the education of the head of the household. In view of the powerful role of the STIM scale it would have been interesting to have had the variable included. To do that, however, would have violated the prospective nature of the data set.

Findings in the *Somatic* domain have a modest value, since even the longer predictor series generated only modest accounts of variance. Some of the results summarized in Tables 7.9 and 7.10 provide little basis for generalizing. The reasons lie no doubt in several things: the nature of the criterion instruments and the domain; the age of the children; and the general lack of a strong relationship between predictors and predictor sets on the one hand, and the criterion domain and its components on the other. The desultory nature of this observation is not without positive aspects. In its own way it represents a polarity from the tendency to generalize about early child development and its influences. In this instance, and for quite good reasons, we see that only quite specific influences within particular aggregates stand out as vectors of influence on somatic development.

Social Development

8

Introduction

As a matter of priorities in longitudinal studies in young children, it is helpful to recall that some aspects of development are more important than others. In this program of studies cognitive and physical development are given higher priority than social or motor development. Indeed, we present in this work no data whatsoever that one might label "personality." To omit such considerations is not to deny their role in development. In Chapter 3 we stated that our formulation of childhood includes growth towards competence, that is, progress towards being a person whose potentials for living an enlightened life are realized. In addition to this element of self-realization there is the reciprocal topic of social compentence—our ability to negotiate human transactions skillfully and competently. The relatively modest amount of data we present on social development in this monograph is the consequence of ordering priorities, given finite resources and a modest degree of access to homes. In retrospect one might wish for some personality measures and more social information. Such data exist, but they are at ages beyond the scope of this work and are analyzed and reported elsewhere. We have, for example, information on locus of control in the children, and measures of behavior and achievement in classrooms at ages when social variables have a higher priority.

Even so, we have information on social development at ages 2 years and 4 years, gathered because it is important to try to understand how social skills grow, and what causes youngsters to reach specific levels. Considered as a separate topic, social development interacts with major domains such as language and intellect. Such is its importance in the preschool years that attempts to promote general development invariably stress the contribution of social context, and so social development, as a medium for growth.

Indeed, the eventual level of effectiveness which children reach in various skills may be highly modulated by the degree of social development—social facility and social sensitivity—that they attain. For these reasons we have gathered and analyzed data on social development in approximately 700 children at age 2, and on slightly more for selected variables at age 4 years.

Assessment of social development is not without its problems when children are young. Social behaviors are contingent on social cues, and the act of inquiring into social behavior as a part of child study often occurs in unfamiliar settings. In this investigation inquiry has taken place in homes; however, this still leaves the question of standardized procedures. In this chapter we present information obtained by talking to mothers at age 2, and by testing directly at age 4 years.

Social Development

Social development begins in the processes of nurture which mothers apply to their infants. Feeding and bathing are interactions in which mothers and babies talk, establish eye contact, and generate mutually rewarding contingencies. Such are the plasticity and responsiveness of infants that they can be influenced by mothers very easily. In saying this we point out that the patterns of behaviors mothers exhibit are themselves quite contingent on the infants. A placid infant constitutionally reassures a young mother and creates a rewarding context for mothering. A tense baby makes nurturing equally tense. Obviously there is a chicken-and-egg problem in such relationships. Even so, we glimpse in the contingent nature of mothers' behaviors the social dimension of babies' behavior.

In some respects social development is learning a role. Such a process is greatly influenced by the range of people who are models for children. Mothers, and with the passage of time, brothers, sisters, and fathers, constitute the basis for learning to be, and for learning how to conduct oneself, in various contexts. Simultaneously, children are absorbing values from their models and acquiring the fundamental orientations that their social status or ethnic group stresses. In middle-class homes this process is aided because most mothers are teaching mothers and see informal, incidental situations as occasions to teach little social lessons. Obviously, boys learn to be boys and girls learn to be girls, although these stereotypes are under attack in some quarters. Normally, a child has a pretty good sense of identity by the end of the preschool period and has acquired a set of skills for transactions with other children and with adults.

No small part of this process is moral development, a topic recently coming under scrutiny, for example, in the work of Kohlberg (1971). Piaget has shown that a sense of justice evolves through several stages in the young, and of course continues well beyond the scope of the time period considered here. However, virtually all later stages of childhood, and some aspects of how we behave as adults may well be foreshadowed in the years from birth to 5.

The importance of social behavior is evident when children are retarded. *Adaptive behavior,* as it is called, is the process of coping with the natural and social demands of the environment. Together with tested intelligence it is requisite to ascertaining the status of a person as retarded, in the view of the American Association of Mental Deficiency. For a broader consideration of this matter the reader is referred to the author's discussion of the topic (Jordan, 1976b).

Hypotheses

The hypotheses proposed to structure inquiry into comparative influences on social development reflect the nature of the predictor groups and the context of the criterion measures. With regard to the latter the *Responsibility* scale of the Preschool Attainment Record, the social criterion at 2 years, presents items of behavior occurring in social contexts and contingent on the behavior of others, usually caregivers. Some of the items demonstrate incorporation of other-centered norms of conduct. In the use of the *Personal–Social–Responsiveness (P–S–R)* component of the Preschool Inventory, which has a high number of items in the scale administered, the behaviors and tasks the child is asked to perform by the test administrator, such as saying "hello" very loudly, demonstrate acquisition of names of parts of the body and following complex directions. The test authors summarize the domain as "knowledge about the child's own personal world and his ability to get along with and respond to communications of another person [Caldwell, 1970, p. 34]."

The hypotheses reflect the salience of the predictor elements for these aspects of development in children at ages 2 and 4 years. For this reason we hypothesize that the greatest form of influence will be the Maternal predictor series, because the criterion elements seem most likely to emerge in mother–child interaction. As second most influential predictor series we hypothesize the Social variables. In third place come the Family variables, noting that this set has only one element, birth order, antecedent to the 2 year criterion. Finally, we hypothesize that the least influential set of predictors will be the Biological set. In the case of the hypothesis, we are led to this position in part by an analysis of perinatal influences made earlier (Jordan, 1971). In this matter of hypotheses, influence is formulated as the relative proportion of criterion variance associated with a predictor set at a given age.

Measures

The *Social* domain contains one measure at age 2, and one measure at age 4 years. At age 2 a refinement of the Vineland Social Maturity Scale, the Preschool Attainment Record, was used. We have cited this instrument in previous chapters and note that the *Responsibility* scale was used in conference with mothers. In the case of the 4-year-olds a subscore based on the first 18 items of the Preschool Inventory was extracted from its protocol, the *Personal–Social–Responsiveness* group.

This is not a large set of measures, and it samples the narrowest span of development, 24 months, to 48–54 months. With the hindsight longitudinal study so exquisitely refines, one can only regret the absence of at least 3-year data; but longitudinal analyses express priorities, and social development was not a priority at 36 months.

Results

(A) BIOLOGICAL SERIES

In order to assess the influence of the Biological predictor set, a corpus of data was assembled from the records of 699 children. That is, the data set was scrutinized to retrieve all cases providing information on the four predictors, birthweight, biological risk, Apgar score, and sex, plus the criterion score from the *Responsibility* subscale of the Preschool Attainment Record. As with other PAR criteria, the information providing scores comes from mothers as well as from their children.

In Table 8.1 we see descriptive characteristics comparable to those presented for other 24 month criteria and the Biological predictor set. Birthweights are good, on the average, and even down at the minus one standard deviation level birthweights are 5.39 lb. This is well above critical levels, developmentally speaking, and also above the WHO standard, which is clearly too high to be of clinical significance. Biological risk is low, and Apgar scores reveal that children were generally in good condition in the

TABLE 8.1

DESCRIPTION OF THE SUBJECTS: BIOLOGICAL SERIES AND TWO-YEAR PAR *RESPONSIBILITY*,

AND THREE-YEAR PRESCHOOL INVENTORY *PERSONAL-SOCIAL-RESPONSIVENESS*

Variable	24 Mos.			36 Mos.			42 Mos.		
	$\overline{M}$	%	σ	$\overline{M}$	%	σ	$\overline{M}$	%	σ
	(N=696)			(N=396)			(N=376)		
Sex (% M)		53			51			51	
Race (% W)		61			65			62	
SES	53.98		15.95	55.91		16.32	54.12		14.85
Birth Weight	7.06		1.26	7.09		1.22	6.93		1.30
BioRisk	.49		1.09	.35		.84	.63		1.28
Apgar	8.72		1.46	9.06		1.15	8.51		1.64
PAR *Responsibility*	8.00		2.74						
Preschool Inventory *P-S-R*				11.42		3.43	13.39		3.20

first few minutes after delivery in this subset containing slightly more boys than girls. Scores on the criterion PAR *Responsibility* scale had a mean of 8.0, which is very similar to the means reported in the remaining descriptive tables.

In Table 8.2 we see that the analysis of PAR *Responsibility* scores did not find birthweights, risk, and Apgar scores useful, while sex differences favoring girls were a significant source of variance. The model explained 2% of the variance, and sex explained much of that. The 4 year data set included *Personal–Social–Responsiveness* scores from nearly 800 boys and girls ($N = 772$). At 48 months Apgar scores were influential in a full model whose $R^2 = .03$. Apgars explained 1% of the variance ($F = 6.29$, $p = .01$). Sex differences were only slightly less pronounced ($F = 5.73$, $p = .01$). In the 54 month analysis, also summarized in Table 8.2, only sex differences were evident. At 48 months higher $P-S-R$ scores were found in girls.

(B) SOCIAL SERIES

The next analyses applied the Social predictor series to social criteria from 700 2-year-olds ($N = 718$) and 500 4-year-olds ($N = 482$). The children described in Table 8.3 resemble other study groups, and the low pro-

TABLE 8.2

MULTIPLE LINEAR REGRESSION ANALYSIS OF BIOLOGICAL INFLUENCES ON SOCIAL ATTAINMENT

Variable	Models Compared	24 Mos. (N=696) PAR Responsibility			48 Mos. (N=396) P.I. Personal-Social			54 Mos. (N=376) P.I. Personal-Social		
		R^2	F	P	R^2	F	P	R^2	F	P
Birth Weight	Full Model 1	.02		.001*	.03		.002*	.02		.04*
	Model 2	.02	.23	.63	.02	2.84	.09	.01	2.52	.11
				.001*			.008*			.14*
Biological Risk	Full Model 1	.02		.001*	.03		.002*	.02		.04*
	Model 2	.02	.08	.77	.03	.78	.73	.01	.71	.39
				.01*			.01*			.20*
Apgar	Full Model 1	.02		.001*	.03		.002*	.02		.04*
	Model 3	.01	2.37	.12	.02	6.29	.01	.01	1.91	.10
				.005*			.04*			.11*
Sex (M)	Full Model 1	.02		.001*	.03		.002*	.02		.04*
	Model 5	.008	9.55	.002	.02	5.73	.01	.01	4.05	.04
				.34*			.11*			.57*

*Significance of the difference from zero.

TABLE 8.3

DESCRIPTION OF THE SUBJECTS: SOCIAL SERIES AND TWO YEAR PAR RESPONSIBILITY

AND FOUR YEAR PRESCHOOL INVENTORY *PERSONAL-SOCIAL-RESPONSIVENESS*

Variable	24 Mos. (N=718)			48 Mos. (N=193)			54 Mos. (N=289)		
	$\bar{M}$	%	σ	$\bar{M}$	%	σ	$\bar{M}$	%	σ
Sex (% M)		54			50			53	
Race (% W)		61			94			66	
SES	54.06		15.86	48.05		15.24	53.20		14.72
Paternal Occup.				40.08		17.89	45.28		18.49
Maternal Work									
- *Full time*					17			24	
- *Part time*					11			5	
- *Home*					72			71	
Maternal Education									
- *Elementary*					5			6	
- *Part H.S.*					17			24	
- *H.S.*					47			43	
- *Part College*					22			17	
- *College*					9			10	
PAR *Responsibility*	8.03		2.76						
P.I. *P-S-R*				11.67		3.17	13.23		3.35

175

portion of black children in the 48 month data set has been observed in preceding analyses of the birthday group. The mean SES level is higher in that group at 48 months than in other two groups. In Table 8.4 we see that the two-predictor model of SES and ethnic group explained 1% of the variance, and was statistically significant from zero. Within that model SES explained most of the variance ($F = 10.31$, $p = .001$). At 48 months the three parental traits were incorporated, but none of the set of five predictors accounted for variance in a comparatively robust model ($R^2 = .10$). At 54 months a still larger R^2 was generated, .15. Maternal degree of employment outside the home was the prime influence, explaining 20% of the full model's $R^2 = .15$; higher scores were associated with mothers working. This was followed by race, explaining 2% of the variance ($F = 7.81$, $p = .005$) with higher scores in white children. Mothers working outside the home were associated with higher social development scores.

(C) FAMILY SERIES

Table 8.5 gives the descriptive data for the data set of two predictors at age 2, five predictors at age 4, and the criteria. The number of cases at 2 years is 311, and at 4 years there are 571 cases.

Applied to the 2 year criterion, using PAR *Responsibility* scores, the sole Family predictor of birth order was not a significant influence. Addition of the number of siblings and specification of the father figure at age 3 raised the predictive model's R^2 to .06, with 48 months P–S–R scores as the criterion. All three predictors were significant, the greatest being the number of siblings; statistically most important, the number of siblings accounted for most criterion variance. High criterion scores were associated with more brothers and sisters in the family. Very close were birth order and the father figure, each accounting for one-third of the variance, and significant at the .01 level. The other half of the 571 subjects were at 54 months, an age at which STIM and type of dwelling were added to the predictor series, extending the R^2 to .15. At 54 months the STIM was the sole, powerful source of variance, accounting for .12 of the .15 of the full model ($F = 40.26$, $p < .00001$). Higher STIM scores were associated with higher socioeconomic status.

(D) MATERNAL SERIES

In contrast to the cumulative nature of the Family variables, all four Maternal variables were present for all three criteria. Once more, there were 600 cases ($N = 618$) at 2 years and slightly more ($N = 671$) at age 4. As Table 8.7 indicates, all three sets of data are quite similar. None of the Maternal traits—marital status, age AFI_{68}, or social risk—influenced PAR *Responsibility* scores at age 2 in a model whose $R^2 = .01$. In contrast, two

TABLE 8.4

MULTIPLE LINEAR REGRESSION ANALYSIS OF SOCIAL INFLUENCES ON SOCIAL ATTAINMENT

Variable	Models Compared	24 Mos. (N=718) PAR *Responsibility*			48 Mos. (N=193) P. I. *Personal-Social*			54 Mos. (N=289) P. I. *Personal-Social*		
		R^2	F	P	R^2	F	P	R^2	F	P
SES	Full Model 1	.01	10.31	.004* / .001	.10	1.33	.0006* / .24	.15	.04	<.00001* / .83
	Model 2	.0005		.52*	.10		.0004*	.15		<.00001*
Race (B)	Full Model 1	.01	1.79	.004* / .17	.10	1.58	.0006* / .20	.15	7.81	<.00001* / .005
	Model 3	.01		.002*	.10		.005*	.13		<.00001*
Paternal Occupation	Full Model 1				.10	1.49	.0006* / .22	.15	.002	<.00001* / .96
	Model 4				.10		.0005*	.15		<.00001*
Maternal Employment	Full Model 1				.10	.00	.0006* / 1.00	.15	9.06	<.00001* / .002
	Model 5				.10		.0002*	.12		<.00001*
Maternal Education	Full Model 1				.10	.17	.0006* / .68	.15	2.11	<.00001* / .14
	Model 6				.10		.0002*	.14		<.00001*

*Significance of the difference from zero.

TABLE 8.5

DESCRIPTION OF THE SUBJECTS: FAMILY SERIES AND TWO-YEAR PAR *RESPONSIBILITY*, AND FOUR-YEAR PRESCHOOL INVENTORY *PERSONAL-SOCIAL-RESPONSIVENESS* SCORES

Variable	24 Mos.			48 Mos.			54 Mos.		
	$\overline{M}$	%	σ	$\overline{M}$	%	σ	$\overline{M}$	%	σ
	(N=718)			(N=293)			(N=278)		
Sex (% M)		54			51			51	
Race (% W)		62			61			59	
SES	54.05		16.39	54.60		16.36	55.15		14.39
Birth Order	2.88		2.30	3.24		2.39	3.12		1.96
N Siblings				2.78		2.22	2.69		1.85
Father Figure									
- *father*					76			73	
- *f. figure*					12			7	
- *none*					12			20	
STIM							32.26		6.23
Dwelling									
- *house*								65	
- *apartment*								35	
- *trailer*									
PAR *Responsibility*	8.05		2.72						
P.I. *P-S-R*				11.34		3.35	13.21		3.27

TABLE 8.6

MULTIPLE LINEAR REGRESSION ANALYSIS OF FAMILY INFLUENCES ON SOCIAL ATTAINMENT

Variable	Models Compared	24 Mos. (N=718) PAR *Responsibility*			48 Mos. (N=293) P. I. *Personal–Social*			54 Mos. (N=278) P. I. *Personal–Social*		
		R^2	F	P	R^2	F	P	R^2	F	P
Birth Order	Full Model 1	.002			.06		.00001*	.15		<.00001*
			.86	.35*		6.10	.01		.35	.55
	Model 2				.04		.0007*	.15		<.00001*
N Siblings	Full Model 1				.06		.001*	.15		<.00001*
						9.10	.002		.50	.47
	Model 3				.03		.003*	.15		<.00001*
Father Figure	Full Model 1				.06		.001*	.15		<.00001*
						6.19	.01		.02	.87
	Model 4				.04		.0007*	.15		<.00001*
STIM	Full Model 1							.15		<.00001*
									40.26	<.00001*
	Model 5							.03		.05*
Dwelling	Full Model 1							.15		<.00001*
									.00	1.00
	Model 6							.15		<.00001*

*Significance of the difference from zero.

TABLE 8.7

DESCRIPTION OF THE SUBJECTS: MATERNAL SERIES AND TWO-YEAR PAR *RESPONSIBILITY* AND

FOUR-YEAR PRESCHOOL INVENTORY *PERSONAL-SOCIAL-RESPONSIVENESS*

Variable	*24 Mos.*			*48 Mos.*			*54 Mos.*		
	$\bar{M}$	%	σ	$\bar{M}$	%	σ	$\bar{M}$	%	σ
	(N=618)			(N=337)			(N=334)		
Sex (% M)		52			50			53	
Race (% W)		65			60			64	
SES	53.15		15.75	54.37		16.32	53.34		14.87
Married		88			87			88	
Delivery Age	25.67		6.54	25.10		6.55	25.77		6.52
AFI$_{68}$	26.15		8.05	27.60		7.44	25.85		8.30
Social Risk	1.10		1.63	1.28		1.72	1.05		1.56
PAR *Responsibility*	8.03		2.79						
P.I. *P-R-S*				11.54		3.36	13.42		3.19

predictors accounted for variance at 48 months in a model explaining 6% of the *P*–*S*–*R* variance. Social risk explained one-third of the variance ($F = 8.66$, $p = .003$). One-sixth of the 6% (R^2) was explained by AFI$_{68}$ ($F = 5.63$, $p = .01$). In all four cases, higher child attainments were associated with lowered authoritarianism and lesser levels of social risk. At 54 months the same two variables prevailed in a model accounting for 8% of the *P*–*S*–*R* variance. However, the order was reversed, and AFI$_{68}$ was more significant ($F = 7.31$, $p = .007$), and AFI$_{68}$ scores were slightly less influential ($F = 6.47$, $p = .01$).

Discussion

So far in this chapter we have reported the results of applying a predictor series of variables in four subgroups, Biological, Social, Family, and Maternal sets, to three social criteria at 2 and 4 years of age. At 2 years, data were assembled on 600 children and at age 4 on 700 children. At both ages subtests of the Preschool Attainment Record and the Preschool Inventory were used as criteria in multiple regression analyses.

TABLE 8.8

MULTIPLE LINEAR REGRESSION ANALYSIS OF MATERNAL INFLUENCES ON SOCIAL ATTAINMENT

Variable	Models Compared	24 Mos. (N=618) PAR Responsibility			48 Mos. (N=337) P. I. Personal-Social			54 Mos. (N=334) P. I. Personal-Social		
		R^2	F	P	R^2	F	P	R^2	F	P
Married	Full Model 1	.01		.11*	.06		.0001*	.08		.00001*
	Model 2	.009	1.18	.27	.06	1.28	.25	.07	.77	.38
				.10*			<.0001*			.00001*
Delivery Age	Full Model 1	.01		.11*	.06		.0001*	.08		.00001*
	Model 3	.007	2.43	.11	.06	1.48	.22	.07	.96	.32
				.17*			<.0001*			.00001*
AFI_{68}	Full Model 1	.01		.11*	.06		.0001*	.08		.00001*
	Model 4	.006	3.37	.06	.05	5.63	.01	.06	7.31	.007
				.26*			.0005*			.00001*
Social Risk	Full Model 1	.01		.11*	.06		.0001*	.08		.00001*
	Model 5	.01	.62	.43	.04	8.66	.003	.06	6.47	.01
				.08*			.002*			<.00001*

* Significance of the difference from model zero.

In Table 8.9 are the R^2 values or proportion of criterion variance generated by the predictor sets for the three criteria. The range of R^2 values is from .01 to .15; within the R^2 values in the table, the lowest are those generated in study of the 2-year criterion, and the highest are associated with the 54-month criterion. The consistently least useful predictor series is the Biological group, but no predictor series is clearly the best for all three criteria. When the question is addressed to the two 4-year criteria, only the Social model is comparatively effective. Looked at from the point of view of which criterion is most analyzable or predictable, the P–S–R criterion at 54 months seems the best, and the 2-year criterion seems the worst.

HYPOTHESES

It may help to recall that earlier in this chapter we hypothesized that predictor sets would influence the *Social* domain in the order Maternal, Social, Family, and Biological groups of predictors. The clearest test comes in the case of the last of these predictor sets, as Table 8.9 indicates. We see that low accounts of criterion variance were generated at both ages 2–4. Thus, our hypothesis of least influence by Biological factors is sustained. In contrast, R^2 values tended to arise across the developmental span with the other three predictor sets. In the case of the hypothesized major influence, Maternal traits, the mean R^2 is .05 for the three Social criteria; this is the

TABLE 8.9

R^2 VALUES OF SOCIAL DOMAIN ANALYSES

	R^2 VALUES			CRITERIA	
Biological Model	Social Model	Family Model	Maternal Model		Mean R^2
.02	.01	.002	.01	24 M. PAR *Responsibility*	.01
.03	.10	.06	.06	48 M. Preschool Inventory *P-S-R*	.06
.02	.15	.15	.08	54 M. Preschool Inventory *P-S-R*	.13
Mean .02	.08	.07	.05		.07

TABLE 8.10

PREDICTORS IN ORDER OF STATISTICAL CONTRIBUTION IN MULTIPLE REGRESSION ANALYSES TO FULL MODEL R^2

Biological and Social Models

CRITERION	BIOLOGICAL MODEL				SOCIAL MODEL					
	Weight	Biological Risk	Apgar	Sex (M)	SES	Race	Pop Occup.	Mom's Employ.	Mom's Educat.	Head of Househ. Educat.
Child Age (Yrs.)	*Birth*	*Birth*	*Birth*	*Birth*	*Birth*	*Birth*	*Three*	*Three*	*Five*	*Five*
24 M. PAR *Responsibility*				1	1					
48 M. Preschool Inventory *P-S-R*			1	2						
54 M. Preschool Inventory *P-S-R*				1		2		1		

Family and Maternal Models

CRITERION	FAMILY MODEL					MATERNAL MODEL				
	Birth Order	N Siblings	Father Figure	Dwelling Type	STIM	Married	Age	AFI 68	Social Risk	Birth
Child Age (Yrs.)	*Birth*	*3 Years*	*3 Years*	*5 Years*	*5 Years*	*Birth*	*Birth*	*Birth*		*Birth*
24 M. PAR *Responsibility*	3	1	2							
48 M. Preschool Inventory *P-S-R*								2		
54 M. Preschool Inventory *P-S-R*					1			1	2	

third best. Hypothesized as second best in influence, the Social model was in fact the best, with a mean R^2 of .08. The Family model, hypothesized as third in influence turned out to be exactly that with an $R^2 = .07$. Thus the hypothesized role of Biological and Family influences are supported, and the posited Maternal and Social degrees of influence are not supported.

DISCRETE INFLUENCES

We now turn to a consideration of the role of particular variables within predictor models as influences on social development. As with previous chapters we note the dynamic, expanding nature of two predictor sets as the children grow in age from birth to age 5. This means that the salience of a variable in relation to a predictor is contingent on the variables included at a given child age.

In Table 8.10 we first consider the Biological predictors, all of which are concurrent with birth. Sex of the children is clearly the salient influence, and higher Social scores are associated with girls. In the case of the Family predictors, birth order is not an influence, but the number of brothers and sisters is. The identity of the father figure is relevant, and the STIM, while only used at 54 months, is very influential. An interesting aspect of the entire set of predictors is the number quite lacking in influence. In particular several of the Social predictors and the Biological predictors are absent from the Table 8.10 list of statistically significant variables.

Summarizing, we hazard that social attainment at the child ages 2 and 4 years are particularly influenced by the sex of children (especially being a boy), socioeconomic status, maternal employment, birth order, AFI_{68}, and social risk.

Among the social predictors, social class, ethnic group, and being a working mother influences social development. Average or better SES level, being white, and have a working mother are associated with higher scores. The latter may be due to enrollment of the children in day care centers.

Physical Development

9

Introduction

In recent decades, especially the 1960s, social scientists implicitly formulated childhood as a disembodied state that contains aptitude, motivation, adjustment, and other functional traits. It is as if empiricists were really Platonists discussing so many propositions in a world of nonmaterial forms. The fact is that children have bodies, and much of the important material developmentalists have studied in recent years have a correlate in physical well-being and healthy growth. Indeed, the evidence is clear that weight at birth, if low, sets the stage for a variety of *risks* to the subsequent development of a range of child behaviors (Drillien, 1964). Postnatal increments in weight and in height reflect the circumstances of life and the course of the body's path toward maturity.

Measures

There is something misleadingly obvious about height and weight. On the face of it one simply measures a child using some chosen unit, avoirdupois or metric, and that is that. In practice there are several methodological niceties to be observed, and they merit attention. The first is that procedures must be standardized; that is, all measurements must be taken by identical steps. As a result, one specifies that outer garments or all garments are discarded, or that shoes must be removed as well as socks.

A second point is that measuring instruments must be identical. That is, all examiners use the same scale, or when different scales are used their calibrations must be checked. Obviously, scales must be carefully selected instruments and examiners are given both oral and written directions in their use. In this regard, the accuracy of measurement requires consideration. Three sources of error are obvious. One is the grossness of error, a topic manageable by specifying that height be recorded to within some degree, for example, one-eighth of an inch, one-half centimeter, or one-quarter pound. Van t'Hof, Roede, and Kowalski's (1977) examination of error of measurement led to the observation that Nymegen data gathered under a careful regimen of anthropometry yielded a 2 mm error in height. A 5 mm error was estimated by Van der Linden, Hirschfield, and Miller (1970). Still another problem is missing data and the question of whether to interpolate missing values in the series on any given subject. Such measurements can be calculated, and Karlberg and Taranger (1976) have done so in their studies of somatic development in Swedish children. A third problem is that dimensions of the body fluctuate during the 24 hour day. The ulna, larger of the two bones in the forearm, is longest in early morning and shortest at noon (Valk & Van Den Busch, 1978), for example.

In this investigation standing height[1] (*stature–NCHS, 1977*) was recorded to one-quarter inch and weight to one-quarter pound under standardized procedures supervised by a nurse. No weights or heights in the data set were obtained by interpolation. The temptation to do so is considerable when height and weight data on a child exist over a decade. However, we have not done so on the grounds that the procedural validity of the data as prospective would be violated by interpolation. The net effect is to reduce Ns at times, but that is less of a problem than invalidity of measurements due to interpolation. We have, however, used physicians' and nurses' measurements in the few cases when they have been available and also timely.

The weight and height series covers the developmental span from 6 to 66 months and is accordingly the longest, containing 10 measures at 6-month intervals. The maximum set of data points for any child is seven, but the 30-month group was small for procedural reasons, and so six measures per child is a realistic way to talk about any given child in this chapter. As a final comment we point out that the criterion heights and weights are pooled for boys and girls. This has been done for consistency with the previous chapters, and of course sex differences are appraised in the Biological model for all criteria.

---

[1]Recumbent length at birth and at 6 months.

Physical Development

The process of physical growth is dynamic in many ways. The basic contribution of genetic materials at conception determines one vector of growth. Also a list of specific elements as yet not finally counted interacts with genetic instructions until maturity is reached.

The general picture of development in children is one of increasing height and weight over past generations. This *secular* trend is evident in increases in height and weight, since such data were systematically gathered for the Parliamentary Factory Inquiries Commission in 1833 by Samuel Stanway. At that time boys were comparatively short at maturity; the reason for that state of affairs is easily found in reports on conditions of life and conditions of child labor (Engels, 1845/1968). Improvements over the generations are evident, with a few exceptions, in the greatly increased height and weight of children today. According to data assembled by Meredith (1963), birth length increased by .8 cm between 1865 and 1961 in North America. From 1875 to 1965 the height of 10-year-old boys increased by about one-half inch per decade, according to Sullivan (1971). Data reported from Holland indicate that the secular trend to increasing height is still evident, even in a well nourished population (Van Venrooij-Ysselmuiden & Van Ipenberg, 1978). Menarche, Tanner (1961) informs us, occurs perhaps 10 months earlier in girls than in their mothers, and about 3 years ahead of women in 1820. Swedish data reported in 1974 by Ljung, Bergsten-Brucefors, and Lindgren indicate that age of menarche continues to decline by about 4 months per decade.

Within the overall picture of increasing height and weight, there continue to be systematic differences due to the social contexts in which children grow (Eveleth & Tanner, 1978). Analyzing data from over 5000 British children born in 1947, Douglas and Blomfield (1958) found that young children's heights, grouped by parental occupation from professional to unskilled, ranged generally from high to low; for example, children of the highest group were about 1 in. taller than children from the lowest group. They also reported regional differences favoring children living in Southeast England over those living in Wales at age 4 years. Obviously, the circumstances of life are a source of variation; comparative data assembled by Chamla and Demoulin (1976) show that Algerian children fall well below Belgian and Sicilian children in stature. The effect of the range of influences are in some respects more relevant at certain ages. Prenatal and infant growth provide a baseline for subsequent development. Being the child of Chicano migrant workers, for example, places a baby at risk for survival, let alone for increments in stature (Chase *et al.*, 1971).

In this chapter we take the developmental span 6–66 months and use height and weight at 6-month intervals as criteria. The question addressed in this chapter is the effect of three kinds of influence, each a set of several variables, on height and weight.

Hypotheses

In this and previous chapters the purpose is to examine the hypothetical influence of sets of predictor variables on criteria of development. For the work as a whole there are the four sets of predictor variables presented in Table 3.6. There we see that the theme of development in the criteria was paralleled longitudinally by extension of the predictor series. That is, the study of growth in some domains of child development is paralleled by acquisition of more information about the predictor domains. In all cases there are predictor variables acquired at the time of birth, or earlier in some cases of biological risk.

One of the prime virtues of prospective study is that not all data need be baseline (i.e., perinatal) factors. The prospective approach allows variables to be added on two bases. First, the problem of excessively long initial interviews which can compromise subsequent data taking is avoided. Second, information of a delicate nature can be acquired when sufficient interviews have been held to establish rapport. In that climate successful contacts predispose families to future contacts, and success builds on success. At the time of writing the nineteenth contact has been made with the birth cohort; some families volunteer information which, if not useable in the total computer-based file, is quite valuable in the context of specific case studies. In this work some of the data sets grow as the children grow.

The predictor sets are three. The first is Biological, and since the criteria in this chapter are also biological we hypothesize that the Biological predictor series will be the most influential; that is, it will explain more variance in height and weight at criterion ages than other predictor sets across the developmental span.

Our hypothesis for second most predicting model is based on the corpus of studies which relate the general strata of society in which children live to their growth. For example, studies dealing with perhaps the largest data set on the subject of influences on development is that of Stein, Susser, Saenger, and Marolla (1972). In their study of Dutch archival data on 19-year-olds born in the period of famine at the end of the war years (1944–1946), they found no persisting effects of prenatal malnutrition. On the other hand, socioeconomic status exerted a persistent influence on growth beginning in the prenatal period. Sand and Emery-Hauzear (1962) have documented social influences on development from birth to age 2. Miller, Billewicz, and Thomson (1972) have identified a substantial effect due to social factors in the weight of females at the age of 5 years and subsequently. Topp, Cook, Holland, and Elliot (1970) have demonstrated social influences on weight at 5 years and later. For these reasons we hypothesize that the social predictors will be the second most influential vector, in the sense of accounting for criterion variance.

We hypothesize the vector of least influence, comparatively speaking, will be the set of Family variables. The reason is that there seems little basis beyond birth order for relating the number of children and the kind of dwelling to the domain of growth in this chapter, although its relevance as a hypothesized influence was evident selectively in previous chapters. Our phrasing of these hypothesized influences applies to both height and to weight.

We have spoken earlier of four models of influence. The fourth model, Maternal traits, is not used as a hypothetical influence. The reason is that previous research (Jordan & Spaner, 1972, 1974) has shown the irrelevance of maternal traits to physical development across the developmental span of interest in this study. Given data at hand, no red-blooded investigator could resist the urge to confirm or refute the earlier findings. In our Technical Report series, we confirm the irrelevance of the Maternal predictor series of this investigation. In 80 comparisons of full and restricted models of height and weight, there were eight scattered findings of statistical significance. Only one of them occurred after age 2 years, and five dealt with height.

Results—Height

(A) BIOLOGICAL SERIES

At 6 months of age, the data set of four perinatal measures plus the criterion height in inches was assembled on 640 children. About half (51%) were males, and the mean birthweight was 6.58 lb. One-half to two-thirds were white, and the rating for biological risk was .5 on the average, which is a low score on a scale from zero to five. Not surprisingly, the Apgar scores average 8.75, which is quite good and represents little departure from a desirable score of 10 representing desirable pulse, skin color, muscle tone, reflex irritability, and respiratory effort.

In Table 9.1 those scores are given, plus the same measures for other criterion groups to age 66 months. Table 9.1 shows that the children studied in 10 data sets are quite comparable versions of the 637 originally studied at age 6 months. We point out that there are slightly different but consistent values for Apgar scores in the birthday (36, 48, and 60 months) and half-year (42, 54, and 66 months) groups. This phenomenon has been seen in other descriptive tables.

TABLE 9.1

DESCRIPTION OF THE SUBJECTS: BIOLOGICAL SERIES AND HEIGHT FROM SIX TO SIXTY-SIX MONTHS

Variable	6 Months (N=637)			12 Months (N=536)			24 Months (N=688)			30 Months (N=182)			36 Months (N=366)		
	$\bar{M}$	%	σ	$\bar{M}$	%	σ	$\bar{M}$	%	σ	$\bar{M}$	%	σ	$\bar{M}$	%	σ
Sex (% M)		51			54			54			59			53	
Race (% W)		56			72			61			67			56	
SES	54.81		16.06	51.20		15.98	53.99		15.95	53.26		16.73	55.86		16.18
Birth Weight (lb.)	6.99		1.26	7.15		1.22	7.07		1.25	7.05		1.30	7.09		1.25
Bio Risk	.50		1.11	.51		1.14	.49		1.09	.60		1.17	.40		.92
Apgar	8.75		1.50	8.59		1.51	8.72		1.46	8.65		1.55	9.02		1.21
Height (in.)	26.38		1.51	29.67		1.65	33.64		2.47	35.64		1.92	37.56		1.92

Variable	42 Months (N=356)			48 Months (N=402)			54 Months (N=379)			60 Months (N=401)			66 Months (N=373)		
	$\bar{M}$	%	σ	$\bar{M}$	%	σ	$\bar{M}$	%	σ	$\bar{M}$	%	σ	$\bar{M}$	%	σ
Sex (% M)		52			52			52			53			52	
Race (% W)		57			53			61			53			62	
SES	55.30		14.82	56.55		16.14	54.18		14.77	56.21		16.20	54.19		14.62
Birth Weight	6.95		1.29	7.10		1.24	6.92		1.31	7.06		1.24	6.94		1.26
Bio Risk	.61		1.27	.37		.88	.64		1.30	.35		.87	.61		1.23
Apgar	8.57		1.62	9.06		1.18	8.50		1.64	9.04		1.18	8.54		1.59
Height (in.)	39.14		1.74	40.64		1.93	41.97		1.92	43.47		2.03	44.68		2.21

In Table 9.2 the Biological predictor set of four elements—birthweight, biological risk, Apgar score, and sex of the child—are analyzed into sources of criterion variance. Neither Apgar nor biological risk scores were a source of variance from 6-month weight. The prime source was weight at birth 6 months before ($F = 75.26$, $p < .00001$), with heavier newborns being proportionately longer at 6 months. A much less influential source of variance in the regression model, explaining 16% of the 6-month weight variance, was the sex of children. This variable explained 3% of the variance of about 20%, and the finding was that boys were longer than girls ($F = 23.00$, $p < .00001$). At 12 months the same two Biological variables were influential, but in a slightly less robust regression model ($R^2 = .12$). The proportion of variance due to sex differences rose to one-third, but the order of influence and direction did not change; that is, at 6 months greater height was associated with being a boy, and having been average rather than light at birth.

At 2 years weight at birth remained influential, in a far less robust model ($R^2 = .04$), accounting for three-fourths of the variance in almost 700 measures of height ($N = 682$). Sex differences were not apparent, but Apgar scores achieved statistical, if not empirical, significance while explaining .006 of the variance ($F = 4.73$, $p = .02$). The Apgar direction associated heights at 24 months with lower Apgars, a finding we have noted in previous occasions. If one keeps in mind the actual decline in R^2 from .044 to .037, the empirical significance fades, despite the statistical significance probably contingent on the large number of degrees of freedom.

At 30 months there is a consistently small study group for all criteria; height was no exception ($N = 182$), and none of the four predictors accounted for variance in this, the least robust of the regression models ($R^2 = .02$).

At 36 months the slight trend of preceding ages for birthweight and sex differences to be significant reappeared in 700 child measurements ($N = 722$), and in the previous order of birthweight first, followed by sex. The direction of influence was the same; boys were taller ($F = 3.64$, $p = .05$), and the greater influence was weight at birth, which accounted for two-thirds of the variance ($F = 15.48$, $p < .00001$) in a typically not too robust model ($R^2 = .06$). In the second group of 3-year-olds, the half-year group started at 42 months, the trend for influence by both birthweight and sex persisted, and in the previous fashion. Babies not light at birth were tallest $3\frac{1}{2}$ years later ($F = 15.77$, $p = .00009$), and boys were a little taller than girls ($F = 4.58$, $p = .03$). Within a model explaining 6% of the variance, two-thirds of the variance was due to birthweight, and one-sixth was due to sex differences.

At age 4 sex differences—never large as an influence—dropped out, as Table 9.2 shows. Birthweight continued as an influence, in a weak model explaining 3% of the variance in heights ($F = 15.48$, $p = .0001$) from nearly 800 boys and girls ($N = 781$). At 54 months virtually all the variance associated with height was due to birthweight in a model whose $R^2 = .06$. Deletion of birthweight, in regression Model 2 dropped R^2 to .006 ($F = 23.66$, $p < .00001$). Statistical, if not empirical significance was associated with biological risk at birth; regression model 3 had an $R^2 = .05$, 20% less than the full model's .065, and low risk was associated with taller children.

Among nearly 800 5-year-olds ($N = 774$), birthweight remained the prime source of variance in height. At 60 months birthweight was the sole influence and explained virtually all the R^2 of .03. In regression Model 2, the R^2 dropped from .03 to .01. In the 66 month group, birthweights explained a higher proportion of variance in height, as evident in the R^2 values of the first two regression models. A slight effect was associated with biological risk, which explained 1% of the full model's 5% value of R^2 ($F = 4.25$, $p = .03$).

(B) SOCIAL SERIES

As a reminder we note that the Social series of predictors begins at birth with SES and race, adds three parental traits at child age 3—father's occupation, mother's education, and extent of work outside the home—and incorporates a check on the education of the head of the household at age 5 years.

The two-term predictor set was applied at 6 months to over 600 ($N = 658$) children's lengths. Despite the attributed influence of social class, generally speaking the full model explained only 1% of the variance ($R^2 = .01$). Within that context race was statistically significant, and lengths were greater in white children.

In about 100 less children at their first birthdays ($N = 555$), race remained the significant variable in the presence of the SES score, which was not significant. Race accounted for virtually all the variance in the small full model; its absence dropped the R^2 of the regression model from .01 to .006.

At 2 years the same finding occurred in 700 measurements of height ($N = 709$). However, the model was much more robust, explaining 11% of the variance. When race was deleted the R^2 dropped by a half from .11 to .05 ($F = 48.82$, $p < .00001$).

As we have noted, the 30 month group is not typical. It has, for example, fewer black children than other groups. This may have a bearing on the absence of a race effect and the presence of an SES effect in the regression model ($R^2 = .08$). Five of the 8% of variance were associated with the SES

TABLE 9.2: MULTIPLE LINEAR REGRESSION

Variable	Models Compared	6 Mos. (N=637)			12 Mos. (N=536)		
		R^2	F	P	R^2	F	P
Birth Weight	Full Model 1	.16	75.26	< .00001* < .00001	.12	37.61	< .00001* < .00001
	Model 2	.06		< .00001*	.05		< .00001*
Biological Risk	Full Model 1	.16	.007	< .00001* .93	.12	.24	< .00001* .61
	Model 3	.16		< .00001*	.11		< .00001*
Apgar	Full Model 1	.16	.94	< .00001* .33	.12	.30	< .00001* .98
	Model 4	.14		< .00001*	.11		< .00001*
Sex (M)	Full Model 1	.16	23.00	< .00001* < .00001	.12	21.87	< .00001* < .00001
	Model 5	.16		< .00001*	.08		< .00001*

		42 Mos (N=356)			48 Mos. (N=402)		
		R^2	F	P	R^2	F	P
Birth Weight	Full Model 1	.06	15.77	.00004* .00009*	.04	15.48	.0004* .0001
	Model 2	.02		.05*	.007		.40*
Biological Risk	Full Model 1	.06	3.13	.00004* .07	.04	.35	.0004* .55
	Model 3	.05		.001*	.04		.003*
Apgar	Full Model 1	.06	1.64	.00004* .20	.04	.75	.0004* .38
	Model 4	.05		.00009*	.04		.0005*
Sex (M)	Full Model 1	.06	4.58	.00004* .03	.04	.59	.0004* .44
	Model 5	.05		.002*	.04		.003*

*Significance of the difference from zero.

ANALYSIS OF BIOLOGICAL INFLUENCES ON HEIGHT

24 Mos. (N=688)			30 Mos. (N=182)			36 Mos. (N=366)		
R^2	F	P	R^2	F	P	R^2	F	P
.04		<.00001*	.02		.22*	.06		.00002*
	19.68	<.00001		2.79	.09		15.48	.00001
.01		.009*	.008		.67*	.02		.02*
.04		<.00001*	.02		.22*	.06		.00002*
	.02	.88		.22	.63		.12	.72
.04		<.00001*	.02		.53*	.06		.0001*
.04		<.00001*	.02		.22*	.06		.00002*
	4.73	.02		.32	.57		.16	.68
.04		<.00001*	.02		.26*	.06		.00002*
.04		<.00001*	.02		.22*	.06		.00002*
	.92	.33		.28	.59		3.64	.05
.04		<.00001*	.02		.54*	.05		.0008*

54 Mos. (N=379)			60 Mos. (N=401)			66 Mos. (N=373)		
R^2	F	P	R^2	F	P	R^2	F	P
.06		.00001*	.03		.006*	.05		.0005*
	23.66	<.00001*		7.44	.006		20.77	.00001
.006		.48*	.01		.18*	.006		.51*
.06		.00001*	.03		.006*	.05		.00005*
	4.23	.04*		.20	.64		4.25	.03
.05		.007*	.03		.35	.04		.002*
.06		.00001*	.03		.006*	.05		.0005*
	.67	.41		3.04	.08		2.80	.09
.06		.00002*	.02		.02	.05		.0001*
.06		.00001*	.03		.006*	.05		.00005*
	.64	.42		.60	.43		.35	.55
.06		.00001*	.02		.04*	.05		.00004*

TABLE 9.3

DESCRIPTION OF THE SUBJECTS: SOCIAL SERIES AND HEIGHT FROM SIX TO SIXTY-SIX MONTHS

Variable	6 Mos. (N=658)			12 Mos. (N=555)			24 Mos. (N=709)			30 Mos. (N=186)			36 Mos. (N=199)		
	$\bar{M}$	%	σ	$\bar{M}$	%	σ	$\bar{M}$	%	σ	$\bar{M}$	%	σ	$\bar{M}$	%	σ
Sex (% M)		52			54			54			59			51	
Race (% W)		56			72			61			66			93	
SES	54.89		15.96	51.32		15.90	54.04		15.86	53.54		16.62	48.32		15.36
Pop's Occupation													40.53		17.85
Criterion (in.)	26.38		1.51	29.65		1.64	33.63		2.49	35.63		1.91	37.55		1.82

Variable	42 Mos. (N=312)			48 Mos. (N=193)			54 Mos. (N=290)			60 Mos. (N=197)			66 Mos. (N=282)		
	$\bar{M}$	%	σ	$\bar{M}$	%	σ	$\bar{M}$	%	σ	$\bar{M}$	%	σ	$\bar{M}$	%	σ
Sex (% M)		53			52			53			50			52	
Race (% W)		65			94			67			93			68	
SES	53.88		14.86	48.71		15.13	53.31		14.70	48.43		15.23	52.25		14.72
Pop's Occup.	46.10		18.55	40.47		17.82	45.36		18.44	40.53		17.92	45.10		18.38

Mom's Employ. (%)					
– Full Time	24	18	23	17	24
– Part Time	5	11	5	11	5
– At Home	71	71	72	72	73
Mom's Educat. (%)					
– College	9	8	10	9	9
– Part College	17	22	17	21	17
– High School	42	48	43	48	44
– Part H. School	24	17	24	17	23
– Element. School	8	5	6	5	7
Head of Household's Education (%)					
– Graduate School				–	1
– 4 Yrs. of College				12	8
– 2+ Yrs. of College				12	14
– H.S. Graduate				19	13
– 9th Grade Educat.				34	33
– 8th Grade Educat.				14	25
– Below 8th Grade				9	8
Criterion (in.)	39.14	40.58	41.95	43.21	44.62
	1.77	1.68	1.97	1.99	2.29

variables; the β-weight for SES was negative, meaning that McGuire and White scores were in inverse proportion to height. Since low SES scores means higher social status, the relationship is what one would expect.

Five hundred boys and girls ($N = 511$) provided measures of height at age 3, the age at which three parental variables of education and occupation data were added. At 36 months none of the five variables influenced the regression analysis. However, at 42 months race was significant for the fourth time. It accounted for half the variance in the weak regression model ($R^2 = .02$). SES was a secondary influence in the regression model ($F = 3.87$, $p = .04$).

Race repeated its role in the 48 month data set, the smaller of the 4 year sets of data from nearly 500 4-year-olds ($N = 483$). Its deletion in regression Model 2 dropped the R^2 from a weak .04 to .02. A secondary influence was the extent that mothers work outside the home ($F = 3.71$, $p = .05$); taller children are associated with mothers not working outside the home. We note in passing that the correlation between socioeconomic status and mothers working outside the home is $-.22$ ($p < .0001$), meaning that it is lower class women who tended to work outside the home. At 54 months none of the five predictors were associated with the criterion variance, in a model explaining 2% of the variance ($R^2 = .02$).

(C) FAMILY SERIES

In the case of the height data examined by means of the Family predictor set, the first four criterion ages have only one predictor variable, birth order. At 6 months data on this variable and length came from under 300 cases ($N = 272$). The R^2 of this one predictor model was .009 ($p = .11$), which is statistically insignificant. In the case of one-variable models it is helpful to point out that the square root of R^2 yields $r = .09$, a correlation between birth order and length at 6 months after delivery that is also statistically insignificant. At the first birthday birth order yielded an R^2 of .02 in a data set from 240 children. This is not statistically significant ($p = .07$). At the second birthday, when heights of 300 boys and girls were available ($N = 308$), the predictive model composed of data on birth order explained .01 of the height variance and was statistically insignificant ($p = .07$). In all three of these sets it is interesting to note that the range of birth orders goes up to thirteenth.

At 30 months, a smaller group for all variables, there were 91 height measures plus birth order data. As a one-predictor model, birth order explained a virtually nonexistent .001 of the variance ($p = .73$). Inspection of the distribution of this variable shows that 10% were in the ordinal position of seventh-born or higher.

When the cohort reached 3 years of age, the Family predictor set added the number of siblings and the identity of the father figure to birth order. In

300 cases ($N = 308$) at 36 months the R^2 value of the three variable predictor model was .01, which is statistically insignificant ($p = .35$). None of the predictors were associated with criterion variance. In a slightly larger group at age $3\frac{1}{2}$ years ($N = 317$) the R^2 dropped to .003, indicating a virtually nonexistent relationship between the predictor and criterion scores. Not surprisingly, none of the predictors accounted for criterion variance.

In the case of the 4-year-olds, a group of 300 boys and girls ($N = 296$) at age 48 months, the three predictor sets explained 3% of the variance in height ($R^2 = .03$), which is statistically significant ($p = .01$). In that modest but more promising context, the number of siblings was a source of variance ($F = 8.66$, $p = .003$). It was followed by birth order ($F = 6.86$, $p = .009$). At 54 months the predictor STIM and dwelling were added.

At 66 months one of the five predictors, STIM, was associated with the criterion of height. Between STIM and SES there is a correlation of .45 ($p < .0001$), with a correlation of height and SES of .07.

Results—Weight

In Table 9.7 the reader may inspect the descriptive characteristics of the data sets based on weight at 10 ages plus the Biological predictor sets. The data are quite comparable to what we have presented previously.

(A) BIOLOGICAL SERIES

Applied to over 600 measures of weight ($N = 668$) at 6 months the Biological series of perinatal variables showed that birthweight was a substantial influence. About one-third of the variance in a model explaining 28% (R^2) was due to weight 6 months before ($F = 156.29$, $p < .00001$). The sex of children explained about one-fifth of the variance ($F = 52.24$, $p < .00001$). The β-weight for this variable was positive, indicating greater weights in boys.

On the first birthday a smaller group of toddlers ($N = 555$) provided data for analysis of Biological influences. Weight at birth 1 year before was the prime influence in a model whose R^2 was .16. Regression Model 2 that deleted birthweight reached $R^2 = .07$, which is less than half the variance of the full model. Substantial sex differences, favoring greater weights in boys, were also observed ($F = 33.14$, $p < .00001$).

The 2-year-old group was comparable in size to the 6-month group, with data from nearly 700 toddlers ($N = 687$). The R^2 of the Biological regression model of weights was .09. The same two variables, birthweight and sex, were influential but the degree of influence, in the sense of proportion of the R^2 value, was about the same. Birthweight was slightly more

Predictor	Models Compared	6 Mos. (N=658)			12 Mos. (N=555)		
		R^2	F	P	R^2	F	P
Race	Full Model 1	.004		.24*	.01		.02*
			.008	.93		3.96	.05
	Model 2	.004		.09*	.006		.05*
SES	Full Model 1	.004		.24*	.01		.02*
			1.83	.17		.41	.51
	Model 3	.001		.31*	.01		.008*
Paternal Occup.	Full Model 1						
	Model 4						
Maternal Employm.	Full Model 1						
	Model 5						
Maternal Educ.	Full Model 1						
	Model 6						

Predictor	Models Compared	42 Mos. (N-312)			48 Mos. (N=193)		
		R^2	F	P	R^2	F	P
Race	Full Model 1	.02		.13*	.04		.11*
			5.45	.02		3.79	.05
	Model 2	.009		.56*	.02		.27*
SES	Full Model 1	.02		.13*	.04		.11*
			3.87	.04		.009	.92
	Model 3	.01		.33	.04		.06*
Paternal Occup.	Full Model 1	.02		.13*	.04		.11*
			.28	.59		.19	.65
	Model 4	.02		.08*	.04		.06*
Maternal Employm.	Full Model 1	.02		.13*	.04		.11*
			.00	1.00		3.71	.05
	Model 5	.02		.07*	.02		.26*
Maternal Educ.	Full Model 1	.02		.13*	.04		.11*
			.03	.85		1.91	.19
	Model 6	.02		.07*	.03		.12*
Head of Househ. Education	Full Model 1						
	Model 7						

*Significance of the difference from zero.

ANALYSIS OF SOCIAL INFLUENCE ON HEIGHT

24 Mos. (N=709)			30 Mos. (N=186)			36 Mos. (N=199)		
R^2	F	P	R^2	F	P	R^2	F	P
.11		<.00001*	.08		.0002*	.01		.61*
	48.87	<.00001*		.00	.97		.66	.41
.05		<.00001*	.08		.00005*	.01		.57*
.11		<.00001*	.08		.0002*	.01		.61*
	1.65	.19		10.92	.001		.18	.60
.11		<.00001*	.03		.01*	.01		.49*
						.01		.61*
							.08	.76
						.01		.48*
						.01		.61*
							1.98	.66
						.001		.81*
						.01		.61*
							1.34	.24
						.01		.69*

54 Mos. (N=290)			60 Mos. (N=197)			66 Mos. (N=287)		
R^2	F	P	R^2	F	P	R^2	F	P
.02		.24*	.03		.35*	.02		.26*
	1.32	.25		4.49	.03		.83	.36
.01		.25*	.01		.82*	.02		.23*
.02		.24*	.03		.35*	.02		.26*
	5.41	.02		.06	.80		3.11	.07
.004		.86*	.03		.25*	.01		.46
.02		.24*	.03		.35*	.02		.26*
	2.35	.12		.22	.63		1.40	.23
.01		.36*	.03		.26*	.02		.27*
.02		.24*	.03		.35*	.02		.26*
	.003	.95		.94	.33		.05	.82
.02		.15*	.02		.33*	.02		.17*
.02		.24*	.03		.35*	.02		.26*
	.01	.90		.80	.36		2.24	´.13
.02		.15*	.02		.32*	.01		.36*
			.03		.35*	.02		.26*
				.07	.78		.94	.33
			.03		.25	.02		.23*

201

TABLE 9.5: DESCRIPTION OF THE SUBJECTS: FAMIL

Variable	6 Mos. $\overline{M}$	%	σ	12 Mos. $\overline{M}$	%	σ
	(N=272)			(N=240)		
Sex (% M)		52			53	
Race (% W)		61			73	
SES	54.39		16.62	51.25		16.46
Birth Order	2.88		2.32	2.82		2.29
N Siblings						
Father Figure						
- Father						
- Father Figure						
- None						
Criterion (in.)	26.38		1.59	29.59		1.65

Variable	42 Mos. $\overline{M}$	%	σ	48 Mos. $\overline{M}$	%	σ
	(N=317)			(N=296)		
Sex (% M)		52			53	
Race (% W)		58			59	
SES	55.41		14.70	55.31		16.22
Birth Order	3.14		2.01	3.27		2.42
N Siblings	2.72		1.92	2.87		2.27
Father Figure						
- Father		73			76	
- Father Figure		7			11	
- None		20			13	
Dwelling Type						
- Trailer						
- Apartment						
- House						
STIM						
Criterion (in.)	39.00		1.76	40.58		1.81

SERIES AND HEIGHT FROM SIX TO SIXTY-SIX MONTHS

24 Mos.			30 Mos.			36 Mos.		
$\overline{M}$	%	σ	$\overline{M}$	%	σ	$\overline{M}$	%	σ
(N=308)			(N=91)			(N=308)		
	54			58			52	
	62			70			59	
54.08		16.38	53.87		16.55	55.09		16.47
2.90		2.32	2.83		2.21	3.22		2.46
						2.77		2.25
							76	
			↗				12	
							12	
33.56		2.56	35.84		1.81	37.83		1.97

54 Mos.			60 Mos.			66 Mos.		
$\overline{M}$	%	σ	$\overline{M}$	%	σ	$\overline{M}$	%	σ
(N=323)			(N=292)			(N=269)		
	51			53			52	
	59			62			60	
54.80		14.25	54.73		16.29	54.85		14.29
1.94		.97	3.22		2.39	3.09		1.92
2.80		1.94	2.76		2.25	2.67		1.83
	72			77			74	
	8			11			7	
	20			12			19	
	1							
	36			30			34	
	63			70			66	
32.47		6.15	33.20		5.54	32.54		6.02
41.98		1.95	43.39		2.12	44.47		2.13

TABLE 9.6

MULTIPLE LINEAR REGRESSION ANALYSIS OF FAMILY INFLUENCES ON HEIGHT

Variable	Models Compared	36 Mos. (N=308) R^2	F	p	42 Mos. (N=317) R^2	F	p	48 Mos. (N=296) R^2	F	p
Birth Order	Full Model 1	.01		.35*	.0003		.99*	.03		.01*
	Model 2	.01	.0002	1.00	.0003	.0002	.99	.01	6.86	.009
				.19*			.94*			.19*
N Siblings	Full Model 1	.01		.35*	.0003		.99*	.03		.01*
	Model 3	.01	.10	.74	.0003	.003	.95	.005	8.66	.003
				.20*			.95*			.46*
Father Figure	Full Model 1	.01		.35*	.0003		.99*	.03		.01*
	Model 4	.005	1.59	.20	.0008	.0003	.97	.03	.12	.72
				.43*			.98*			.006*

Variable	Models Compared	54 Mos. (N=323) R^2	F	p	60 Mos. (N=292) R^2	F	p	66 Mos. (N=269) R^2	F	p
Birth Order	Full Model 1	.01		.50*	.04		.02*	.02		.31*
	Model 2	.01	.86	.35	.03	3.22	.07	.01	1.12	.28
				.48*			.05*			.31*
N Siblings	Full Model 1	.01		.50*	.04		.02*	.02		.31*
	Model 3	.01	.35	.55	.02	5.35	.02	.01	2.09	.14
				.41*			.11*			.43*
Father Figure	Full Model 1	.01		.50*	.04		.02*	.02		.31*
	Model 4	.01	.005	.93	.04	.04	.83	.02	.12	.72
				.36*			.13*			.21*
Dwelling Type	Full Model 1	.01		.50*	.04		.02*	.02		.31*
	Model 5	.01	.66	.41	.03	4.01	.04	.02	.71	.39
				.45*			.07*			.81*
STIM	Full Model 1	.01		.50*	.04		.02*	.02		.31*
	Model 6	.008	1.61	.20	.04	.03	.85	.005	4.36	.03
				.60*			.01*			.26*

*Significance of the difference from zero.

TABLE 9.7

DESCRIPTION OF THE SUBJECTS: BIOLOGICAL SERIES AND WEIGHT FROM SIX TO SIXTY-SIX MONTHS

Variable	6 Mos. (N=668)			12 Mos. (N=555)			24 Mos. (N=687)			30 Mos. (N=184)			36 Mos. (N=359)		
	$\bar{M}$	%	σ	$\bar{M}$	%	σ	$\bar{M}$	%	σ	$\bar{M}$	%	σ	$\bar{M}$	%	σ
Sex (% M)		51			54			53			59			53	
Race (% W)		57			72			61			68			56	
SES	54.69		16.06	51.15		16.07	54.00		15.91	53.28		16.67	55.59		16.23
Birth Weight (lb.)	7.01		1.23	7.16		1.22	7.07		1.25	7.05		1.30	7.08		1.26
Bio Risk	.50		1.11	.52		1.14	.49		1.10	.60		1.17	.40		.92
Apgar	8.75		1.49	8.60		1.50	8.73		1.46	8.66		1.54	9.01		1.21
Weight (lb.)	16.83		2.38	22.27		2.73	27.79		3.55	29.20		3.26	31.77		4.20

Variable	42 Mos. (N=356)			48 Mos. (N=405)			54 Mos. (N=379)			60 Mos. (N=401)			66 Mos. (N=373)		
	$\bar{M}$	%	σ	$\bar{M}$	%	σ	$\bar{M}$	%	σ	$\bar{M}$	%	σ	$\bar{M}$	%	σ
Sex (% M)		52			52			51			53			52	
Race (% W)		58			53			61			54			62	
SES	55.27		14.77	56.40		16.25	54.18		14.77	56.21		16.20	54.19		14.62
Birth Weight (lb.)	6.95		1.27	7.10		1.24	6.92		1.31	7.09		1.24	6.94		1.26
Bio Risk	.60		1.25	.36		.88	.64		1.30	.35		.87	.61		1.23
Apgar	8.58		1.58	9.06		1.88	8.50		1.64	9.04		1.18	8.54		1.59
Weight (lb.)	33.37		4.39	35.91		4.41	38.30		5.29	41.55		5.79	43.26		6.68

TABLE 9.8: MULTIPLE LINEAR REGRESSION

Variable	Models Compared	6 Mos. (N=668) R^2	F	P	12 Mos. (N=555) R^2	F	P
Birth Weight	Full Model 1	.28	156.29	<.00001* <.00001	.16	37.06	<.00001* <.00001
	Model 2	.16		<.00001*	.07		<.00001*
Biological Risk	Full Model 1	.28	.03	<.00001* .85	.16	58.80	<.00001* <.00001
	Model 2	.28		<.00001*	.16		<.00001*
Apgar	Full Model 1	.28	.05	<.00001* .81	.16	.23	<.00001* .63
	Model 4	.28		<.00001*	.16		<.00001*
Sex (M)	Full Model 1	.28	52.24	<.00001* <.00001	.16	33.14	<.00001* <.00001
	Model 5	.22		<.00001*	.11		<.00001*

Variable	Models Compared	42 Mos. (N=356) R^2	F	P	48 Mos. (N=405) R^2	F	P
Birth Weight	Full Model 1	.11	28.86	.00001* <.00001*	.09	31.14	<.000001* <.000001*
	Model 2	.04		.0009*	.02		.01
Biological Risk	Full Model 1	.11		.00001* .003	.09	.10	.000001* .74
	Model 3	.09		.00001*	.09		.003*
Apgar	Full Model 1	.11	4.43	.00001* .03	.09	.77	.00001* .38
	Model 4	.10		.00001*	.09		.000001*
Sex (M)	Full Model 1	.11	10.83	.00001* .001	.09	2.42	.00001* .12
	Model 5	.09		.00001*	.09		.000001*

*Significance of the difference from zero.

influential, accounting for .04 of the variance ($F = 30.48$, $p <.00001$) as Table 9.8 shows, while sex explained about one-third ($F = 26.25$, $p <.00001$).

In the small 30-month group of 184 cases the R^2 was .04. None of the four Biological predictors gave a statistically significant account of variance. This model provided the least R^2 value of the 10 in the weight series.

ANALYSIS OF BIOLOGICAL INFLUENCES ON WEIGHT

24 Mos. (N=687)			30 Mos. (N=184)			36 Mos. (N=359)		
R^2	F	P	R^2	F	P	R^2	F	P
.09		<.00001*	.04		.05*	.08		.00001*
	30.48	<.00001		3.04	.08		20.79	.00001
.05		.00001*	.02		.20*	.02		.02*
.09		<.00001*	.04		.05*	.08		.00001*
	.23	.62		.002	.95		.04	.82
.09		<.00001*	.04		.18*	.08		.00001*
.09		<.00001*	.04		.05*	.08		.00002*
	1.65	.19		.60	.43		.59	.44
.08		<.00001*	.03		.07*	.07		.00002*
.09		<.00001*	.04		.05*	.08		.00002*
	26.25	<.00001		2.61	.10		4.30	.08
.06		<.00001*	.02		.42*	.06		.0008*

54 Mos. (N=379)			60 Mos. (N=401)			66 Mos. (N=373)		
R^2	F	P	R^2	F	P	R^2	F	P
.09		<.00001*	.06		.000001*	.06		.0001*
	33.95	<.00001		21.33	.00001		20.66	.00001
.01		.08*	.01		.05*	.01		.14*
.09		<.00001*	.06		.000001*	.06		.00001*
	8.87	.003		.01	.90		6.32	.01
.07		.00001*	.06		.00003*	.05		.001*
.09		<.00001*	.06		.000001*	.06		.0001*
	4.37	.03		1.70	.19		4.46	.03
.08		<.00001*	.06		.00001*	.05		.0001*
.09		<.00001*	.06		.000001*	.06		.00001*
	2.56	.11		.95	.33		1.84	.55
.09		<.00001*	.06		.00005*	.06		.0002*

At 3 years the 715 cases were almost equally divided between the birthday group at 36 months and the half-year group at 42 months. In the 36 month set, the previous trend to influence by birthweight and sex was maintained within a model that explains 8% of the variance. Weight at birth was still an influence 3 years later, accounting for three-quarters of the variance of the model ($F = 20.79$, $p < .00001$). Sex, still favoring greater weight in boys, explained 2 of the 8% of the variance in the regression model ($F = 4.30$, $p = .03$). In the 42 month data the R^2 was a little larger, $R^2 = .11$. Still the prime source of variance in the model birthweight explained two-thirds of the variance ($F = 28.86$, $p < .00001$). Sex, favoring boys, was the second influence ($F = 10.83$, $p = .001$). However, the other two variables in the predictor set were influential in this, the sixth of the weight analyses using Biological predictors. Biological risk explained 2 of the 11% of the variance ($F = 8.58$, $p = .003$), and Apgar scores also played a part. The direction of the Apgars' influence was positive, with higher scores associated with higher weights.

Just under 800 4-year-olds provided data ($N = 784$); one more instance of the size of data sets rising as well as falling in longitudinal study. Curiously, the significance of the Biological set of variables dropped to nothing with a model in which $R^2 = .09$. However, in the 54 month data set, in which the R^2 was an identical .09, three of the four variables were significant. Not surprisingly, birthweight was the prime influence, accounting for 8 of the 9% ($F = 39.95$, $p < .00001$), followed by biological risk ($F = 8.87$, $p = .003$). Apgars remained in third place, explaining one-ninth of the variance ($F = 4.37$, $p = .03$). For the first time there were no sex effects, and as we shall see, sex differences do not appear again.

The 5-year-olds were almost as numerous as the 4-year-olds. This data set was large ($N = 724$), and there were slightly more children in the birthday series. In a full regression model explaining 6% of the variance, 5% were attributable to birthweight ($F = 21.33$, $p = .00001$). None of the other three Biological predictors (including sex) were influential. At 66 months the R^2 was .06, as at 60 months. Birthweight remained the prime source of variance, accounting for 5 of the model's 6%. It was accompanied by biological risk ($F = 6.32$, $p = .01$), and at a lower level of probability by Apgar scores ($F = 4.86$, $p = .03$). As Apgars rose towards the theoretical normal of 10, so weights increased.

(B) SOCIAL SERIES

Race and perinatal social class are, it will be recalled, the Social series of predictors to age 3. At the first three criterion ages no differentials in weight were traceable to either race or sex. The regression models at these ages had R^2 values of .01, .006, and .006. In the small 30-month group of just under 200 cases ($N = 188$), racial differences emerged in a model that explained 2% of the variance ($F = 5.09$, $p = .02$). The β-weight for race was negative, indicating that higher weights at 30 months were observed in white children.

The 3 year data set from 500 children ($N = 505$) created identical R^2

values of .02 at 36 and at 42 months. None of the social predictors, including three parental traits added at this age, were significant.

At 4 years identical R^2 values of .03 were generated by the regression models in fair sized groups of children (Ns = 197 and 290). At 48 months none of the Social variables was an influence on weight. At 54 months there was a slight effect due to race. Heavier children were white rather than black.

The 5-year-olds provided an equally substantial data set (N = 484), with the addition of another variable of the educational level of the head of the household. Within the six-predictor model, none of the variables was an influence on weight among the 5-year-olds.

(C) FAMILY SERIES

The Family series of predictors to age 3 consists merely of birth order. Applied to weight at 6 months, this variable's R^2 was not statistically significant from zero (F = 2.52, p = .11) within a data set of almost 300 cases (N = 285). Using data from 250 children at 12 months, birth order remained irrelevant (R^2 = .0006, F = .15, p = .69). At 24 months birth order explained .01 of the weight variance, a statistically significant model (F = 4.84, p = .03). Higher weights were associated with lower birth order. At 30 months 92 cases provided data, and birth order explained 2% of the variance. This model was not statistically significant from zero (F = 1.58, p = .21).

At child age 3 years, the three-term predictor group in Table 9.12—birth order, number of siblings, and father figure—were applied to a data set from 600 youngsters (N = 619). The regression model at 36 months had an R^2 = .005 (p = .64), and at 42 months the model's R^2 = .01 (p = .22); both models were statistically insignificant from zero. None of the predictors was a significant source of variance in either the birthday or half-year analyses.

A slightly smaller number of 5-year-olds provided the data set in Table 9.12 (N = 580). None of the predictors accounted significantly for criterion variance (R^2 = .01) in the birthday group. Relatively modest accounts of variance arose in the half-year group at 54 months, however. In order of the magnitude of the effects, the variables of influence were STIM (F = 5.70, p = .02), father figure (F = 4.92, p = .03), and birth order (F = 4.62, p = .03). Influence was in the expected direction; that is, high criterion scores were associated with high STIM scores, presence of the biological father, and low rather than high birth order, as interpretations of β weights within the 6% of variance of the full model.

The 5-year data set of five predictors and weights came from a slightly

TABLE 9.9

DESCRIPTION OF THE SUBJECTS: SOCIAL SERIES AND WEIGHT FROM SIX TO SIXTY-SIX MONTHS

Variable	6 Mos.			12 Mos.			24 Mos.			30 Mos.			36 Mos.		
	$\bar{X}$	%	σ	$\bar{X}$	%	σ	$\bar{X}$	%	σ	$\bar{X}$	%	σ	$\bar{X}$	%	σ
		(N=690)			(N=574)			(N=709)			(N=188)			(N=193)	
Sex (% M)		51			53			54			59			52	
Race (% W)		57			72			61			68			93	
SES	54.73		15.96	51.27		15.98	54.07		15.82	53.55		16.60	47.74		15.14
Paternal Occup.													39.96		17.83
Maternal Work															
- Full-time														17	
- Part-time														11	
- Home														72	
Maternal Education															
- Elementary														5	
- Part H.S.														16	
- H.S.														48	
- Part College														22	
- College														9	
Weight (lb.)	16.83		2.39	22.25		2.75	27.79		3.58	29.15		3.26	31.48		3.52

Variable	42 Mos.			48 Mos.			54 Mos.			60 Mos.			66 Mos.		
	$\bar{M}$	%	σ	$\bar{M}$	%	σ	$\bar{M}$	%	σ	$\bar{M}$	%	σ	$\bar{M}$	%	σ
		(N=312)			(N=197)			(N=290)			(N=197)			(N=287)	
Sex (% M)		53			51			53			50			53	
Race (% W)		65			94			66			94			68	
SES	53.84		14.82	48.45		15.30	53.31		14.70	48.43		15.23	53.25		14.72
Paternal Occup.	46.00		18.50	40.39		17.87	45.36		18.44	40.53		17.92	45.10		18.38
Maternal Employm.															
- Full-time		25			17			24			17			24	
- Part-time		4			11			5			11			5	
- Home		71			72			71			72			71	
Maternal Education															
- Elementary		8			5			7			5			7	
- Part H.S.		24			16			24			16			23	
- H.S.		42			48			43			48			43	
- Part College		16			22			17			22			17	
- College		9			9			9			9			10	
Education H. of H.															
- To 9th grade														32	
- H.S.														33	
- Part College														14	
- College														21	
Weight (lb.)	33.41		4.45	35.55		3.95	38.24		5.46	41.37		5.34	43.32		7.31

Variable	Models Compared	6 Mos. (N=690)			12 Mos. (N=574)		
		R^2	F	P	R^2	F	P
SES	Full Model 1	.01		.006*	.006		.14*
			2.48	.11		2.40	.12
	Model 2	.01		.006*	.002		.22*
Race (B)	Full Model 1	.01		.006*	.006		.14*
			1.32	.25		.07	.78
	Model 3	.01		.003	.006		.05*
Paternal Occup.	Full Model 1						
	Model 4						
Maternal Employm.	Full Model 1						
	Model 5						
Maternal Educ.	Full Model 1						
	Model 6						

Variable	Models Compared	42 Mos. (N=312)			48 Mos. (N=197)		
		R^2	F	P	R^2	F	P
SES	Full Model 1	.02		.19*	.03		.30*
			.31	.57		.19	.65
	Model 2	.02		.13*	.03		.21*
Race (B)	Full Model 1	.02		.19*	.03		.30*
			3.43	.06		.00	1.00
	Model 3	.01		.41*	.03		.19*
Paternal Occup.	Full Model 1	.02		.19*	.03		.30*
			.53	.46		.03	.85
	Model 4	.02		.14*	.03		.20*
Maternal Employm.	Full Model 1	.02		.19*	.03		.30*
			.04	.82		3.35	.06
	Model 5	.02		.11*	.01		.62*
Maternal Educ.	Full Model 1	.02		.19*	.03		.30*
			.14	.70		1.77	.18
	Model 6	.02		.12*	.02		.37*
Head of Househ. Education	Full Model 1						
	Model 7						

*Significance of the difference from zero.

24 Mos. (N=709)			30 Mos. (N=188)			36 Mos. (N=193)		
R^2	F	P	R^2	F	P	R^2	F	P
.006		.10*	.02		.07*	.02		.49*
	.002	.96		.84	.35		.41	.51
.006		.03*	.02		.03*	.04		.40*
.006		.10*	.02		.07*	.02		.49*
	3.08	.07		5.09	.02		.23	.63
.002		.23*	.001		.59*	.02		.38*
						.02		.49*
							1.50	.22
						.01		.57*
						.02		.49*
							2.66	.10
						.009		.78*
						.02		.49*
							.33	.56
						.02		.39

54 Mos. (N=290)			60 Mos. (N=197)			66 Mos. (N=287)		
R^2	F	P	R^2	F	P	R^2	F	P
.03		.08*	.02		.71*	.02		.54*
	1.72	.16		.00	1.00		.40	.49
.02		.09*	.02		.58*	.01		.47*
.03		.08*	.02		.71*	.02		.54*
	4.00	.04		1.33	.24		3.00	.08
.02		.21*	.01		.79*	.006		.85*
.03		.08*	.02		.71*	.02		.54*
	1.33	.24		1.14	.28		.35	.55
.02		.07*	.01		.76*	.01		.46*
.03		.08*	.02		.71*	.02		.54*
	.36	.54		1.47	.22		.25	.61
.03		.05*	.01		.81*	.01		.45*
.03		.08*	.02		.71*	.02		.54*
	.09	.75		.12	.72		.20	.60
.03		.04*	.01		.60*	.01		.44*
			.02		.71*	.02		.54*
				.31	.57		1.77	.16
			.02		.60*	.01		.70*

TABLE 9.11

DESCRIPTION OF THE SUBJECTS: FAMILY SERIES AND WEIGHT FROM SIX TO SIXTY-SIX MONTHS

Variable	6 Mos. (N=285)			12 Mos. (N=250)			24 Mos. (N=307)			30 Mos. (N=92)			36 Mos. (N=302)		
	$\bar{M}$	%	σ	$\bar{M}$	%	σ	$\bar{M}$	%	σ	$\bar{M}$	%	σ	$\bar{M}$	%	σ
Sex (% M)		53			53			54			57			52	
Race (% W)		61			72			62			70			59	
SES	54.32		16.72	51.33		16.59	54.20		16.31	54.05		16.55	54.78		16.52
Birth Order	2.86		2.30	2.90		2.32	2.91		2.32	2.81		2.20	3.22		2.39
N Siblings													2.77		2.75
Father Figure															
- *Father*														75	
- *F. Figure*														12	
- *None*														13	
Weight (lb.)	16.92		2.37	22.26		2.68	28.02		3.62	29.49		3.38	31.54		3.83

	42 Mos. (N=317)			48 Mos. (N=300)			54 Mos. (N=280)			60 Mos. (N=291)			66 Mos. (N=269)		
	$\overline{M}$	%	σ	$\overline{M}$	%	σ	$\overline{M}$	%	σ	$\overline{M}$	%	σ	$\overline{M}$	%	σ
Sex (% M)		52			52			51			52			52	
Race (% W)		58			60			58			62			60	
SES	55.38		14.67	55.05		16.39	55.28		14.33	54.84		16.21	54.85		14.29
Birth Order	3.15		2.01	3.26		2.41	3.12		1.96	3.23		2.39	3.09		1.92
N Siblings	2.72		1.92	2.80		2.26	2.70		1.86	2.76		2.25	2.67		1.83
Father Figure															
- *Father*					76			73			77			74	
- *F. Figure*					11			7			11			7	
- *None*					13			20			12			19	
STIM							32.25		6.23	33.19		5.55	32.54		6.02
Dwelling															
- *House*								65						66	
- *Apartment*								35						34	
- *Trailer*															
Weight (lb.)	33.21		4.28	35.67		4.27	37.91		5.26	41.49		5.73	42.84		6.92

TABLE 9.12   MULTIPLE LINEAR REGRESSION ANALYSIS OF FAMILY INFLUENCES ON WEIGHT

Variable	Models Compared	36 Mos. (N=302)			42 Mos. (N=317)			48 Mos. (N=300)		
		R^2	F	P	R^2	F	P	R^2	F	P
Birth Order	Full Model 1	.005		.64*	.01		.22*	.01		.25*
	Model 2	.004	.19	.65	.008	1.71	.19	.01	.41	.52
				.47*			.25*			.15
N Siblings	Full Model 1	.005		.64*	.01		.22*	.01		.25*
	Model 3	.004	.37	.54	.006	2.33	.12	.009	1.23	.26
				.52			.35*			.24*
F. Figure	Full Model 1	.005		.64*	.01		.22*	.01		.25*
	Model 4	.003	.005	.41	.005	2.83	.01	.01	.006	.93
				.60*			.45*			.12*

Variable	Models Compared	54 Mos. (N=280)			60 Mos. (N=291)			66 Mos. (N=269)		
		R^2	F	P	R^2	F	P	R^2	F	P
Birth Order	Full Model 1	.06		.001*	.02		.23*	.03		.16*
	Model 2	.05	4.62	.03	.02	1.98	.15	.03	.16	.68
				.005*			.30*			.10*
N. Siblings	Full Model 1	.06		.001*	.02		.23*	.03		.16*
	Model 3	.05	3.31	.06	.01	2.93	.08	.03	.007	.93
				.003*			.42*			.09*
F. Figure	Full Model 1	.06		.001*	.02		.23*	.03		.16*
	Model 4	.05	4.92	.03	.02	.56	.45	.03	.74	.38
				.006*			.18*			.13*
Dwelling Type	Full Model 1	.06		.001*	.02		.23*	.03		.16*
	Model 5	.04	1.33	.24	.02	1.61	.20	.02	1.99	.15
				.009*			.26*			.21*
STIM	Full Model 1	.06		.001*	.02		.23*	.03		.16*
	Model 6	.06	5.70	.02	.02	.98	.32	.02	3.58	.06
				.001*			.21*			.37*

*Significance of the difference from zero.

smaller group of children ($N = 560$). At neither 60 nor 66 months did the five predictor variables account for a statistically significant portion of the variance.

Discussion

This investigation stresses the value of multiple regression analysis as a way to explicate relationships between predictors and criteria. Of special interest is the fact that regression analysis draws attention to the proportion of variance explained by a predictor set. In behavioral–developmental inquiries, as Cohen (1977) has pointed out, the connection between a criterion and its putative influences is necessarily less than what we would like, and less than is regularly encountered in the physical sciences. Given modest expectations for relations between variables, it is important to see how much explanation is justified by the magnitude of the regression effects. The proportion of criterion variance assigned to a predictor set is R^2, and in Table 9.13 we see the R^2 values of three models for height and weight at 10 ages from 6 to 66 months after birth.

HEIGHT

The range of R^2 values in Table 9.13 for height is from virtually zero to .16, with a mean $R^2 = .06$. Most powerful, in the sense of the proportion of variance accounted for, is the Biological model in which R^2 values range from .02 to .16, around a mean of .06. Less powerful, but with a comparable range are the Social models of height, ranging from .01 to .11, around a mean $R^2 = .04$. In the case of the third, Family model of height, the range is much narrower, ranging from a virtual zero (.001) to .04 at best, with a mean $R^2 = .01$. From these values we see that the range among the three values is wide, in the relative sense, with the best model half again as powerful as the next and six times more powerful than the least useful. Examined across the developmental span of 6–66 months, no real trend to more effective prediction is evident for any of the three regression models. The mean R^2 for all models, that is, the row means, tend to be higher at 6, 12, and 24 months, but the range is narrow. In general we may say that predictor variables in three arrays, or models, do not tell us very much about variations in height measured at 10 ages in the preschool years.

HYPOTHESES

Earlier in the chapter we hypothesized that the influence of the three predictor sets would be in order: first, Biological data; second, Social; and, finally, Family data. Recalling the R^2 values of the preceding section and keeping Table 9.13 in mind, we examine the hypothetical order of influence.

TABLE 9.13

R^2 VALUES OF HEIGHT AND WEIGHT ANALYSES

Biological Model	Social Model	Family Model	Criteria	Mean R^2
.16	.01	.01	6 M. Height	.06
.12	.01	.01	12 M. Height	.05
.04	.11	.01	24 M. Height	.05
.02	.08	.001	30 M. Height	.03
.06	.01	.01	36 M. Height	.03
.06	.02	.003	42 M. Height	.03
.04	.04	.03	48 M. Height	.04
.06	.02	.01	54 M. Height	.03
.03	.03	.04	60 M. Height	.03
.05	.02	.02	66 M. Height	.03
Mean .06	.04	.01		.04
.28	.01	.008	6 M. Weight	.10
.16	.006	.0006	12 M. Weight	.05
.09	.006	.01	24 M. Weight	.03
.04	.02	.02	30 M. Weight	.02
.08	.02	.005	36 M. Weight	.03
.11	.02	.01	42 M. Weight	.05
.09	.03	.01	48 M. Weight	.04
.09	.03	.06	54 M. Weight	.06
.06	.02	.02	60 M. Weight	.03
.06	.02	.03	66 M. Weight	.04
Mean .11	.02	.02		.05

For the developmental span of interest the mean R^2 of the Biological model is clearly the highest, and on that basis we confirm the hypothesis.

There are only two ages, 12 and 24 months, at which the Social model is more influential, and only one at which the Family model is more influential. In the case of the second degree of influence for the Social model, the hypothesized order is upheld. At ages 24–30 months the Social model of SES and race was most powerful, comparatively speaking. The Family model, as hypothesized, was least powerful. Of the 10 R^2 values, 5 are .01; only one reaches .04, which is the mean of the Social model, and which is exceeded by 6 of the Biological R^2 values. For height our hypothesized order of relative influence is completely supported. However, the degree of influence is within models which generally leave 95% of the variance unexplained.

DISCRETE INFLUENCES

At a more analytic level we turn now to consideration of the 19 predictor variables and call attention to Table 9.14. It is clear that one developmental variable, weight at birth, influences height at all ages from 6 to 66 months. At only one age, 30 months, is it not the prime source of variance, but no other variable is at that age. While we can discern a secondary influence in the sex of the child—boys being heavier—it exists only to age 42 months, and there are no statistically significant sex differences after that. The remaining two potential influences of biological risk and Apgar are quite unpatterned in their scarcely observed influence.

Within the Social model racial differences in height are almost equally discernable, with greater heights in white boys and girls. Of the remaining four variables of this model, the three of maternal employment, maternal education, and the education of the head of the household, simply do not appear in regression analysis as influences. Maternal employment plays a secondary role at age 4 years.

Within the Family set of predictors no influences on height are apparent until age $4\frac{1}{2}$ years. The first six ages of the children are quite untouched by the predictor birth order, for example. At ages 4 and 5 there is some support for associating height with the number of boys and girls in the family, tallness being more likely when the sibship is small. Birth order plays a subsidiary role in the data set, followed by a minor effect due to dwelling in a house rather than an apartment. Once more we see that STIM scores are positively associated with the criterion.

Generalizing on the matter of discrete influences in height (see Table 9.15) among the 19 predictor variables, and acknowledging the several child ages at which variables were available and the size of the R^2 values, we see that a few variables stand out. In the positive sense we surmise that being a

TABLE 9.14

PREDICTORS IN ORDER OF STATISTICAL CONTRIBUTION

IN MULTIPLE REGRESSION ANALYSES TO R^2 OF FULL MODELS - *HEIGHT*

	BIOLOGICAL MODEL						SOCIAL MODEL	
	Weight	Biological Risk	Apgar	Sex	SES	Race	Pop's Occup.	Mom's Employ.
CRITERION								
	Birth	*Birth*	*Birth*	*Birth*	*Birth*	*Birth*	*Three*	*Three*
6 M. Height	1			2		1		
12 M.Height	1			2		1		
24 M. Height	1		2			1		
30 M. Height					1			
36 M. Height	1			2				
42 M. Height	1			2	2	1		
48 M. Height	1					1		2
54 M. Height	1	2						
60 M. Height	1					1		
66 M. Height	1	2						

white male of good birthweight in a small family is probably the best way to be tall, comparatively speaking. In the negative, we report that some variables in all three predictor domains have little to offer in the search for why some children are tall and others short. Inspection of Table 9.14 shows that Apgar scores, biological risk, parental traits, and birth order affect height very little; this is, in selected instances, confirmation by multivariate means of a relationship not hard to frame. Yet, would one be unreasonable to discount SES effects on height, or expect consistent sex differences? Such influences do not occur. While recalling the earlier reference to the secular trend in height still observed in boys and girls in Holland, we speculate that Old Man River's Children are above minimal nutrition levels, and that both

			FAMILY MODEL				
Mom's Educat.	Head of Household Education	Birth Order	N Siblings	Father Figure	Dwelling Type	STIM
Five	*Five*	*Birth*	*3 Years*	*3 Years*	*5 Years*	*5 Years*

		2	1			
			1		2	
						1

sexes consequently grow well. In this regard the data confirm Lindgren's (1976) report from a Swedish population, a condition in which society's state in relation to height is referred to by Tanner (1978) as "classlessness of society." However, we do not discount the racial difference; its source may yet be found in the gene pool, and we recall our brief review of research on development in children in Chapter 4. However, our fundamental generalization springs from the regression data themselves. The error or unassigned variance in the dozens of regression models we have reported is staggering, despite use of 19 predictor variables in three domains. Our speculations, although based on empirical data, are advanced modestly on the topic of variations in height in the preschool years.

TABLE 9.15

PREDICTORS IN ORDER OF STATISTICAL CONTRIBUTION

IN MULTIPLE REGRSSION ANALYSES TO R^2 OF FULL MODELS - *WEIGHT*

| CRITERION | BIOLOGICAL MODEL | | | | | | SOCIAL MODEL | |
| | Weight | Biological Risk | Apgar | Sex (M) | SES | Race | Pop's Occup. | Mom's Employ. |
	Birth	*Birth*	*Birth*	*Birth*	*Birth*	*Birth*	*Three*	*Three*
6 M. Weight	1			2				
12 M. Weight	1			2				
24 M. Weight	1			2				
30 M. Weight						1		
36 M. Weight	1			2				
42 M. Weight	1	3	4	2				
48 M. Weight								
54 M. Weight	1	3	2			1		
60 M. Weight	1							
66 M. Weight	1	2	3					

WEIGHT

In general, the robustness of the regression models of weight, that is, the proportion of criterion variance accounted for, is similar to that for height, and slightly higher at $R^2 = .05$ by 1%. The overall range of robustness is from $R^2 = .0006$ to .28. The most predictive model is the set of Biological predictors in which R^2 values range from .04 to .28, with a mean (as Table 9.14 shows) of .11, highest of the six values in the table. When we move to the second, Social, model of weight, the R^2 values drop steeply, ranging merely from a microscopic .006 to .03, and averaging .02. From

Mom's Educat.	Head of Household Education	Birth Order	N Siblings	FAMILY MODEL Father Figure	Dwelling Type	STIM
Three	Five	Birth	Three	Three	Five	Five

		1				
		3		2		1

child ages 30–60 months, the Social R^2 values are all either .02 or .03. In the case of the Family models of weight, the proportions of variance go no higher than .06 and average .02. Comparatively speaking the Social and Family models are equally weak, and well behind the Biological predictor series in analysis of the criterion variance in height. These two models are also similar in the tendency for R^2 values to rise from near-meaningless .006s to .03s. In contrast, the Biological model's effectiveness is evident in statistical significance from zero at all 10 ages and at a high statistical level. Across the developmental span, the minimum Biological R^2 is equalled by only 1 of the 20 Social and Family R^2 values for weight. We conclude that the Biological model tells us a good deal about variation in weight from 6 to 66 months, and that the other two models of Social and Family data tell us very little.

HYPOTHESES

Initially, we asserted comparative degrees of influence for the three models in the order, Biological, Social, and Family data. Inspection of the data in Table 9.15 shows that indeed the Biological data set is most influential overall; this support for the hypothesized influence is evident both by mean R^2 and by R^2 values at all 10 child ages. Unlike height, where the three regression models for certain ages such as 48 months seem comparable, there are no such instances in the case of weight. In the matter of the second hypothesis of influence, from the Social data it is upheld, but not in a too enlightening way. That is, the mean R^2 value of .02 is well below that of the Biological predictor set, but it is matched by the R^2 value of the Family set; this equality is expressed both by grand mean for the columns in Table 9.13, and also for the means Child age $\times$ Child age. Equally, we can support the hypotheses of tertiary influence by the Family data. The phenomenal $R^2 = .0006$ at age 1 year shows how unrelated predictors and criteria can be (recalling that birth order is the sole predictor).

DISCRETE INFLUENCES

The role of the 19 variables within the three predictor sets can be approached by disposing of predictors quite unrelated at any age to children's weights. Within the Social model it is evident that parental traits are not relevant, nor is perinatal SES level. Within the Family predictors the number of siblings is equally irrelevant. There are several variables which curiously achieved statistical significance at 54 months. In Table 9.15 we see that biological risk at birth, Apgars, race and birth order, father figure and STIM were relevant, with occasional duplications of significance for biological risk, Apgar, and birth order at earlier ages. The variables of interest are clearly weight at birth, sex, and race, based on ordinal degree of influence and frequency.

In the case of weight at birth it is apparent that optimal birthweight has implications for good weight across the preschool years. It is also apparent that boys are heavier than girls, although that effect is absent beginning at age 4. At a far lesser degree of frequency, but primarily when observed at 30–54 months, heavier weights are identified in white children. No such influence is apparent at other ages. We caution that there were less than 200 children in the 30-month study group.

Sketching the meaning of the analysis, we start by observing that the only variable among the 19 with a clear influence on weight at 10 years is weight at birth. Beyond that, and at a lesser degree of influence, is sex favoring boys for the first 3 years of life. Beyond that age sex differences are not apparent. Slight, inconsistent, racial differences occur in a fragmentary way. In some respects the nonsignificant variables tell more about influences on weight. For 18 of the analyses of weight no variable, within its relevant predictor set, was significant, and this applies especially to the nonbiological variables. The meaning is clearly that most of the predictor variables have little to do with weight.

HEIGHT AND WEIGHT

This chapter deals with physical development, therefore it is appropriate to try to synthesize some comments from the two physical measures. At the most particular level we conclude that weight at birth is the most important variable in our search for influences on physical attainment. In 18 of 20 age-criterion analyses, it is the prime source of variance; in one of the other two instances no variable was influential. After birthweight the race of the child, favoring greater development in white children, is the next influence, followed by sex differences, favoring boys.

However, we feel that the more provocative findings are in the nonsignificant results. That is, it seemed not unreasonable to hypothesize a degree of influence for nonbiological variables which are commonly held to influence growth. No such influence was found, for example, in SES level. This means that knowing the SES level that is basic to subsequent influence does not improve our explanation for growth at 10 ages in two dimensions, height and weight. As interpretation we conclude that socioeconomic status no longer distinguishes the haves from the have-nots in the matter of basic physical growth. There are differences between children, but those differences are not traceable to the circumstances of life. That is, we no longer have the case in which some children fall below a minimum social level with the consequence that their somatic growth is stunted. In this regard we feel a finding of great importance as an index of social welfare has been observed. It does not mean that every child is without nutritional hazard, but it does mean Old Man River's Children as a group are indistinguishable in height and weight from each other by social class level.

When placed in historical perspective this state of affairs is quite striking; for purposes of comparison we draw on data from 1878 reported to Galton's Committee of the British Association in 1883. Data gathered by a Mr. Roberts on prepubertal children revealed that "a difference of five inches exists between the average statures of the best and the worst nurtured classes of children of corresponding ages ... [Galton, 1884, p. 281]." Our data are reported 100 years later and give testimony to the generally satisfactory state of child health today.

However, we identify a minor but evident racial difference favoring greater height and weight in white children as opposed to black. In noting this we recall that there is a difference in SES level for whites and blacks, with blacks less likely to have higher socioeconomic status. However, a brief return to Figure 3.1 shows that there are black boys and girls at SES levels from high to low, although there are proportionately more with high McGuire and White (*low*) status scores. We cannot simply equate black as meaning lower socioeconomic status and thereby a better social marker than SES scores. It is necessary to recall that race, although used here as an ethnic variable, is not insensitive to constitutional considerations. Differences in body morphology due to genetic differences cannot be ruled out as an explanation of height and weight differences. In asserting this we recall that the differences due to race are less frequent, and less powerful, than the differences due to birthweight, regardless of sex.

It is apparent that physical growth is a far less determinate matter than one might suspect, even given a matrix of predictor variables within which to examine the matter. Were it determinate, more of our full regression models would have been statistically significant, and at a higher level. We place a benign interpretation on the relative nonassociation of some models' nonbiological predictors. It may be that we have reached a state of society in which differences in physical attainment, as never before, stem less from arbitrary social circumstances than from morphogenic elements in the backgrounds of children.

Discussion

10

Regression Models and Variance

We being discussion by presenting a summary of what we have reported so far. In a context of prospective longitudinal study, we have reported multiple regression analyses of development in a cohort of newborns. Using four predictive aggregates, two of which expand through the developmental span from birth to age $5\frac{1}{2}$ years, we have analyzed measures of development in six domains. The last of them, physical attainment, consisted of height—*stature*—and weight at 10 ages. The briefest criterion domains consisted of three measures at several ages. Data have been presented by reporting in the preceding six chapters each of the four predictor series by age of criterion measures. That is, some predictor sets grew longer as the children grew older. In that organization, chapter by chapter, we saw the influence of the four predictor groups, Biological, Social, Family, and Maternal, within regression analyses that progressively incorporated more predictive data, and saw criterion measures also evolve.

In discussion we alter the time frame in order to sift the comparative influences at given child ages, and refer the reader back to Tables 3.6 and 3.7 (see page 37 and 40) in order to recall which variables were contemporary at any given age. Before that major aspect of discussion begins, however, it is useful to get an overall picture of what the analysis has to show

Table 10.1

MEAN R^2 VALUES OF FOUR PREDICTOR MODELS IN SIX DOMAINS

Biological Model	Social Model	Family Model	Maternal Model	(Speculative Sum)	Criterion Domains	Criterion Mean R^2
.05	.15	.10	.25	(.55)	Motor	.14
.05	.17	.14	.13	(.50)	Intellectual	.12
.07	.21	.14	.20	(.62)	Linguistic	.16
.01	.09	.03	.17	(.30)	Somatic	.08
.04	.12	.07	.11	(.34)	Social	.08
.07	.05	.03		(.15)	Physical - Height	.05
.09	.11	.03		(.23)	- Weight	.07
.05	.14	.07	.17			

about the value of the regression models' accounts of criterion variance at the generalized level of the domains. In Table 10.1 we report the R^2 values generated by the four predictor models against the criterion sets. It can be seen that the highest account of criterion variance from the measures of child development comes from the Social model, which has the highest mean R^2, and that for the linguistic measures between child ages 24–66 months. On the other hand, the most powerful model consistently is the Maternal model, applied to all but the physical criteria. Viewed in another way, the data summarized in Table 10.1 tells us that the criteria varied in predictability from $R^2 = .01$ to .18. Height was the least predictable criterion, and language the most analyzable, when all four predictor series are combined.

In this regard conservatism prevails; we generalize by saying that even multivariate analyses using comparatively long predictor sets leave much variance unassigned. One respectable strategy to obtain a better fit for the data would have been to square criterion values and so make data more predictable. We chose to keep the criterion in their regular form recalling that regression models have more value than is at first apparent. Cohen (1977) has demonstrated that R^2 values conventionally deemed small, actually more *powerful* than they seem. That is, the potential for avoiding a Type I error, in view of a given value for R^2, is actually considerably larger than it might appear at first glance, due to the presence of several independent or predictor variables. As a consequence, we generalize that the R^2 values in Table 10.1 are useable, and provide a basis for looking within the total data set in an analytic and comparative fashion.

On that premise we turn to an examination of the regression data within the developmental skein that builds predictor and criterion measures. In particular, we examine the array of R^2 values when set out primarily across the child ages used for testing, and secondarily by criterion domain. In Table 10.2 we see the means of R^2 values for any number of analyses at a particular age. In most cases this is simply one test at any age in a domain; there are exceptions, such as the use of three Intellectual criteria at 24 months, summated as PAR *Intellectual* score. A second critical observation is that criteria are diverse, and amalgamating R^2 values into arithmetic means is intended as a superordinate, expository device. However, in Table

Table 10.2

MEAN R^2 BY CHILD AGE FOR ALL CRITERIA

Child Age	Criterion Domains							All Domains
	Motor	Intellectual	Linguistic	Somatic	Social	Height	Weight	
6 Mos.			.03			.06	.09	.06
12 Mos.						.05	.06	.05
24 Mos.		.05	.02		.03	.06	.03	.06
30 Mos.			.19			.05	.05	.10
36 Mos.	.09	.19	.20	.14		.03	.06	.11
42 Mos.	.10	.21	.13	.03		.04	.05	.08
48 Mos.	.18	.25	.21		.13	.05	.05	.12
54 Mos.	.18	.15	.19		.13	.03	.06	.12
60 Mos.		.17	.28			.08	.06	.15
66 Mos.		.13	.20			.05	.03.	.10

10.2 we see that 45 domain R^2 values are set forth. Interestingly, they show some consistency at any given age, excepting the physical R^2s. This is especially the case as the age of the cohort increases, and particularly from 48 months on. With equal consistency the R^2 values are low from 6–24 months. At age 3 there is a good deal of variability, with highest values being six times the lowest, at least. The mean R^2 values for domains by child age, as given in the last column of Table 10.2, show an observable trend to rise from the first to the sixth year of life. The last five mean R^2s for all domains in the last column average .10, which is double the average value of the first five values, .05. The grand mean R^2 by child age and criterion domains is .07. Interestingly, the column means for domains arrange themselves as .10, .11, and .02 and as .03, .04, and .05 around the grand mean, which is also the median value.

From the point of view of coherent, theoretical views of influences on early child development, this is welcome news. Yet, even so, we are led to observe that an empirical examination of influences on children shows how much is yet to be learned about the vectors that sway the course of early development. Even multivariate analysis leads to modest speculation. While influences may be fairly supportable, in the sense of Cohen's reasoning of *power* in research, the amount of unassigned variance is considerable in all domains of development. It means that criterion test scores cannot be assigned unreservedly to the predictors employed. This is not surprising when the earliest ages are considered, because the predictor sets are brief. Even the Biological predictor set of four perinatal traits, however, leaves a large proportion of test variance unassigned. When the predictor sets are longest, and the R^2 values the highest, the proportion of unassigned variance is substantial. However, the enterprise of research does not employ a theory of truth in which findings correspond isomorphically to the way things *really are*, once we pierce the veil of nature. Rather, the enterprise attempts to exceed a knowledge state of zero information at some empirically generated degree of probability. It is clear that even multivariate analyses leave much to be desired; those reported in this investigation so far tend to exceed chance as a level of probability, while falling substantially below a metaphysically desirable level (e.g., $R^2 = .99$).

Stages of Development

The data-reporting Chapters 4 to 9 presented information in the sequence of development, that is, as the children grew older. Our object in this section is to discuss these findings with a view to defining comparative influences at 10 ages, across six domains. By way of introduction, recall that not every criterion domain was examined at every age due to the obvious problem of taking data from small children and in their homes. Domains studied and reported express the writer's priorities among domains of attainment. Reference to specific variables in this section is drawn from the matrix of variables listed in Table 3.6 and presented in detail in Chapters 4 to 9.

We preface this consideration of growth by describing the status at birth of the cohort from which the subgroups to be discussed were derived. At birth the mean weight of 1000 babies was 6.96 lb ($\sigma = 1.31$), and their mean length was 19.60 in. ($\sigma = 1.41$ in.).[1] The mean Apgar rating was 8.79 ($\sigma = 1.48$). The sexes were evenly divided, and 53% of the babies were white. The average mother was 25 years old ($\sigma = 6.75$), and 85% of the mothers were married.

AGE 6 MONTHS

By this time the average baby had gained 10 lb and was nearly 8 in. longer at 16.38 lb and 26.38 in. The child was taking an interest in the surroundings, anticipated being picked up, and knew how to attract mother's attention. In the matter of influences on physical growth clear importance can be attached to being male and to weight at birth. The importance of this index of development at the end of gestation is clear from a body of research by Wiener (1965), Drillien (1970), and Neligan, Neligan, Kolvin, Scott, and Garside (1976).

In the case of aspects of development recorded by the Ad Hoc Development Scale perinatal social class is an important influence as is the degree of liberalism in mothers' child rearing values. We find that higher levels of attainment in 6-month-old babies are reported by mothers of less priviledged social background who also tend to be authoritarian in outlook, these two variables being highly correlated ($p < .0001$).

[1]Correlation of growth in height and weight from 6 to 66 months has been as follows:

Age of child	r	df	p
6 Mos.	.55	1/658	<.0001
12 Mos.	.43	1/552	<.0001
24 Mos.	.24	1/709	<.0001
30 Mos.	.53	1/186	<.0001
36 Mos.	.54	1/365	<.0001
42 Mos.	.67	1/372	<.0001
48 Mos.	.63	1/411	<.0001
54 Mos.	.71	1/397	<.0001
60 Mos.	.63	1/412	<.0001
66 Mos.	.64	1/390	<.0001

AGE 1 YEAR

On the first birthday the infants weighed 22.25 lb ($\sigma = 2.75$) and were 29.65 in. in length ($\sigma = 1.64$). Initial weight at birth 12 months before seems identifiable as an influence on height, as is the sex difference favoring greater length in boys. White children tend to be taller by the end of the first year. Weight is affected by both birthweight and sex, but not by race.

AGE 2 YEARS

On the second birthday the average toddler weighed 27.79 lb ($\sigma = 3.58$) and stood 33.63 in. high ($\sigma = 2.49$). The sole identifiable influence on weight was original weight at birth. In the case of height, perinatal socioeconomic level is perhaps the greatest influence, together with birthweight, being white, and being male. Our data shed some light on mothers' reports of social development. Boys are ahead of girls in assuming responsibility, and higher social scores are more likely in children living in more favored circumstances. Influences on language development are apparent: girls have higher scores than boys, and low degrees of biological and social risk; and being early in birth order is associated with high rather than low language attainment. Curiously, mothers of children with low Apgar scores at birth report higher scores. Since this persists throughout the language domain it merits further consideration. One idea which may be entertained is Zuk's (1959) concept of autistic distortion, as he termed it; a process by which parents' perceptions of nonphysical problems, for example, delayed development, compensate for low attainments.

AGE 3 YEARS

At age 3 children are about 4 in. taller than on the previous birthday, averaging 31.77 lb ($\sigma = 4.20$) and 37.56 in. ($\sigma = 1.92$). Weight and height continues to be influenced by birthweight, and to a lesser degree by sex. At this age our picture of child development and related influences broadens due, obviously, to the greater responsiveness of the children to standardized procedures. In the matter of motor development at age 3, birthweight is a minor influence, while SES level and the extent to which mothers work outside the home are consistently major influences within the Family. Presence of the real father appears to be an influence, as does the degree of maternal authoritarianism. With the exception of birthweight, it is evident that the other significant influences express social forces. The intellectual attainment of 3-year-olds is influenced by Apgar scores, but in a fashion we have found perplexing. Biological risk and birthweight are slightly influential. Both of these elements are far less important than SES level, mother's years of schooling, and father's presence. Finally, we note the influence of maternal liberalism in children's ideology as a positive influence on mental growth. In language, a cognitive area continuous with what we have called intellect, perinatal Apgar scores are influential, but less so than SES level, presence of the father, and a liberal attitude on the part of the mother, and that she be married. In somatic growth at age 3 we detect, curiously, no biological influence from our data, but note a selective but powerful SES effect. Minor influences due to the presence of the father, and mothers being married, and liberal, are also present.

AGE 4 YEARS

At 4 the typical child is 39 in. tall ($\sigma = 1.74$ in.) and weighs 32 lb ($\sigma = 4.20$ lb), and weight at birth and sex, are influences to a lesser extent. Birth order, favoring an early arrival, is an identifiable but not a large influence. Influences on fine motor-perceptual skill are birthweight and SES as substantial influences, and Apgar scores to a lesser degree. Family environment (STIM) and mothers' values are important, while family characteristics play a lesser role. Influencing intellectual attainment at a consistent level is birthweight, with lesser influence due to biological risk, Apgars, and last of all, sex. We have noted earlier the ambiguous role of sex differences in item selection for standardized tests. Among social factors consistent influence comes, at age 4, from SES, race, and maternal level of education. Within the range of family variables the effect of class and home culture is substantial and consistent, as is maternal child rearing orientation. In the related language area at this age, there are minor but perceptible influences from perinatal biological status. Maternal employment outside the home and education, plus race, are lesser influences, while the influence of the father's presence is substantial and consistent. A minor but consistent influence is the number of brothers and sisters, and the influence of maternal values tends to be consistent and evident.

AGE 5 YEARS

At age 5 children then start their sixth year at 33 lb ($\sigma = 4.39$ lb) and 39 in. ($\sigma = 1.74$ in.), and end it at 46 lb ($\sigma = 7.17$ lb) and 46 in. ($\sigma = 1.89$ in.). At age 5 years major correlates other than home environment and birthweight are not evident in our data. Vocabulary, an index of mental maturity, is slightly influenced by perinatal status; social factors, especially the home situation (STIM), is a powerful influence. Other social influences appear, but they are less powerful—maternal work and education, age, and child rearing orientation.

In offering this descriptive summary we wish to present the results of our analyses in narrative fashion and appraise the consistency and primacy of effects. In our next section we report an attempt to reduce the variables which are most salient within a single model, thereby refining the comparative quality of findings to this point.

Comparative Influences

To the picture of development we have just described we now add a final analysis based on the preceding analyses. It is clear that each domain of development is influenced by some of our 19 predictor variables, but not by others. In order to give a summatory picture of the influence of salient variables, we have generated regression models of each domain at the latest level of maturity analyzed. From the various analyses of the last criterion we assembled sets of predictors, allowing one predictor per domain, four in all, except for height and weight criteria for which only three predictor sets were used. As Table 10.3 indicates, three predictors were used with the 42 month PAR *Physical* criterion from the somatic domain with none identified from the Biological predictor set. In the case of the Social domain measure at 54 months, Preschool Inventory *P–S–R* scores, four predictors were used. In the case of the motoric criterion, at 54 months four predictors were indicated, by a slight margin in some instances. Two predictors were used to study height at 66 months. In the case of weight only one variable was indicated, and no regression analysis was necessary. Two quite similar sets of four predictors, differing only in use of maternal education or race as the Social predictor, were used for study of the linguistic and intellectual criteria at 66 months. The data sets employed have a mean SES score of 54 on the McGuire and White scale, are typically one-half male and one-third black. All are quite comparable; for example, the proportion of males in six subsets ranges from 50 to 54%, the proportion of white children from 60 to 67%, with mean SES scores of 53 or 54.[2] As with previous analyses the role of any given variable is a function of the set of predictors and its R^2 value, rather than an absolute role.

Beginning with the somatic criterion at the youngest child age, we consider the comparative influence of SES, AFI_{68}, and father figure variables on PAR *Physical* scores at 42 months. The requisite data came from a

[2]Description of subjects using empirically derived predictor series.

| Criterion | N | Sex | Race (W) % | $\overline{M}$ SES | Criterion | |
					M	σ
66 m IPTA A–A	345	53	62	54.11	18.36	5.06
66 m Ht	368	52	63	54.27	44.60	2.18
54 m Copy F	318	52	66	53.30	36.91	13.01
54 m P.I. P–S–R	280	53	64	54.00	13.37	3.17
42 m PAR Phys	316	54	62	54.31	19.72	4.09
66 m WPPSI V.	274	54	65	53.84	16.25	5.10

$\overline{M}$ sample $N=321$

substantial group of children, as Table 10.3 shows. Only one variable, AFI_{68}, was significant in a regression model whose $R^2 = .03$ ($F = 5.01$, $p = .02$). Next we report the motoric domain results in which birthweight, SES, AFI_{68}, and STIM were applied to 54 month Copy Forms. In the regression analysis the full model had an $R^2 = .28$, which is quite high comparatively. One-half of the variance was associated with SES ($F = 62.20$, $p < .00001$), and only slightly less with STIM scores ($F = 41.05$, $p < .00001$). In the case of the Social criterion, the P–S–R score of the Preschool Inventory at 54 months, the four factor model of sex, AFI_{68}, maternal employment, and STIM accounted for 28% of the variance. The most substantial influence was the STIM score ($F = 44.23$, $p < .00001$), accounting for about one-third of the variance. A far lesser influence was maternal employment outside the home. In the matter of height, birthweight and STIM accounted for .06 of the variance at child age 66 months. Birthweight was the greater influence, as Table 10.3 shows ($F = 17.86$, $p < .00003$), with a slight but statistically significant effect associated with STIM ($F = 5.08$, $p < .02$). In the intellectual domain the full model of social risk, Apgar, birthweight, and STIM produced a robust regression model, $R^2 = .17$. Maternal level of education was the prime influence ($F = 14.38$, $p = .0001$) and accounted for about one-third of the variance. It was followed by a lesser association with the STIM score ($F = 11.26$, $p = .0009$). A similar model, differing only in substitution of race for maternal education, generated a model of the linguistic criterion, ITPA *Auditory Association*, at 66 months. Only race was not an influence, with Apgars, STIM, and social risk scores being salient influences. With the exception of maternal liberalism, AFI_{68}, the criterion maternal reports of *Physical* attainment at 42 months, Apgars, and ITPA A–A high levels of predictors are associated with high levels of criterion measures.

What we have just reported is an analysis in which the predictor series is derived empirically from all four predictor domains. The analysis is powerful in the sense of being the culmination of analyses in previous chapters, but it is also a brief, derived series. Essentially, the analysis concentrates the predictive variables on the latest criterion for each domain by child age. Overall, the analysis shows that Family influences, especially in the form of home environment as measured by Professor Bettye Caldwell's STIM, is the most important influence within the set of variables we have assembled. We augment this observation by pointing out that the frequency with which STIM is an overwhelming influence is attenuated in this data set by its late arrival. That is, we would have used the STIM in the perinatal phase of longitudinal study had it existed. Even with its arrival in the scene at age 4–5 in this cohort, the effect of the STIM score in regression analyses is powerful. Inspection of Table 10.3 shows the frequency of statistical significance

TABLE 10.3: MULTIPLE LINEAR REGRESSION ANALYSES

Models Compared	Predictor	R^2	F	P	Predictor
		66 Mos. WPPSI *Vocabulary* (N=274)			
Full Model 1		.17		<.00001*	
			.01	.91	
Model 2	Social Risk	.17		<.00001*	Birthweight
Full Model 1		.17		<.00001*	
			.84	.35	
Model 3	Apgar	.17		<.00001*	SES
Full Model 1		.17		<.00001*	
			14.38	.0001	
Model 4	Maternal Educ.	.12		<.00001*	AFI_{68}
Full Model 1		.17		<.00001*	
			11.26	.0009	
Model 5	STIM	.13		<.00001*	STIM
		66 Mos. ITPA *A-A* (N=345)			
Full Model 1		.24		<.00001*	
			11.96	.0006	
Model 2	Social Risk	.21		<.00001*	Birthweight
Full Model 1		.24		<.00001*	
			41.60	<.00001	
Model 3	Apgar	.15		<.00001*	STIM
Full Model 1		.24		<.00001*	
			.02	.87	
Model 4	Race	.24		<.00001*	
Full Model 1		.24		<.00001*	
			40.78	.00001	
Model 5	STIM	.15		<.00001*	

*Significance of the difference from zero.

USING EMPIRICALLY DERIVED PREDICTOR SETS

Motoric-54 Mos. Copy Forms (N=318)			Predictor	54 Mos. P.I. $P\text{-}S\text{-}R$ (N=280)		
R^2	F	P		R^2	F	P
.28		<.00001*		.18		<.00001*
	1.28	.25			1.85	.17
.28		<.00001*	Sex	.17		<.00001*
.28		<.00001*		.18		<.00001*
	62.20	<.00001*			.51	.47
.14		<.00001*	AFI_{68}	.18		<.00001*
.28		<.00001*		.18		<.00001*
	3.27	.07			4.00	.04
.27		<.00001*	Maternal Employm.	.17		<.00001*
.28		<.00001*		.18		<.00001*
	41.05	<.00001*			44.23	<.00001
.19		<.00001*	STIM	.05		.002*

Height - 66 Mos. (N=368)				42 Mos. PAR $Physical$ (N=316)		
R^2	F	P		R^2	F	P
.06		<.00001*		.03		.008*
	17.86	.00003			.10	.74
.02		<.002*	SES	.03		.002*
.06		<.00001*		.03		.008*
	5.08	.02			5.01	.02
.06		<.00001*	AFI_{68}	.02		.03*
				.03		.008*
					2.32	.12
			Father Figure	.03		.009*

of STIM scores through significant F-ratios. Other predictor variables are significant, but only once; STIM scores are significant in all five analyses where they appear.

In calling the reader's attention to the STIM scale as the salient variable, we note the hazard of over-reductionism. That is, the predictor series for each criterion domain began with 19 predictors in four sets. Our attention was then focused on more parsimonious predictor subsets derived empirically from the analyses in preceding chapters. Now we report the salience of one of the 19, the STIM. In separately published research, written before the analyses of this work and using a different data subset, we have looked at factors correlated with STIM scores (Jordan, 1978b). In these analyses we identified maternal traits as most important, especially mothers' level of schooling. The effect of those findings is to support our view of the primacy of mothers and homes in child development, and to demonstrate empirically that the process of early development is less opaque than we think. The hazard is that the generalization could be carried beyond the data, and we recall the low R^2 values of the regression models and proportionately large amounts of unexplained variance.

Influences on Child Development

The goal of empirical study is to attempt generalization about the object of inquiry, in this case development in the preschool years. In some respects the empirical investigator is at a disadvantage since he is limited by the data chosen for analysis and by the qualities of the data once analyzed. In contrast, the ideologue, or clinician dealing with a sample of one case, is in a much better position; in that orientation one can assert that 3-year-olds are trusting, and that large segments of our child population are at risk of malnutrition and that they are evidently lighter and shorter than they should be. In such discourse, which has a grain of truth for particular children, generalizations are broad, and often arise from premises which are rhetorical and philosophical. For example, it is intolerable to some theoreticians that there be differences in levels of attainment; the concept of range, in their thinking, necessarily means that the child at the bottom of a range is proof of a problem, an unmet need, a scandal in a democratic society. In many cases the empiricist and the ideologue agree in all respects; however, there are occasions when they do not agree. As an example of how the range of a variable, with someone inevitably at the bottom, can be misused we consider overcrowding.

In the findings of this study we learn that about 25% of all 3-year-old children do not live in a conventional family structure with two parents, a finding similar to that reported from Stockholm by Curman and Nylander (1976). This descriptive outcome is depressing to people interested in the welfare of children, whatever their philosophical stance. On the other hand, the number of rooms per person in families has a wide range today. Among our St. Louis children it varies from .37 to 3.54 rooms per person. The smaller of these numbers is clearly far less desirable; interestingly, this aspect of childrens lives turns out to be insignificant by itself, a finding we have reported elsewhere (Jordan, 1978b) in a study of language in preschoolers. What is needed to understand this kind of observation is a larger perspective than what is observed. In the case of home density, the ratio of people and rooms, the present situation is generally highly favorable. For example, the data set from which this investigation is drawn generally shows that the number of rooms per person is 1.03 ($\sigma = .51$). Other reports of the numbers of room and people are as follows:

1. Clark (1952) reported that the incidence of tuberculosis in Edinburgh in 1946 rose by a statistically significant amount when the proportion of one person per room was exceeded. Richards, McIntosh, and Sweenie (1979) reported 1.5 occupants per room as the criterion of overcrowding in Glasgow.
2. Cartwright (1976) reported less than 1 person per room in approximately 80% of a sample of British homes.
3. Smith (1934) reported 2.5 people per bedroom as the threshold of overcrowding.
4. Duke (1915) reported .38 people per room in Pennsylvania.
5. Booth reported instances of 2–10 people per room among the poor in London in 1903 (Fried & Elman, 1971).
6. Engels (1845) reported 1 family per room, in 46% of Bristol families.
7. Christiansen, Mora, and Herrera (1975) report at least 3–5 persons per bedroom among the poor in Bogota, Columbia.

Clearly, overcrowding means different things at different times. Put in perspective, circumstances of life today in regard to home density are infinitely better than in the past; the lack of significance for this variable as an influence, for example, on language development is due to the enormous improvements of the last half century, and century. The variable of people-to-rooms, as analyzed by Gall, Gove, and McPherson (1972) remains salient for rates of mortality, fertility, public assistance, and delinquency. It seems not salient in our study population for child development, especially in language (Jordan, 1978b). Thus, it follows that those at the low end of a distribution are at a disadvantage in so far as we believe that the low end of distributions is inherently bad, or is unacceptable by a contemporary standard, as in the case of our worst-off children.[3]

This point is useful when considering some of the data reported in preceding chapters. In the case of weight and height, we found in the previous chapter that the regression models accounted for little of the variance, and that within less than robust models few variables out of 19, beyond birthweight and sex, were relevant. We suspect that the data sets of Chapter 9 reveal a positive thing in a negative way. That is, we feel that children's weights and heights are, on the average, quite good. For example, the lack of association with socioeconomic status may well mean that Society now has a minimal level of nutrition which vitiates former demonstrable effects of social realities in the community. It is a fact that one cannot distinguish the shortest from the tallest, the lightest from the heaviest, by their differing social levels, as a statistically supported generalization. In addition, one cannot explain variance in height through two models composed of social data; such social variables simply do not account as a full regression model for measures of height and weight to a substantial, statistically significant degree.

Put another way we assert that physical development of Old Man River's Children may no longer be a marker of social disadvantage. Their bodies are above the minimum level of discriminating nutritional status. (To the statistician it will be clear we are concentrating on unassigned or error variance, for which there can be other explanations.) In this regard, our St. Louis data may be compatible with Lindgren's (1976) Swedish data which show that a number of aspects of development, generally held to distributed as a function of SES—the haves and have-nots—are now independent of SES. If this is the case, and it is not improbable, it is not evidence that the Millenium has arrived; rather it suggests that Society may be closer to attainment of some of its goals than popular opinion suggests.

It may well be that standards of nutrition have risen in the last few generations to an extent we had not realized. While there are sections of the population who are malnourished and misnourished we have made progress, generally speaking. The writer can recall as a boy seeing the bow-legs of small men—miners—whose malnourishment as children led to ricketts and permanent damage. A respect for social history suggests that in nourishment as in housing, we are far from perfect, but far from the wide-

---

[3] It may be that there are environmental correlates of home density which merit attention. Cohen, Glass, and Singer (1973) have shown that the level of highway noise affects children's process of auditory discrimination. Children living on upper floors of high rise buildings experienced less loss of discrimination than those on lower floors. Adaption to ambient noise levels was only partial.

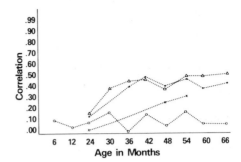

Figure 10.1. Correlation of perinatal SES with four major aspects of development (O = weight, ● = intellectual, × = social, △ = linguistic).

spread conditions our forefathers sought to remedy. In the matter of nutrition enormous advances have been made. Boyd-Orr (1936) reported enormous increases in consumption of nutritionally important food since 1909. Consumption of fruit, vegetables other than potatoes, eggs, and meat rose by proportions up to 188%. Braudel (1975) reported that the family of a man in Berlin in 1800 spent 44.2% of its weekly income on bread. In Lancashire in 1841 working class families spent up to 39% of their weekly incomes on bread. This percentage, according to the Mayor of Manchester, William Neild (1841), did not drop below 12%, a most unfortunate pattern of eating. Obviously, we have made substantial progress as consumers in choice of foods for child nutrition in the last 150 years. Social and economic progress has occurred, and is reflected in the *secular* trend to reach selected levels of growth at progressively earlier ages (Sullivan, 1971).

On the other hand, there are within the data set indicants of social influences on nonphysical aspects of growth in preschool boys and girls. This should not be surprising, coinciding as it does with a large body of research findings. For the most part, the significant biological influences can be grouped as matters of social class and family subculture. In the case of social class we are referring to the composite score of family data developed using McGuire and White's (1955) three-factor technique in the first several years of study. What social status scores represent, and we have several others in the data file on each family (see Figure 10.1),[4] is a set of objective pieces of data which place people in some position relative to other people. Conceptually, we are dealing with a set of perceptions of childhood and expectations for what children may aspire to and what one may reasonably expect of them. The totality is an attitude to life and a view of the world. In our data set the range of social status scores, from high status to low is from

---

[4] In addition to the McGuire and White SES scores based on weight and occupation, education and income, we also have SES scores based on Duncan, Hollingshead, and NORC scorings.

14 to 84, a spread of 70 points, and the theoretical range in the McGuire and White scoring system.

The house sits on a little knoll and there are no close neighbors. White columns are at the front, a widow's walk at the back. All floors are parquet, and several rooms are panelled in a rich, dark wood. But the furnishings are the outstanding attraction, mostly antiques, with a beautiful stained glass window in an oval at the top of the stairs, and old, gas light-type chandeliers. (Caseworker)

Contrast this family with another family.

Mary lives in a poor neighborhood, and whenever I visit her she is dressed in dirty clothes, hair unkempt, and no shoes or socks on. Her mother uses several names and moves back and forth between the city and a small, shabby town to the southwest. Each year the mother is difficult to locate. As I leave the house I wonder sadly where I will see Mary next year. (Caseworker)

Obviously, we are presenting extremes in order to make a point sharply. Not surprisingly, these two levels of social class suggest different patterns of health care, shelter, and prospects.

However, there is a second construct which has an explanatory value, the orientation of the primary caregiver. In this case the picture is far more complex, and what might appear an unprepossessing social stratum can be illuminated by a mother's care.

I was much impressed by what Bobby's mother did after answering my preliminary questions. She sat on the floor, while holding a four or five month old baby in her lap, to assist one of her small children who was working with an educational toy—a puzzle box. (Caseworker)

Sue's mother told me that she became aware of what she was not doing for Sue. This resulted in her purchasing a set of encyclopedias, records, educational toys, games, tables, and chairs, chalkboard and etc., all of which they make use of. (Caseworker)

Mrs. Braun is an intelligent, soft-spoken woman whose quiet manner is reflected in the four of her seven children I have seen. There appears to be much interaction between this mother and her children. She shows an awareness of and concern for about what Jimmy is doing in school. She visits the school to have conferences with his teacher. (Caseworker)

All three of these women were poor, and live in unprepossessing circumstances, and yet express their personal value systems in showing an enlightened interest in child developing procedures within their very modest homes.

In these observations on the data and in the data-presenting chapters we have said relatively little about fathers. The reason has its roots in procedures. In the hospital phase of study we obtained the ccooperation of several hundred mothers more than we subsequently studied. In most instances energy invested in initial interviews and data taking, for example the AFI_{68} measure of authoritarian family ideology, was wasted; that is, fathers refused to participate in the study despite wives' interest. Similarly, we lost some cooperative mothers and their children at later dates when father recalled or were reminded that "The Baby Study Lady" was here today. As best we can tell the mulishness of some fathers was a combination of generalized hostility to the vague "them" of the Establishment, plus resistance to "their" prying. Much of our success in data taking, at this point perhaps 10,000 family contacts, has been due to visiting when fathers are at work. Occasionally, a father has been home:

I had been in this apartment located over a store only a few minutes when a man staggered up the stairs—using very foul, abusive language—striking a small child in the process, and demanding his dinner. Mrs. Smith . . . asked him to calm down . . . his reply was vulgar and offensive. He then entered the room . . . and stood directly behind me . . . went back into the kitchen, got a beer and returned to the room where tests were being administered. He turned on the television and then walked in front of me to turn on a radio . . . muttering to himself.

As I went downstairs and reached the sidewalk this man leaned out of a window. I quickly moved across the sidewalk feeling that he might drop something on my head! (Caseworker)

In fairness, many fathers have been cooperative, but we have limited our data taking within the family to what we could learn about fathers from wives. In that sense family as a subculture is less fully explored than we would have liked. To have dealt only with families whose total cooperation was never in doubt would have been to make the common mistake of studying a partially representative set of family subcultures. Such practice has long been the weakness of longitudinal studies which, in effect, look for the missing object only under the streetlight.

The point to the illustrations we have just given is that family as a subculture emerges from the data as a critical influence on child attainment. In particular, mothers' liberalism–authoritarianism, as measured by Ernhart and Loevinger's Family Problems Scale AFI_{68}, is a relatively important expression of the values guiding child development. AFI_{68} is an influence in three domains of child development, and exerts its influence benignly when mothers are liberal; its influence extends to age 4, for example in the Intellectual domain.

In contrast to physical development, where it seems society has generally crossed the threshold of minimum levels of growth in height and weight for children, other aspects of development have a long way to go. If one considers eating habits as aspects of subculture, it may be that generations of education through schooling and rising income have wrought the necessary changes. In contrast, the things within families which influence the course of growth in, for example, language or social development, are less responsive to social change. They may also be less the target of change with the exception of preschooling in the late 1960s and early 1970s.

What needs to be changed in families to optimize development in areas beyond physical growth is the way of life. In many ways it is the routines of daily living and the sense of identity with the ways of the world that are quietly significant. To change such elements of culture is to change much of the course of peoples' lives. Research tells us that even colossal unheavals in the way people live, nominally intended to reach the narrow and specific objective of bettering their way of life, do not succeed very quickly. In particular, we refer to the study from Warsaw by Firkowska *et al.* (1978) who report that "social policy has indeed resulted in the even distribution of school and district variables across the population. . . . Despite this social policy of equalization the association (with family education and occupation) persists in a form characteristic of more traditional societies [p. 1362]." Similarly, Halperin, Rao, and Martin (1975) demonstrated that 30 years of social change after the Russian revolution of 1917 did not eliminate the effects of socioeconomic status in a nominally classless society.

The matter of putting a minimal level of nutrition under children, thereby achieving a degree of growth not linked to social circumstances, is relatively simple, if only because the criteria of success are relatively easy to establish. We wish that children of all backgrounds be indistinguishable from one another in height and weight. More focally, there is unanimity that being as tall and robust as possible is a good thing. In the case of nonphysical growth, to put the matter at its broadest, the problem is precisely the lack of agreement on the cultural accomplishments we wish to see children attain, regardless of their backgrounds. The current phrase "social disadvantage" is in part a soft euphemism for being poor, but it is also recognition that some ways of life equip people for life at different levels. As a matter of public philosophy, to use Lippmann's term, one question is (to paraphrase Parsons [1975]), a matter of how to change our social institutions to help those born into less favored families; a second question is the more difficult matter of whether that is desirable. This last point is a sharp one because changing our institutions, for example schools and families, requires that people give up what is near and dear to them; in the death of the neighborhood school as a legal concept we have clear testimony to the resistance social change can bring.

For our discussion here the relevant institution is the family. What people do within families varies enormously. The descriptive data of this study show that by child age 3—recalling our study child is roughly the third child—about one-quarter of the families lack a father. The regression analyses show that the presence of a father is not insignificant, while also not a primary influence. Presumably, social policy might address that matter on grounds of child welfare. However, that evokes the countertheme of stability of family ties and, indeed, the coolness towards legal union evident in some quarters. A declining birth rate makes it clear that children are no longer the overriding theme of men and women living together, with or without legal ties. Equally, emancipation of women is still a long way from tidy formulation in most respects.

Even when the conventions of family arrangements exist, there remain the elements of family culture and the explosive question of what counts. Some families value the silent machismo of the nonfluent male and others value the equality of parental rights and obligations in a setting where full fluency, indeed lack of inhibition, is important. To ask some parents, especially fathers, to talk to little children seems undignified. In that case we see, but only implicitly, that family values are perhaps more adult than child-centered. Ideally, a respect for education should be inculcated early in youngsters. For it to move beyond a mere verbalism it requires that parents are self-consciously, and in a fashion they can articulate, teaching parents in a teaching family. From our anecdotes we recall that the mothers of Billy, Sue, and Jimmy are all teaching mothers.

For such people there is always the question of what to teach. In this period of ethnic pride it may be self-devaluing to use conventional English grammar, or even more devaluing to use English at all. To those who have made it or, perhaps, whose parents or grandparents made it, it is self-evident that thrift, washing one's hands, and wearing clean pajamas is the only thing to do. To those less well favored the pressures of the moment may make it impossible to plan very far ahead, and to delay gratification.

Summing up, we suggest that putting a minimum level of attainment under children is a difficult thing to do, even if as in Poland and Russia total control is available to a State that has resolved by dialectic the contradictions of traditional social values. To those no less interested in a better life, prescriptive solutions are harder to come by, since compromise and consensus are modes of social change. We have the means to produce higher levels of attainment in all boys and girls. If we decide that 10 more IQ points on a standardized test in a given year is the minimum, we can probably help disadvantaged children reach that goal. Implicitly, the level of attainment in favored children will probably rise also. This brings us back to the inescapable questions of whether differences in levels are inherently a bad thing, and whether bringing all but those held back by organic factors to a maximum level becomes a good thing, when differences exist above that level as a consequence of genetic endowment. Clearly, we can aspire to improve minimum levels of attainment by all children. As with universal literacy, once considered a goal with revolutionary import, differences above an agreed minimum are inescapable, and not unworthy; our prime is obligation to raise the universal minimum.

We return, finally, to the broad question at the opening of this work, one which remains fascinating as we plan data taking at age 13 years on our group of children growing up on the banks of Old Man River. As we write, the seasons are changing, and the rolling hills are golden in the pale light of Fall. The seasons evolve and the children mature; their progress is in the hands of those who love them. In some cases this is a certain and true bond, and in others it is in unstable homes, with thoughtless, foolish, and irresponsible parents. Some children will fare well through inner resources which are their heritage, while others will move less certainly towards responsibility and maturity. As we write the children have ended their earliest years, and stand on the threshold of the great adventure of schooling. As Nature threw the dice at birth so now the children face another great allocation. Quality of schooling, interaction of aptitude and opportunity, and personal qualities not yet evident will rise, but that is another study.

Bibliography

Ammons, R. B. & Ammons, C. H. *Full Range Picture Vocabulary Scale.* Missoula, Mont: Psychological Test Specialists, 1958.

Ammons, R. B. & Ammons, C. H. *The Quick Test.* Missoula, Mont: Southern University Press, 1962.

Anastasi, A. *Differential Psychology.* New York: MacMillan, 1958.

Andres, R. *The Normality of Aging: The Baltimore Longitudinal Study.* Washington, D.C.: U.S. Public Health Service, 1978.

Apgar, V. & James, L. S. Further Observations on the Newborn Scoring System. *American Journal of Diseases of Children,* 1962, *104,* 419–428.

Babson, S. G., Gorham, W. B., & Clark, W. M. *The Preschool Intelligence of Oversized Newborns.* Paper presented to the American Psychological Association, 1970.

Baltes, P. B. Longitudinal and Cross-Sectional Sequences in the Study of Age and Generation Effects. *Human Development,* 1968, *11,* 145–171.

Barrai, I., Moroni, A., & Cavalli-Sforza, L. Further Studies on Record Linkage from Parish Books. In Acheson, E. D. (ed.), *Record Linkage in Medicine.* Edinburgh: E. & S. Livingston, 1968.

Baulant, M. Le Prix des Grains à Paris. *Annales,* 1968, *3,* 520–540.

Beal, V. A. Nutrition in a Longitudinal Growth Study. *Journal of the American Dietetic Association,* 1965, *46,* 457–461.

Bell, R. Q. Convergence: An Accelerated Longitudinal Approach. *Child Development,* 1953, *24,* 145–152.

Belmont, L., Wittes, J., & Stein, Z. Relation of Birth Order, Family Size, and Social Class to Family Functions. *Perceptual and Motor Skills,* 1977, *45,* 1107–1116.

Bendig, A. The Development of a Short-Form of the Manifest Anxiety Scale. *Journal of Consulting Psychology,* 1945, *20,* 384.

Bereiter, C. & Engelmann, S. *Teaching Disadvantaged Children in Preschool.* Englewood Cliffs, N.J.: Prentice Hall, 1966.

Berendes, H. W. The Structure and Scope of the Collaborative Project on Cerebral Palsy, Mental Retardation, and Other Neurological Sensory Disorders of Infancy and Childhood. In Chipman, S., Lilienfeld, A., Greenberg, B. G., & Donnelly, J. F. (eds.), *Research Methodology and Needs in Perinatal Studies.* Springfield, Ill.: Thomas, 1966.

Bernstein, B. Aspects of Language and Learning in the Genesis of the Social Process. *Journal of Child Psychology and Psychiatry,* 1960, *1,* 313–324.

Birch, H., Richardson, S. A., Baird, D., Horobin, G., & Illsley, R. *Mental Subnormality in the Community.* Baltimore: Williams & Wilkins, 1970.

Bjarnason, O., Fridrikson, S., & Magnusson, M. Record Linkage in a Self-Contained Community. In Archeson, E. D. (ed.), *Record Linkage in Medicine.* Edinburgh: E. & S. Livingstone, 1968.

Bjarnason, O. & Magnusson, M. Linkage of the Icelandic Cancer Registry to an Icelandic Population File. In Grundmann, E. & Pedersen, E. (eds.), *Recent Results in Cancer Research.* Berne, Germany: Springer–Verlag, 1975.

Bleuler, M. A 23-Year Longitudinal Study of 208 Schizophrenics and Impressions in Regard to the Nature of Schizophrenic. In Rosenthal, D. & Kety, S. (eds.), *The Transmission of Schizophrenia.* New York: Pergamon Press, 1968.

Block, J. *Lives Through Time.* Berkeley: Bancroft Books, 1971.

Boehm, A. E. *Boehm Test of Basic Concepts.* New York: Psychological Corporation, 1969.

Bottenberg, R. A. & Ward, J. H. *Applied Multiple Linear Regression.* Aerospace Medical Division, United States Air Force, 1963.

Boyd-Orr, J. *Food, Health, and Income.* London: MacMillan, 1936.

Bradshaw, P. W., Ley, P., Kincey, J. A. & Bradshaw, J. Recall of Medical Advice: Comprehensibility and Specificity. *British Journal of Social and Clinic Psychology,* 1975, *14,* 55–62.

Braudel, F. *Capitalism and Material Life 1400–1800.* New York: Harper Colophon Books, 1975.

Brazelton, T. B. *Neonatal Behavioral Assessment Scale.* London: Heinemann Medical Books, 1971.

Brekstad, A. Factors Influencing the Reliability of Anamnestic Recall. *Child Development,* 1966, *37,* 603–612.

Brown, J. A. & Houart, G. C. Application of an Archaeological Site Survey Retrieval System to the Lower Illinois River Valley Research Program. In Mittman, B. & Borman, C. (eds.), *Personalized Data Base Systems.* Los Angeles: Melville, 1975.

Broman, S. H., Nichols, P. L., & Kennedy, W. A. *Preschool IQ: Prenatal and Early Developmental Correlates.* New York: Wiley and Sons, 1975.

Bruch, H. & Cottington, F. A Detailed Diary of the Early Years of a Schizophrenic Boy. *Nervous Child,* 1942, *1,* 232–249.

Bryant, F. B. & Wortman, P. M. Secondary Analysis: The Case for Data Archives. *American Psychologist,* 1978, *33,* 381–387.

Burstein, L. Secondary Analysis: An Important Resource for Educational Research and Evaluation. *Educational Researcher,* 1978, *7,* 9–12.

Burton, R. V. Validity of Retrospective Reports Assessed by the Multitrait-Multimethod Analysis. *Developmental Psychology,* Monograph, 1970, *3,* 3, Part 2.

Caldwell, B. M. *The Preschool Inventory.* Princeton, N.J.: Educational Testing Service, 1970.

Carmichael, L. (ed.). *Manual of Child Psychology.* New York: Wiley, 1954.

Carrow, E. *Elicited Language Inventory.* 1974.

Cartwright, A. *How Many Children?* London: Routledge and Kegan Paul, 1976.

Chamla, M. C. & Demoulin, F. *Croissance des Algeriens de l'Enfance à l'Age Adulte (Region de L'Aures)*. Paris: Centre National de la Recherche Scientifique, 1976.

Chase, H. P., Kumar, V., Dodds, J. M., Saoberlich, H. E., Hontes, R. M., Burton, R. S., & Spalding, V. Nutritional Status of Mexican-American Migrant Farm Children. *American Journal of Diseases of Children*, 1971, *122*, 316–324.

Chomsky, N. *Syntactic Structures*. The Hague: Mouton, 1957.

Clark, W. G. Housing and Tuberculosis. *Public Health* 1952, *65*, 113–119.

Christiansen, N., Mora, J. O., & Herrera, M. G. Family Social Characteristics Related to Physical Growth of Young Children. *British Journal of Preventive and Social Medicine*, 1975, *29*, 121–130.

Cohen, J. Multiple Regression as a General Data-Analytic System. *Psychology Bulletin*, 1968, *70*, 426–443.

Cohen, J. *Statistical Power Analysis for the Behavioral Sciences*. New York: Academic Press, 1977.

Cohen, S., Glass, D. C., & Singer, J. E. Apartment Noise, Auditory Discrimination, and Reading Ability in Children. *Journal of Experimental Social Psychology*, 1973, *9*, 407–422.

Colborn, D. W. & Salzman, M. The Apgar Scoring System in the Evaluation of the Newborn Infant. *New York State Journal of Medicine*, 1960, *60*, 246–249.

Cratty, B. J. *Movement Behavior and Motor Learning*. Philadelphia: Lea & Febiger, 1967.

Cratty, B. J. *Motor Activity and the Behavior of Retardates*. Philadelphia: Lea & Febiger, 1969.

Crider, D. M., Willits, F. K., & Bealer, R. C. *Locating People in Longitudinal Studies: A Research Report and Suggested Guidelines*. Bulletin 778, Agricultural Experiment Station, Pennsylvania State University. 1972.

Crystal, D., Fletcher, P., & Garman, M. *The Grammatical Analysis of Language Disability: A Procedure for Assessment and Remediation*. London: Arnold, 1976.

Curman, H., & Nylander, I. A Ten-Year Prospective Follow-up Study of 2268 cases at the Child Guidance Clinics in Stockholm. *Acta Paediatrica Scandinavica Supplementum*, 1976, *260*.

Damon, A. & Bajema, C. J. Age at Menarche: Accuracy of Recall After Thirty Nine Years. *Human Biology*, 1974, *46*, 381–384.

Doll, E. A. *Preschool Attainment Record*. Minneapolis, Minn.: American Guidance Service, 1966.

Douglas, J. W. B. *The Home and the School: A Study of Ability and Attainment in the Primary School*. London: Panther Books, 1967.

Douglas, J. W. B. The Use and Abuse of National Cohorts. In Shipman, M. (ed.), *The Organization and the Impact of Social Research*. London: Routledge and Kegan Paul, 1976.

Douglas, J. W. B. & Blomfield, J. M. *Children Under Five*. London: Allen & Unwin, 1958.

Douglas, J. W. B., Ross, J. M., & Simpson, H. R. *All Our Future*. London: Panther Books, 1971.

Drillien, C. M. *The Growth and Development of the Prematurely Born Infant*. London: E. & S. Livingstone, 1964.

Drillien, C. M. School Disposal and Performance for Children of Different Birthweight Born in 1953–1960. *Archives of Diseases in Childhood*, 1969, *44*, 562–570.

Drillien, C. M. The Small-for-Date Infant: Etiology and Progress. *Pediatrics Clinics of North America*, 1970, *17*, 2–24.

Duke, E. *Infant Mortality: Results of a Field Study in Johnstown, Pa., Based on Results in One Calendar Year*. Washington, D.C.: U.S. Children's Bureau, 1915.

Eastmen, N. J., Kohl, S. G., Maisel, J. E., & Kavaler, F. The Obstetrical Background of 753 Cases of Cerebral Palsy. *Obstetrics and Gynecology Survey*, 1962, *17*, 459–500.

Elder, G. H. *Children of the Great Depression.* Chicago: University of Chicago Press, 1974.

Engels, F. *The Condition of the Working Class in England (1845).* Palo Alto, Calif.: Stanford University Press, 1968.

Epstein, H. T. & Epstein, E. B. The Relationship Between Brain Weight and Head Circumference from Birth to Age Eighteen Years. *American Journal of Physical Anthropology,* 1978, *48,* 471–474.

Ernhart, C. B. & Loevinger, J. Authoritarian Family Ideology: A Measure of Its Correlates and Its Robustness. *Multivariate Behavior Research Monographs,* 1969, *1.*

Eveleth, P. B. & Tanner, J. M. *World-Wide Variation in Human Growth.* Cambridge: Cambridge University Press, 1978.

Falkner, F. Some Physical Growth Standards for White North American Children. *Paediatrics,* 1962, *29,* 467–474.

Ferb, T. E., Larson, J. C., & Napior, D. *Education as Experimentation a Planned Variation Model. Volume IV-D. Part 1: A Longitudinal Study of Follow-Through.* Boston, Mass.: ABT Associates, Inc., 1977.

Ferri, E. & Robinson, H. *Coping Alone.* London: NFER Publishing Co., 1977.

Fetters, W. B. *National Longitudinal Study of the High School Class of 1972—Base Year Study: Student Questionnaire and Test Results by Academic Ability, Socioeconomic Status, and Region.* Washington, D.C.: National Center for Educational Statistics, 1976.

Firkowska, A., Ostrowska, A., Sokolowska, M., Stein, Z., Susser, M., & Wald, I. Cognitive Development and Social Policy: The Contribution of Parental Occupation and Education to Mental Performance in 11-Year Olds in Warsaw. *Science,* 1978, *200,* 1357–1362.

Flax, M. *A Study in Comparative Urban Indicators: Conditions in 18 Large Metropolitan Areas.* Washington, D.C.: Urban Institute, 1972.

Fogelman, K. (ed.). *Britain's Sixteen-Year-Olds: Preliminary Findings from the Third Follow-Up of the National Child Development Study (1958 Cohort).* London: National Children's Bureau, 1976.

Fogelman, K. R. & Goldstein, H. Social Factors Associated with Changes in Educational Attainment Between 7 and 11 Years of Age. *Educational Statistics,* 1976, *2,* 95–109.

Ford, P. D., Patterson, C. S., & Treuting, W. C. Fetal Exposure to X-Rays and Leukemia and Other Malignant Diseases in Childhood. *Journal of National Cancer Institute,* 1959, *22,* 1093–1104.

Foster, T. A., Voors, A. W., Webber, L. S., Frericks, R. R., & Berenson, G. S. Anthropometric and Maturation Measurements of Children, Age 5–14 Years, in a Biracial Community— the Bogalusa Heart Study. *American Journal of Clinical Nutrition,* 1977, *30,* 582–591.

Freund, H. J. & Elardo, R. Maternal Behavior and Family Constellation as Predictors of Social Competence Among Learning Disabled Children. Unpublished manuscript, 1978.

Fried, A. & Elman, R. E. (eds.). *Charles Booth's London.* London: Penguin Books, 1971.

Gall, O. R., Gove, W. R., & MacPherson, J. M. Population Density and Pathology: What are the Relations for Man? *Science,* 1972, *176,* 23–30.

Galton, F. Final Report of the Anthropometric Committee. In *Report of the Fifty-Third Meeting of the British Association for the Advancement of Science.* London: John Murray, 1884.

Gerstenblith, G., Frederiksen, J., Yin, F. C. P., Fortuin, N. J., Lakatta, E. J., & Weisfeld, M. L. Echocardiographic Assessment of A Normal Adult Aging Population. *Circulation,* 1977, *56,* 273–278.

Gleiss, J., & Holdenburg, F. Studies About the Respiratory Regulating Function of the Newborn. 1. *Biologica Neonatorum,* 1963, *5,* 350–378.

Glueck, S. & Glueck, E. *Criminal Careers in Retrospect.* Commonwealth Fund, 1943.

Goldstein, H. Longitudinal Studies and the Measurement of Change. *Statistician,* 1968, *18,* 93–117.

Goldstein, H. & Johnson, F. E. A Method for Studying Shape Change in Children. *Annals of Human Biology,* 1978, *5,* 33–39.

Graham, F. K., Berman, P. W., & Ernhart, C. B. Development in Preschool Children of the Ability to Copy Forms. *Child Development,* 1960, *31,* 339–359.

Graunt, J. *Natural and Political Observations Mentioned in a Following Index, and Made Upon the Bills of Mortality.* London: Martin, Allestry, and Dycus, 1662.

Griffith, F. *The Abilities of Babies.* London: University of London Press, 1954.

Halperin, S. L., Rao, D. C., & Morton, N. E. A Twin Study of Intelligence in Russia. *Behavior Genetics,* 1975, *5,* 83–86.

Hamilton, M. C. & Whitehead, F. I. H. The Treatment of Severe Attrition in a Young Patient: A Case Report. *British Dental Journal,* 1968, *125,* 538–539.

Hardy, J. & Mellitts, E. D. Does Maternal Smoking During Pregnancy Have a Long-Term Effect on the Child? *Lancet,* 1972, 1332–1336.

Harrald, B. & Hauge, M. A Catamnestic Investigation of Danish Twins. *Acta Genetica,* 1958, *8,* 287–294.

Havighurst, R. The Relative Importance of Social Class and Ethnicity in Human Development. *Human Development,* 1976, *19,* 56–69.

Haynes, S. G., Levine, S., Scotch, N., Feinleib, M., & Kannel, W. B. The Relationship of Psychosocial Factors to Coronary Heart Disease in the Framingham Study. I. Methods and Risk Factors. *American Journal of Epidemiology,* 1978, *107,* 362–383.

Heston, L. L. & Denney, D. Interactions Between Early Life Experience and Biological Factors in Schizophrenia. In Rosenthal, D., & Kety, S. (eds.), *The Transmission of Schizophrenia.* New York: Pergamon Press, 1968.

Hollingshead, A. B. *Two-Factor Index of Social Position.* New Haven: Author, 1957.

Illsley, R., Finlayson, A., & Thompson, B. The Motivation and Characteristics of Internal Migrants, Part I. *Milbank Memorial Fund Quarterly,* 1963, *41,* 115–144.

International Classification of Diseases Adapted, Volume 2 Alphabetical Index. Washington, D.C.: U. S. Public Health Service, 1962.

Janson, C. G. *Project Metropolitan—A Presentation; Research Report No. 1.* University of Stockholm, 1975. (a)

Janson, C. G. *Project Metropolitan, the School Study—A Code Book; Research Report No. 3.* University of Stockholm, 1975. (b)

Janson, C. G. *Project Metropolitan, the Family Study—A Code Book; Research Report No. 4.* University of Stockholm, 1975. (c)

Janson, C. G. *The Handling of Juvenile Delinquency Cases: Research Report No. 7.* Project Metropolitan, University of Stockholm, 1977.

Janson, C. G. *Project Metropolitan, the Longitudinal Approach; Research Report Number 4.* Stockholm: University of Stockholm, 1978.

Jekel, J. F., Currie, J. B., Klerman, L. V., McCarthy, C. P. N., Sarvel, P. M., & Greenberg, P. A. An Analysis of Statistical Methods for Comparing Obstetric Outcomes: Infant Health in Three Samples of School-Age Pregnancies. *American Journal of Obstetrics and Gynecology,* 1972, *112,* 9–19.

Jessor, R. & Jessor, S. L. *Problem Behavior and Psychosocial Development: A Longitudinal Study of Youth.* New York: Academic Press, 1977.

John, E. Neurometrics. *Science,* 1977, *196,* 1393–1410.

Joossens, J. F. & Brems-Heyns, E. High Power Polynomial Regression for the Study of Distance Velocity and Acceleration of Growth. *Growth,* 1975, *59,* 535–551.

Jordan, R., John, R., Karmel, B. Z., Corning, W. C., Easton, P., Brown, D., Ahn, I., John, M., Harmony, T., Prichep, L., Toro, A., Gerson, I., Bartlett, F., Thatcher, R., Kaye, H., Valdes, P., & Schwartz, E. The 1972 Cuban National Growth Study As an Example of Population Health Monitoring; Design and Methods. *Annals of Human Biology,* 1975, *2,* 1953–1971.

Jordan, T. E., *Technical Note 3.2 Extension and Validation of the Ad Hoc Child Development Scale.* St. Louis Baby Study, 1967. (a)

Jordan, T. E. Retrospective Versus Prospective Technique in Research on Learning Disability. *Journal of Special Education,* 1967, *1,* 257–265. (b)

Jordan, T. E. The Influence of Age and Social Class on Authoritarian Family Ideology. *Multivariate Behavioral Research,* 1970, *5,* 193–201.

Jordan, T. E. Early Developmental Adversity and the First Two Years of Life. *Multivariate Behavioral Research Monographs,* 1971, *6,* 1.

Jordan, T. E. Developmental Factors Influencing Exceptional Status at Age Six Years. *Contemporary Educational Psychology,* 1976, *1,* 4–16. (a)

Jordan, T. E. *The Mentally Retarded.* Fourth Edition, Merrill Books, 1976. (b)

Jordan, T. E. On the Comparability of Multiple Linear (MULR–05) and Interaction Regression Techniques. *Multiple Linear Regression Viewpoints,* 1978, *8,* 81–89. (a)

Jordan, T. E. Influences on Vocabulary Attainment: A Five-Year Prospective Study. *Child Development,* 1978, *49,* 389–399. (b)

Jordan, T. E. The St. Louis Baby Study: Theory, Practice, and Findings. In Mednick, S. & Harway, M. (eds.), *Longitudinal Research in the United States,* in press.

Jordan, T. E., & Spaner, S. D. Biological and Ecological Influences on Development at 24 and 36 Months of Age. *Psychological Reports,* 1972, *31,* 319–332.

Jordan, T. E., & Spaner, S. D. Biological and Ecological Influences on Development at 48 and 60 Months of Age. *Psychological Reports,* 1974, *34,* 119–126.

Jordan, T. E. & Spaner, S. D. *Effects of Age at Delivery in Juveniles and Older Females on Child Development: Technical Report Number 37.* St. Louis Baby Study, 1978.

Kahl, J. A. Educational and Occupational Aspirations of "Common Man" Boys. *Harvard Educational Review,* 1953, *23,* 186–203.

Karlberg, P. & Taranger, J. The Somatic Development of Children in a Swedish Urban Community: A Prospective Longitudinal Study. *Acta Paediatrica Scandinavica,* Supplementum, *258,* 1976.

Kimbrell, D. L. Comparison of PPVT, FRPVT, RS-B, and Academic Achievement Scores Among Institutionalized Educable Mental Retardates. *Perceptual and Motor Skills,* 1966, *23,* 1178.

Kirk, S. A. & McCarthy, J. *Illinois Test of Psycholinguistic Abilities.* Champaign, Ill.: University of Illinois Press, 1968.

Klackenberg, G. A Prospective Longitudinal Study of Children. Data on Psychic Health and Development Up to 8 Years of Age. *Acta Paediatrica Scandinavica,* Supplement, *224,* 1971.

Klemmetti, A. & Saxen, L. Prospective Versus Retrospective Approach in the Search for Environmental Causes of Malformations. *American Journal of Public Health,* 1967, *57,* 2071–2075.

Kohlberg, L. The Development of Children's Orientations Towards Moral Order. I. Sequential Development of Moral Thought. *Vita Humana,* 1971, *6,* 11–33.

Koplyay, J. B., Gott, C. D. & Elton, J. H. *Automatic Interaction Detector—Version 4 Reference Manual: AFHRL–73–17.* Texas: Air Force Systems Command, Brooks Air Force Base, 1973.

Kukuk, C. R., Levine, D. R., & Meyer, J. K. Neighborhood Predictors of Reading Achievement in Six Big City School Districts: A Path Analysis. *Multiple Linear Regression Viewpoints,* 1978, *8,* 27–43.

Kunter, V. M. Wirbelsaulenbefunde bei Einer Vorderasiatischen Skelettpopulation aus dem 5. Jh.v.Chr. *Homo,* 1976, *27,* 118–127.

Lancet, B. M. Dental Arch Growth Without the Aid of Orthodonic Treatment. *Dental Cosmos,* 1930, *75,* 246–252.

Lee, L. L. *Developmental Sentence Analysis.* Evanston, Ill.: Northwestern University, 1974.

Ley, P. Primary, Rated Importance, and the Recall of Medical Statements. *Journal of Health and Social Behavior,* 1972, *13,* 311–317.

Lindgren, G. Height, Weight, and Menarche in Swedish Urban School Children in Relation to Socioeconomic and Regional Factors. *Annals of Human Biology,* 1976, *3,* 510–528.

Mack, R. W. & Johnston, F. E. Height, Skeletal Maturation and Adiposity in Adolescents with High Relative Weight at One Year of Age. *Annals of Human Biology,* 1979, *6,* 77–83.

McGuire, C. M. & White, G. *The Measurement of Social Status: Research Paper in Human Development Number 3.* Austin: University of Texas, 1955.

McKusick, V. A., Eldridge, R., Hostetler, J. A., & Egeland, J. A. Dwarfism in the Amish. *Transactions of the American Association of Physicians,* 1964, *77,* 151–168.

McKusick, V. A. & Cross, H. E. Genealogical Linkage of Records in Two Isolated Populations. In Acheson, E. D. (ed.), *Record Linkage in Medicine.* Edinburgh: E. & S. Livingstone, 1968.

McNeil, J. E. *The Refinement and Prediction of a Measure of Infant Development.* Unpublished doctoral dissertation, Southern Illinois University, 1974.

McNeil, K. A., Kelly, F. J., & McNeil, J. T. *Testing Research Hypotheses Using Multiple Linear Regression.* Carbondale: Southern Illinois University Press, 1975.

Manning, A. P., Wyman, J. B., & Heaton, K. W. How Trustworthy are Bowel Histories? Comparison of Recalled and Recorded Information. *British Medical Journal,* 1976, *30,* 101–106.

Mantel, N., & Haenszel, W. Statistical Aspects of the Analysis of Data from Retrospective Studies of Disease. *Journal of National Cancer Institutes,* 1959, *22,* 719–748.

Mecham, M. *Verbal Language Development Scale.* Minneapolis, Minn.: American Guidance Service, 1958.

Mednick, S. A. & Baert, B. (eds.). *Prospective, Longitudinal Research in Europe: Implications for Primary Prevention.* Oxford: Oxford University Press, 1979.

Mednick, S. & Witkin-Lanoil, G. H. Intervention in Children at High Risk for Schizophrenia. In Albee, G. W. & Joffe, J. M. (eds.), *Primary Prevention of Psychopathology. Volume I; the Issue.* University Press of New England, 1977.

Meredith, H. V. Changes in the Stature and Body Weight of North American Boys During the Last Eighty Years. In Lipsitt, L. P. & Spiker, C. C. (eds.), *Advances in Child Development and Behavior.* New York: Academic Press, 1963.

Miller, F. J. W., Billewicz, W. Z., & Thomson, A. M. Growth from Birth to Adult Life of 442 Newcastle Upon Tyne Children. *British Journal of Preventive and Social Medicine,* 1972, *26,* 224–230.

Menyuk, P. *Sentences Children Use.* Cambridge, Mass.: M.I.T. Press, 1969.

Moorrees, C. F. A. *The Dentition of the Growing Child: A Longitudinal Study of Dental Development Between 3 and 18 Years of Age.* Cambridge, Mass.: Harvard University Press, 1959.

Morrison, P. A. Urban Growth and Decline: San Jose and St. Louis in the 1960s. *Science,* 1974, *185,* 757–762.

Mowrer, O. H. Hearing and Speaking: An Analysis of Language Learning. *Journal of Speech and Hearing Disorders*, 1958, *23*, 143–152.

Families of the Working Classes in Manchester and Dukinfield, in the Years 1836 and 1841. *Journal of the Royal Statistical Society*, 1841, *4*, 320–324.

Neligan, G. A., Kolvin, I., Scott, O., & Garside, D. F. *Born Too Soon or Born Too Small*. (Clinics in Developmental Medicine No. 61) Philadelphia: Lippincott, 1976.

Nelson, B. *Education as Experimentation A Planned Variation Model. Volume IV-D, Part II: An Academic Risk Study*. Boston, Mass.: ABT Associates Inc., 1977.

Newson, J. & Newson, E. *Infant Care in an Urban Community*. London: Allen and Unwin, 1963.

Newson, J. & Newson, E. *Four Year Olds in an Urban Community*. Chicago: Aldine, 1968.

Newson, J. & Newson, E. *Seven Year Olds in the Home Environment*. London: Allen & Unwin, 1976. (a)

Newson, J. & Newson, E. Parental Roles and Social Contexts. In Shipman, M. (ed.), *The Organization and Impact of Social Research*. London: Routledge and Kegan Paul, 1976. (b)

Niswander, K. R. & Gordon, M. (eds.). *The Women and Their Pregnancies*. Washington, D.C.: National Institute of Health, 1972.

Ohanian, P. B. A Musically and Artistically Talented Family Nearly Half a Century Later. In Stanley, J. C., George, W. C., & Solano, C. H. (eds.), *The Gifted and Creative: A Fifty-Year Perspective*. Baltimore: Johns Hopkins University Press, 1977.

Parnes, H. S. The National Longitudinal Surveys: New Vistas for Labor Market Research. *American Economic Review*, 1975, *65*, 244–249.

Porter, W. T. The Growth of St. Louis Children. *Transactions of the Academy of Science of St. Louis*, 1894, *6*, 263–380.

Prahl-Andersen, B., Pollman, A. J., Raaben, D. J., & Peters, K. A. Automated Anthropometry. *American Journal of Physical Anthropology*, 1972, *37*, 151–154.

Prahl-Andersen, B. & Kowalski, C. J. A Mixed Longitudinal, Interdisciplinary Study of the Growth and Development of Dutch Children. *Growth*, 1973, *37*, 281–295.

Rao, M. N. & Rao, C. R. Linked Cross-Sectional Study for Determining Norms and Growth Rates—A Pilot Survey of Indian School-Going Boys. *Indian Journal of Statistics*, 1966, *Series B*, 237–258.

Richards, I. D. G., McIntosh, H. T., & Sweenie, S. A Hundred Vulnerable Families. *Public Health, 1979, 93*, 16–24.

Richman, A. Peak Year of Onset of Heroin Use: Epidemiologic Fact or Mystic Statistic. In Senay, E., Shorty, V., & Alksne, H. (eds.), *Developments in the Field of Drug Abuse*. New York: Schenkman, 1975.

Robins, L. N. The Reluctant Respondent. *Public Opinion Quarterly*, 1963, *27*, 276–286.

Rous, S. N. & Turner, W. R. Retrospective Study of 95 Patients with Staghorn Calculus Disease. *Journal of Urology*, 1977, *118*, 902–907.

Rowe, J. W., Andres, R., Tobin, J. D., Norris, A. H., & Shock, N. W. Age-Adjusted Standards for Creatinine Clearance. *Annals of Internal Medicine*, 1976, *84*, 456–569.

Rubin, R. A. & Balow, B. Perinatal Influences on the Behavior and Learning Problems of Children, In Lahey, B. B. & Kazdin, A. E. (eds.), *Advances in Child Clinical Psychology*. New York: Plenum Press, 1977.

Rubin, R. A. & Balow, B. Measures of Infant Development and Socioeconomic Status as Predictors of Later Intelligence and School Achievement. *Developmental Psychology*, 1979, *15*, 225–227.

Rubin, R. A., Balow, B., & Hara, C. *Relationship of Apgar Scores to Neonatal Survival and Later Development: A Review*. Interim Report Number 19, University of Minnesota, 1975.

Rutter, M., Graham, P., & Yale, W. *A Neuropsychiatric Study in Childhood.* London: Heinemann Medical Books, 1970.

Rutter, M., Tizard, J., & Whitmore, K. *Education, Health, and Behavior.* New York: Wiley, 1970.

Rutter, M., Tizard, J., Yule, W., Graham, P., & Whitmore, K. Research Report: Isle of Wight Studies, 1964–1974. *Psychological Medicine,* 1976, *6,* 313–332.

Sand, E. A. & Emery-Hauzeur, C. Le Développement Psychomoteur de L'Enfant au Cours des Deux Premières Années. *Acta Neurologica et Psychiatrica, Belgica,* 1962, *62,* 1087–1102.

Sartorius, N., Jablonsky, B., & Shapiro, R. Two-Year Follow-Up of the Patients included in the WHO International Pilot Study of Schizophrenia. *Psychological Medicine,* 1977, *7,* 529–561.

Sears, R. S. Sources of Life Satisfactions of the Terman Gifted Men. *American Psychologist,* 1977, *32,* 119–128.

Sears, R. W. & Barbee, A. H. Careers and Life Satisfactions Among Terman's Gifted Women. In Stanley, J. C., George, W. C., & Solano, C. H. (eds.), *The Gifted and the Creative: A Fifty-Year Perspective.* Baltimore: Johns Hopkins University Press, 1977.

Short, T. *New Observations, Natural, Moral, Civil, Political, and Medical. On City, Town, and Country Bills of Mortality.* London, 1750.

Silva, P. A. *Learning Difficulties in the Preschooler: The Dunedin (New Zealand) Multidisciplinary Child Development Study.* Dunedin, New Zealand: University of Otago Medical School, 1979.

Silva, P. A. & Ferguson, D. M. Socio-Economic Status, Maternal Characteristics, Child Experience and Intelligence in Preschool Children. *New Zealand Educational Studies,* 1976, *11,* 180–188.

Simon, A. & Ward, L. O. Age, Sex, Intelligence, and Religious Beliefs in 11 to 15-Year-Old Pupils. *Irish Journal of Education,* 1975, *9,* 108–114.

Skeels, H. M. Adult Status of Children With Contrasting Early Life Experiences. *Monographs of the Society for Research in Child Development,* 1966, *31,* No. 105.

Skells, H. M. & Skodak, M. Techniques for a High-Yield Follow-Up Study in the Field. *Public Health Reports,* 1965, *80,* 249–257.

Smith, H. L. (ed.). *The New Survey of London Life and Labour. Vol. 1: Forty Years of Change.* London: King and Son, 1934.

Snyder-McLean, L. K. & McLean, J. E. Verbal Information Gathering Strategies: The Child's Use of Language to Acquire Language. *Journal of Speech and Hearing Disorders,* 1978, *43,* 306–325.

Sonnini, C. S. *Histoire Naturelle, Generale, et Particuliére, Par le Clerc de Buffon.* Paris: L'Imprimerie de Bufart, 1799.

Speciale, S. G. Nowaczyk, T., & Jouvet, M. A Longitudinal Study of Bioelectric Activity in the Pre- and Post- Hatch Chick. *Developmental Psychobiology,* 1976, *9,* 539–545.

Spence, J., Walton, W. S., Miller, F. J. W., & Court, S. O. M. *A Thousand Families in Newcastle Upon Tyne.* Oxford: Oxford University Press, 1954.

Stein, Z., Susser, M., Saenger, G., & Marolla, F. Intelligence Test Results of Individuals Exposed During Gestation to the World War II Famine in the Netherlands. *Tijdschrift voor Sociale Geneeskunde,* 1972, *50,* 766–744.

Stone, J. L. & Norris, A. H. Activities and Attitudes of Participants in the Baltimore Longitudinal Study. *Journal of Gerontology.* 1966, *21,* 573–580.

Stott, D. H. Epidemiological Indicators of the Origins of Behavior Disturbance As Measured by The Bristol Social Adjustment Guides. *Genetic Psychology Monographs,* 1978, *97,* 127–159.

Sullivan, W. Boys & Girls are now Maturing Earlier. *New York Times,* January 24, 1971.

Takahashi, S. & Gjessing, L. R. Studies of Periodic Catatonia—IV. Longitudinal Study of Catecholamine Metabolism with and without Drugs. *Journal of Psychiatric Research,* 1972, *9,* 293–314.

Tanner, J. M. Some Notes on the Reporting of Growth Data. *Human Biology,* 1951, *23,* 93–159.

Tanner, J. M. *Education and Physical Growth.* New York: International Universities Press, 1961.

Tanner, J. M. *Fetus into Man: Physical Growth from Conception to Maturity.* Cambridge, Mass.: Harvard University Press, 1978.

Tanner, J. M., Healy, M. J. R., Lockhart, R. D., MacKenzie, J. D., & Whitehouse, R. H. Aberdeen Growth Study: I. The Prediction of Adult Body Measurement from Measurements Taken Each Year from Birth to 5 years. *Archives of Disease in Childhood,* 1956, *31,* 372–381.

Tanner, J. M., Prader, A., Habich, H., & Ferguson-Smith, M. A. Genes on the Y-Chromosome Influencing Rate of Maturation in Men: Skeletal Age Studies in Children with Klinefelter's (XYY) and Turner's (XO) Syndromes. *Lancet,* 1959, *2,* 141–144.

Tanner, J. M., Whitehouse, R. H., & Takaishi, M. Standards from Birth to Maturity for Height, Weight, Height Velocity, Weight Velocity: British Children, 1965. *Archives of Diseases in Childhood,* 1966, *41,* 454–471; 613–635.

Terman, L. S. *Mental and Physical Traits of One Thousand Gifted Children.* Palo Alto, Calif.: Stanford University Press, 1925.

Terman, L. S. & Oden, M. H. *Genetic Studies of Genius: V. The Gifted Group at Mid-Life.* Stanford University Press, 1959.

Thompson, B. Longitudinal Studies in Aberdeen: Overview, In Mednick, S. A. & Baert, A. (eds.), *Prospective Longitudinal Research in Europe: Implications for Primary Prevention.* Oxford: Oxford University Press, 1979.

Thrupp, S. L. A Survey of the Alien Population of England in 1440, In Grew, R. & Steneck, N. H. (eds.), *Society and History: Essays by Sylvia L. Thrupp.* Ann Arbor: University of Michigan Press, 1977.

Topp, S. G., Cook, J., Holland, W. W., & Elliot, A. Influence of Environmental Factors on Height and Weight of School Children. *British Journal of Preventive and Social Medicine,* 1970, *24,* 154.

Valk, I. M. & Van Den Busch, J. S. G. Intradaily Variation of the Human Ulnar Length and Short-Term Growth—A Longitudinal Study in Eleven Boys. *Growth,* 1978, *42,* 107–11.

Van der Linden, F. P. G. M., Hirschfield, W. J., & Miller, R. L. On the Analysis and Presentation of Longitudinally Collected Growth Data. *Growth,* 1970, *34,* 385–400.

Van't Hof, M. A., Roede, M. J., & Kowalski, C. J. A Mixed Longitudinal Data Analysis Model. *Human Biology,* 1977, *49,* 165–179.

Van Venrooij-Ysselmuiden, M. E. & Van Ipenburg, A. Mixed Longitudinal Data on Skeletal Age from a Group of Dutch Children Living in Utrecht and Surroundings. *Annals of Human Biology,* 1978, *5,* 359–380.

Voors, A. W., Webber, L. S., & Berenson, G. S. Time Course Studies of Blood Pressure in Children—The Bogalusa Heart Study. *American Journal of Epidemiology,* 1979, *109,* 320–333.

Wechsler, D. *Wechsler Preschool and Primary Scale of Intelligence.* New York: Psychological Corporation, 1967.

Weiss, A. A. Long-term Psychodiagnostic and Clinical Follow-up of Three Cases of Temporal Lobectomy. *Israel Annals of Psychodiagnostics,* 1975, *13,* 372–378.

Wenar, C. The Reliability of Developmental Histories. *Psychosomatic Medicine,* 1963, *25,* 505–509.

Werner, E., Bierman, J., & French, F. E. *The Children of Kauai: A Longitudinal Study from the Prenatal Period to Age Ten*. Honolulu, Hawaii: University of Hawaii Press, 1971.

Werner, E., Bierman, J. M., French, F., Simonian, K., Connor, A., Smith, R. S., & Campbell, M. Reproductive and Environmental Casualties: A Report on the 10-Year Follow-up of the Children of the Kauai Pregnancy Study. *Pediatrics*, 1968, *42*, 112–127.

Werner, E. & Smith, R. S. *Kauai's Children Come of Age*. Honolulu, Hawaii: University Press of Hawaii, 1977.

Wiener, G., Rider, R. V., Oppel, W. C., Fischer, L. K., & Harper, P. A. Correlates of Low Birth Weight: Psychological Status at Six to Seven Years of Age. *Pediatrics*, 1965, *35*, 434–444.

Wilkins, L. T. *Delinquent Generations*. London: H. M. Stationery Office, 1960.

Williamson, A. P. (ed.). A Special Report: Four-year study of a Boy with Combined Immune Deficiency Maintained in Strict Reverse Isolation from Birth. *Pediatric Research*, 1977, *11*, Part 2.

Wrigley, E. A. Mortality in Pre-Industrial England: The Example of Colyton, Devon, Over Three Centuries. In Glass, D. G. & Revelle, R. (eds.), *Population and Social Change*. London: Arnold, 1972.

Yarrow, M. R., Campbell, J. D., & Burton, R. V. Reliability of Maternal Retrospection: A Preliminary Report. *Family Proceedings*, 1964, *3*, 207–218.

Zajonc, R. B. Family Configurations and Intelligence. *Science*, 1976, *192*, 227–236.

Zajonc, R. B. & Marcus, G. B. Birth Order and Intellectual Development. *Psychological Review*, 1975, *82*, 74–88.

Zazzo, R. Diversité, Realité, et Mirages de la Methode Longitudinale. *Enfance*, 1967, *2*, 131–136.

Zuk, G. H. Autistic Distortions in Parents of Retarded Children. *Journal of Consulting Psychology*, 1959, *23*, 171–176.

Author Index

259

Subject Index

EDUCATIONAL PSYCHOLOGY

continued from page ii

António Simões (ed.). The Bilingual Child: Research and Analysis of Existing Educational Themes

Gilbert R. Austin. Early Childhood Education: An International Perspective

Vernon L. Allen (ed.). Children as Teachers: Theory and Research on Tutoring

Joel R. Levin and Vernon L. Allen (eds.). Cognitive Learning in Children: Theories and Strategies

Donald E. P. Smith and others. A Technology of Reading and Writing (in four volumes).

> *Vol. 1. Learning to Read and Write: A Task Analysis (by Donald E. P. Smith)*
>
> *Vol. 2. Criterion-Referenced Tests for Reading and Writing (by Judith M. Smith, Donald E. P. Smith, and James R. Brink)*
>
> *Vol. 3. The Adaptive Classroom (by Donald E. P. Smith)*
>
> *Vol. 4. Designing Instructional Tasks (by Judith M. Smith)*

Phillip S. Strain, Thomas P. Cooke, and Tony Apolloni. Teaching Exceptional Children: Assessing and Modifying Social Behavior